VIOLA

*The Life and Times
of a Hull Steam Trawler*

ROBB ROBINSON & IAN HART

Lodestar Books

Published 2014 by
Lodestar Books
71 Boveney Road, London, SE23 3NL, United Kingdom

www.lodestarbooks.com

A CIP catalogue record for this book
is available from the British Library

ISBN 978-1-907206-27-6

Typeset by Lodestar Books in Equity

Printed in Spain by Graphy Cems, Navarra

All papers used by Lodestar Books
are sourced responsibly

FSC
www.fsc.org
FSC™ C022692

The mark of
responsible forestry

CONTENTS

FOREWORD

Vessels such as the steam trawler Viola normally had short lifetimes, either through increasing obsolescence, or disaster in that most unforgiving of environments—the sea. Few observers could have expected *Viola* to be any different from the norm on her launch from Cook, Welton and Gemmell's Grovehill shipyard at Beverley, East Yorkshire in January 1906. That she is today marooned at the old whaling station at Grytviken on Cumberland Bay on the remote South Atlantic island of South Georgia, as the last example of her type, with her engine still intact, bears remarkable testament to her varied history under British, Norwegian and Argentinian ownerships.

Robb Robinson and Ian Hart, through meticulous and painstaking research, have produced an evocative and highly readable historical account, which not only successfully sets *Viola*'s history in the wider historical context, but also brings to life the businesses and personalities who owned and crewed her throughout her long career.

Her working history begins with the Humber North Sea boxing fleet up to the outbreak of the Great War, when she was requisitioned by the British Admiralty, fitted with a 3-pounder gun and dispatched to the Shetland Isles on auxiliary patrol duties, before being refitted with a 12-pounder gun and reassigned to the River Tyne in 1916 on minesweeping and escort duties.

She was sold to Norwegian interests in 1920, renamed *Kapduen* and later converted to a whale catcher. As *Dias*, she took part in two whaling expeditions in 1924/25 off the coast of Angola in search of migratory humpback whales. These were commercially unsuccessful and she was laid up in Sandefjord, and in 1927 was sold to the Compañia Argentina de Pesca S.A. Crewed mainly by Norwegians, *Dias* operated out of Grytviken as a sealer, taking elephant seals, and also served as an expedition and exploration ship in the wider South Atlantic. Her triple expansion engine was converted to

8

burn oil instead of coal in 1956, and by 1960 she had been sold to the British firm, Albion Star. Subsequently, the Grytviken Whaling Station was closed in 1964/65 and *Viola/Dias* was laid up with two other whaling vessels, *Albatros* and *Petrel*, in Cumberland Bay.

There she lay, increasingly forlorn, partly submerged and largely forgotten until March 1982 when a group of scrap dealers planted the Argentinian flag on South Georgia—sparking the beginnings of the Falklands conflict between the United Kingdom and the military-junta controlled Argentina.

Post-the Falklands conflict, *Viola/Dias* continued to deteriorate until January 2004 when her hull was patched, and she was re-floated and re-berthed alongside *Albatros*. Her funnel was removed for safety reasons some years ago and has not been refitted. To date, her fate remains uncertain and thus far various attempts to repatriate her to the Humber have failed.

It is my fervent hope that this book reaches a wide and influential audience, and that *Viola/Dias* should return to the Humber for preservation as the last example, although extensively reconverted, of a British steam trawler.

Professor Hugh Murphy
Centre for Business History in Scotland
University of Glasgow
September 2014

I

A GHOST SHIP OF GRYTVIKEN

DEEP IN SOUTHERN LATITUDES, in a desolate corner of Cumberland Bay on the east coast of the sub-Antarctic island of South Georgia, hard by the rotting quays of the abandoned whaling station of Grytviken and almost within a stone's throw of the grave of Sir Ernest Shackleton, lie three forsaken steam ships: rusting remnants of our industrial past, unique survivals from a vanished age of steam at sea. Far from any main shipping lane, the isolation of their anchorage has helped them avoid the scrap-cutter's torch.

Their refuge is certainly remote. Set amongst savage South Atlantic seas, South Georgia ranks high on any list of far-flung places of our earth. A dramatic glacial wilderness of around 120 miles in length, yet no more than twenty or so in width, it lies on the Scotia ridge and can only be reached by ship after a voyage of some 800 miles from Stanley in the Falkland Islands.

A haven for albatross, skuas, petrels and countless other seabirds, its vast snow-streaked peaks of Alpine proportions rise steeply, almost straight from the sea, above colonies of millions of penguins and the herds of huge elephant seals that haul themselves ashore in sparse tussock-strewn bays for a few months each year to give birth. There are no towns, or even villages, only a string of derelict whaling stations that cling where they can to the shores beneath spectacular ice-clad mountains and great glaciers along the island's eastern coast. Although visited by passing cruise ships, much of the island is almost, but not quite, devoid of any permanent human presence. King Edward Point, across Cumberland Bay from Grytviken, is the centre of the island's administration and today home to a sophisticated fisheries research laboratory.[1]

Even when whaling operations were in full swing, much of the wider world knew little of South Georgia, let alone had any idea where it was; except, perhaps, on the two occasions when dramatic events brought it briefly to the attention of the international media. Back in 1916, Ernest Shackleton reached the island after an 800-mile voyage across huge seas in a small open boat, from Elephant Island where the crew of his ill-fated Antarctic expedition was marooned. His party scrambled ashore in King Haakon Bay on the west coast. Although exhausted, Shackleton and two companions had no choice but to become the first people to traverse the glaciers and uncharted mountains of the island's interior in order to reach the comparative safety of the Stromness whaling station. Shackleton subsequently rescued all his crew from Elephant Island but was later to die of a heart attack aboard his ship, *Quest*, in Cumberland Bay on returning to South Georgia, en route for the Antarctic again in 1922.[2]

*   *   *

Some sixty years after Shackleton was buried in Grytviken's cemetery, South Georgia hit the headlines once more. On a cold and wet morning, this time in March 1982, a group of Argentine scrap metal merchants were landed by the naval auxiliary *Bahía Buen Suceso* at Leith Harbour, a few miles from Cumberland Bay. Their remit was to cut up the rusting equipment that littered the old whaling stations, and the three old ships left in the waters of Cumberland Bay.

Yet something was not quite right about the Argentines' arrival. Diplomatic protocol and international law required that the *Bahía Buen Suceso* should not have disembarked people at Leith Harbour before visiting Cumberland Bay and reporting for Customs and Immigration Clearance to the official British Magistrate, a scientist resident at the British Antarctic Survey Base on King Edward Point. This they conspicuously failed to do and instead raised the Argentine flag at Leith Harbour. Thus began the incident that arguably opened the Falklands War.

The British Government, caught off guard by the subsequent escalation of a long-simmering conflict, had less than one hundred marines and the survey vessel HMS *Endurance* in the South Atlantic with which to defend the Falkland Islands and their Dependencies from a full-scale Argentine invasion. Within weeks, the Falkland Islands were in Argentine hands after a spirited defence by the British marines around the Governor's House in Stanley. South Georgia was taken a little later when Argentine soldiers reinforced the original landings at Leith Harbour, but not before they faced a fierce firefight around Grytviken with just eighteen British marines, who eventually surrendered to an overwhelmingly larger force.

History records that these Argentine successes were of short duration. A British Task Force was quickly assembled and within days had set sail for the South Atlantic. A few weeks later South Georgia was back under British control after a series of actions in which UK military helicopters disabled the submarine *Santa Fe* and landed Special Forces on shore. The British Task Force's recapture of South Georgia was a precursor to retaking the Falkland Islands via San Carlos Bay, Goose Green, and battle on the heights above Stanley.

For a few short weeks events on South Georgia attracted world attention. Cumberland Bay was briefly a hive of unaccustomed activity, being visited by various requisitioned vessels including the liners *QE2* and *Canberra*. Today a few remnants, including the wreckage of an Argentine helicopter brought down by British troops, remain around the island as reminders of the war.[3]

International interest soon vanished. Though the dispute over the sovereignty of the Falkland Islands and the Dependencies continues to this day, South Georgia, the forsaken whaling stations and the old ships slipped back into their accustomed obscurity. Much of the island remains largely untouched and unspoilt, a haven for seabirds and seals—an immense natural sanctuary—although the old whaling stations have steadily deteriorated, their scrap metal, which had ostensibly lured the Argentines back in 1982, continuing to rust away.

*   *   *

On another grey and grainy morning back in February 1906, almost seventy-six years before the landings at Leith Harbour, the cold, wet quaysides by the Humber around St Andrew's Dock in the great seaport of Hull were also alive with activity. Light showers and occasional flurries of sleet and snow dusted the docksides as close on fifty steam trawlers prepared to take leave for the North Sea fishing grounds. This was the first full sailing of the new Hellyer Boxing Fleet.[4]

So-called boxing fleets were an early form of industrial fishing. Their name came from the boxes in which the trawler crews packed their newly caught fish. The ships in these fleets worked far from port for weeks on end. Most days fast steam cutters reached the fleets from London, and the boxes of fish were transferred from trawlers to cutter by open rowing boat in every kind of weather. Once laden with all the trawlers' catches, these cutters then dashed for the Thames, at high speed through all sorts of sea, past empty sister ships steaming back out to the fleet. Cutters, trawlers and trawlermen: all played their part in a seemingly unending struggle to service Billingsgate Market and satisfy London's almost insatiable demand for fresh fish.

Three fleets of boxing steamers already hailed from Hull. These were known respectively as the Gamecock, Great Northern and Red Cross fleets. But Charles Hellyer, Hull's leading trawler owner and Managing Director of the Hellyer Steam Fishing Company, thought there was room for another such venture, and in September 1905 he announced plans to build a new North Sea boxing fleet from scratch. The scale and pace of Hellyer's project was staggeringly ambitious, even for an Edwardian British fishing industry that led the world. Almost £450,000 worth of orders with tight delivery dates were quickly placed with, and then turned out by, shipyards on the Humber, Tyne and Clyde. Whilst the earlier boxing fleets had been built up over several years, this one was ready to sail within five months.

As dawn broke on that morning in February 1906, the crews were already trickling through the wide wet subway below the busy railway that separated the dock from the warren of red brick streets and terraces on the southern side of Hull's Hessle Road district. For a time, the trickle approached a torrent as men, young and old alike, dodged around crowded carts, rullies and railway wagons full of fish, and hurried past busy barrow-boys who were bustling boxes and barrels beneath the gaunt structure of the fish market. All headed for the lock pit area, anxious to watch the spectacle and catch a last glimpse of family and friends going to sea.

The district's women were no less interested or anxious about all that the fleet's sailing entailed, but few watched. Women might welcome you home from the sea but it was considered bad luck on Hessle Road to be seen off by a female; farewells had already been made in the crowded 'sham fours,' the terraced houses, across the railway track. Meanwhile, men and boys gathered on the windswept quays below the big skies by the broad, brown mud waters of the Humber estuary to watch the fleet sail. Because of the sheer numbers of vessels involved, some trawlers had already passed through St Andrew's lock gates and out into the Humber roadstead by the time crowds gathered. Almost every vessel in the fleet had a Shakespearian name—Hellyer named all his ships after the Bard's characters—and indeed it seemed that an armada of almost Elizabethan extent was taking leave of the port.[5]

The sailing of a full boxing fleet was a far from common occurrence, for these fleets might remain at sea for years. Individual trawlers returned to port every five or six weeks when coal, provisions and crews were exhausted, but as they left the fleet other vessels took their place, refuelled, revictualled and ready to resume their unrelenting trawl. Unless weather conditions were extremely dire, these fleets kept a constant presence on the far-flung North Sea grounds, trying to meet the demand for fish, not only of London's Billingsgate but also of countless other fish markets across the country. By the Edwardian epoch white fish was a working class staple. The fish and chip shop had emerged in the previous century to help sustain Britain's rapidly growing towns and cities; fish and chips were the first fast food of the new industrial age, almost a maritime McDonalds but without the corporate dimension.

No one owned the fish these fleets sought; the rich grounds they worked had never been appropriated. The trawler crews pursued a common—if fugitive—maritime resource. Deep-sea fishermen were—and are—amongst the last people in the world to hunt for a living. Sea fish may be theoretically free for the taking but the real costs of catching them have always been considerable, to be counted not only in terms of capital expended on vessels and gear but also in pounds of flesh and blood—in fishermen's lives. Throughout the twentieth century, fishing remained Britain's most dangerous industry. Statistics suggest it was four times more dangerous than coal mining. Those whose business was steam trawling often toiled in great seas, far from the comforts of family and home, in cold grey waters and every sort of weather to haul a harvest from the deep. They faced the full force of both natural and human agents of destruction. In just twelve years, between 1906 and 1918, no less than twenty-two of the fifty or so trawlers built for this Hellyer fleet were lost, either to the sea or to enemy action in the Great War. Bereavement remained an all-too-common burden for the families of fishermen throughout the twentieth century.

In much the same way as South Georgia's whaling stations have been abandoned, Hull's once proud St Andrew's Dock—periodically in the media spotlight when at the wrong end of a series of Cod Wars with Iceland between the 1950s and 1970s—has also slipped into an obsolete obscurity, long since forsaken by Hull's fishing vessels, a fleet no longer even a shadow of its former self. Even before the Falklands War this dock, once home to the greatest distant-water trawling fleet in the world, had also been deserted, partly filled in, and many of its surrounding buildings left derelict or demolished, bulldozed into oblivion during the 1960s and 1970s like so many of the adjacent terraces. Huge swathes of the strong Hessle Road community, of a distinct industrially maritime way of life, have been dispersed to the winds.

All physical trace of the once proud Hellyer fishing fleet had disappeared many years before the dock's decline; with one exception. Amongst the multitude of trawlers taking the tide in the Humber on that distant day in 1906 was the newly built steamer, *Viola*. Whilst all her sisters have long since been scrapped or else sunk in storms or war, this one seemingly insignificant craft has survived against all the odds. In 1982, this self-same vessel lay in Cumberland Bay, awaiting the Argentine scrap metal merchants' cutting torch.

Today, accompanied by the former whalers *Albatros* and *Petrel*, she still lies at the ruined township of Grytviken, South Georgia, part of a ghost fleet from a forgotten age.[6]

Throughout most of a career which encompassed almost the entire length of the long Atlantic, through both war and peace, this little ship, this former Hull trawler, remained an everyday working vessel, just one of many apparently mundane, most certainly unsung, craft used by mariners of all persuasions to earn their living in a variety of ways across the world's wide oceans.

Unlike the mighty HMS *Dreadnought* which was launched three weeks later, *Viola* was built not for fighting but for fishing, for the profitable and unending task of taking fish for the London market; but the outbreak of the Great War in 1914 changed all this forever. Hastily requisitioned and armed by the Admiralty, the little ship and her crew of fishermen sailed off from Hull straight into the fogs and uncertainty of a grim war at sea, and to more than four years of voyaging through waters infested with U-boats and mines. HMT *Viola*, as she was by then known, steamed thousands of miles patrolling Britain's maritime front line, far more than any single dreadnought, and her crew had numerous engagements with the enemy; the little armed trawler survived everything the enemy and seas could throw at her. But the return of peace took her in new directions, to different waters, and *Viola* has yet to return to her home port from that Great War voyage.

II

SAIL, STEAM AND STEEL

TAKING FISH IS AN ANCIENT AND UNIQUE OCCUPATION. Sea fishing defies many conventional land-based classifications of economic activity. It cannot really be described as either agriculture or transport, nor is it a typical industry in the strict sense of the word, yet it shares many characteristics of all three pursuits. But there is something much more elemental, perhaps primeval, about fishing. Fishermen are almost the last people in the western world who earn their livelihood through hunting. All fishing vessels, be they basic open boats or modern steel-hulled factory freezer trawlers equipped with the latest electronic technology, are hunting implements in essence. Deep-sea fishermen have always conducted their business in great waters, and knowledge of the haunts and habits of their wild and fugitive prey, and an ability to weather their way over a vast maritime wilderness, remain essential skills for every successful skipper. The waters on which they work and the fish they have always sought have not been appropriated, that is owned by anyone, in the conventional landed sense. It is the process of capture that turns wild sea fish from a common resource into private property. Without such successful hunting and survival skills no fisherman has ever been able to win a consistent livelihood from the sea in any age, and there would never have been any economic sense to commercial fishing.

Until the middle of the nineteenth century many of the varieties of white fish we popularly consume, species such as cod, haddock and their relations, had mainly been taken on long- or hand-lines using baited hooks. Trawling, a technique which typically involves dragging a bag-shaped net over the seabed, was much less common than today and mainly centred on the towns of Brixham in Devon, Barking in Essex and the old Kentish port of Ramsgate.[1]

Line fishing predominated because of transportation problems. It is true that fresh fish could be conveyed quite quickly, quite far inland, even in an age of notoriously slow and uncertain transport, if packhorses and fast carts were used; but these were expensive. High transport costs restricted the inland market for fresh fish. Only the most valuable species, bound for the banquets of the wealthy, could stand the cost of transportation. Whilst trawlers usually made bigger catches than vessels fishing with hooks and lines, and sometimes took some prime species such as sole in reasonable quantities, their trawls were usually less discriminating and a large portion of their catch was of so-called offal fish, cheaper varieties such as haddock or codling that were not worth the cost of transporting overland for any distance. Line fishermen may usually have taken less fish but a larger proportion of their catch was of so-called prime fish, large cod, ling and the like, which could be sold at a good price on inland markets.[2]

So the poorer classes in many inland districts ate little fresh fish. They might consume some cured fish but this had been heavily salted or smoked: a modern kipper is a herring smoked for around six hours, whilst its eighteenth century counterpart, the red herring, could be in the smokehouse for ten days or more. If fresh fish came their way then it had usually been rejected by richer customers because it had begun to 'go off'—past its sell-by date as we would say today—which scarcely made it attractive. It had always been like this. Since time immemorial, fresh fish had been a luxury commodity away from the coasts of the British Isles, but in the mid-nineteenth century, in a little more than twenty years, the arrival of the railway age changed everything.

During the 1840s and 1850s much of Britain's national railway network, as we know it today, was laid out. Numerous railway companies were formed; offering an ostensibly safe means of investment they mobilized the nest-eggs of thousands of small savers and harnessed the skills and ingenuity of some superb Victorian engineers. The hard graft of constructing thousands of miles of railway over almost every type of terrain was carried out by large armies of unskilled labourers—navvies—a remarkable feat when we recall that they were often armed with little more than pickaxe, shovel and wheelbarrow.

By the late 1850s the map of Britain was garlanded in railway track, linking county to county, town to town, the country's interior to its coast.

The railway had a profound impact on almost every aspect of economy and society, and nowhere was this more apparent that in the fishing sector. Railways smashed the transportation bottleneck which had long constrained the fish trade. For the first time there was a relatively cheap, as well as fast, means of conveying fresh fish from the coast to the burgeoning inland industrial towns and cities. This could not have occurred at a more opportune time. As the country industrialized it became increasingly urban in character. The 1851 Census showed that for the first time more people were living in towns and cities than in the countryside, drawn there by job opportunities in industry. Towns and cities desperately needed substantial supplies of cheap nutritious food, and fresh fish, brought by railway, fitted the bill. Sometime between the 1840s and the 1870s some genius, and we still don't really know who, put fried fish with potato chips and a national institution was created. In short, the railway made fish an article of cheap mass consumption.

Not surprisingly, the British fishing industry was revolutionized, and the marketing opportunities created for fresh fish not only led to a rapid expansion of the fish trade, but also had a profound impact on the catching sector. The large catches of fish caught by the trawlers now commanded much better prices on the quayside, the economics of trawling were transformed, and great profits were there to be made by those willing to take up the practice. Back in 1840 the majority of white fish taken off the coasts of England had been caught by baited hook and line. By the 1870s far more fish was being landed and most was brought in by trawlers.[3]

Sailing trawlers soon covered the North Sea but their beam trawls could only work effectively on areas of smooth or sandy ground, and their crews tried to avoid towing gear over rocky bottoms. Sometimes they persuaded local line fishermen, despite their reservations, to help them find the areas they sought. On most occasions they explored the seas for themselves. Often, lacking accurate charts and relevant nautical almanacs, they deployed a variety of methods to get a feel for the bottom beneath their boats. A piece of tallow attached to the base of a sounding lead was a regular way of ascertaining whether the seabed consisted of sand, shells, shingle or rocks, but sometimes less orthodox methods were deployed. James Alward, a leading Grimsby trawler owner in the early twentieth century, remembering his early days on the first smacks off the north-east coast, recalled that the skipper or mate might often bite on to the warp that towed the trawl behind the boat. The vibrations passing through his jaw gave him a feel for the conditions, contours and curves of the seabed the smack was trawling over.[4] Presumably a strong set of teeth was a pre-requisite for this procedure.

Many areas of the bed of the North Sea still retain the names given them by these early smacksmen. Around the middle of the nineteenth century, for example, they came across one particularly profitable place to trawl in the vicinity of Flamborough Head. Although already frequented by local line fishermen, it soon attracted many trawlermen who named it California, presumably because it yielded riches on 1849 Gold Rush lines, although in this case it was the silvery wealth of the North Sea waters that they sought. Indeed, the most famous grounds they discovered were the Silver Pits, a series of depressions in the seabed where sole tended to congregate in extremely cold winters. No one now knows for certain who found and first worked these grounds but many believe it was Thomas Sudds in the late 1830s. Late one year, so the story goes, a lone fishing smack working far out to sea was suddenly beset by a great storm and unable to retrieve its trawl before being blown before high winds for two days and nights. When the shattered crew finally found safety in Scarborough harbour they discovered large numbers of sole in the remnants of their net. They spread out a map, worked out where the storm had blown them, repaired their gear, retraced their passage and found the Silver Pits. They probably kept the location a secret for some time—a practice far from uncommon amongst later fishermen—but the grounds became widely known during the harsh winter of 1844/5, even meriting a mention in *The Times*. Although sole was a much sought-after fish, usually retailing at a high price, the sheer quantities caught during that winter sold at low cost, providing much needed cheap sustenance for large numbers of poor people afflicted by economic depression, in Leeds and other towns along the route of the railway between Hull and Manchester.

Traditional fishing ports grew in size and new players emerged. The railway reached the ancient port of Hull in 1840 and Grimsby in 1857. In 1840 there had been no more than a dozen small fishing vessels operating out of the Humber estuary, but by the end of the 1870s more than a thousand sailing trawlers, known as smacks, were sailing from there. Hull and Grimsby vied with Great Yarmouth for the title of the world's largest fishing port.[5] All were well placed to exploit the North Sea's silvery-scaled bonanza.

The new fish trade at Hull and Grimsby was largely created by incomers who had little previous connection with the ports: trawlermen who gravitated to the Humber and other North Sea ports from the established trawling centres of Ramsgate, Barking and Brixham. Initially, a number voyaged up to try their luck for a few months each year before returning to their home port. Later many migrated north, moving up lock, stock and barrel, settling permanently at either Hull or Grimsby. Amongst the families who made Hull their home and base for fishing were the Hellyers from Brixham.

By the early 1850s Robert Hellyer and his father had become seasonal visitors to Hull.[6] Every October they voyaged from Brixham for the North Sea and fished out of Hull until the following Whitsuntide when they returned to the West Country. Family, household goods and pets, the Hellyer's entire business, were all packed aboard and subject to this annual migration. Everything was shipped back at the end of the season. This was commonplace amongst the Devon visitors in the early years of the Hull fishing industry but in 1855 Robert, his wife and family, decided to join a number of other south-coast fishermen who had settled permanently in the Humber port.

Robert registered a newly built fishing smack, *Excel*, a couple of years later.[7] He prospered and soon acquired several fishing smacks, and by then had probably given up going to sea regularly himself; most owners stayed ashore to manage operations once they owned two or more vessels. He retained his strong south coast connections, as many of the vessels he subsequently built were ordered from yards in Rye and Sandwich.[8] A surviving record book shows Robert to be very exacting in his transactions with builders when it came to the construction of his trawling smacks, and he had an eye for detail. By the mid-1860s the Hellyer household were well established as key players in the Hull trawling trade.

The Hull fishing industry was growing rapidly at this time and there were good profits to be made by those who could acquire a trawler of their own. Many locals, and also workhouse youngsters drawn from far afield who went to sea on these trawlers as apprentices from the age of fourteen or even younger, had aspirations to become smackowners in their own right. If they were sober, industrious and lucky, a combination not commonplace amongst trawlermen, then they could save up a deposit for a vessel, but they usually lacked the connections or background to secure a full loan from a bank or local wealthy individual. But Robert knew the growing Hull fishing community very well and was a good judge of character. He developed a lucrative sideline in placing orders for vessels and then selling them on to such aspiring smackowners by way of mortgages.

He also diversified into importing ice. Today, ice is ubiquitous. We are accustomed to refrigerators and freezers, but artificial ice only became available in commercial quantities in the late nineteenth century. Throughout Victoria's reign the growing demand was satisfied by importing Norwegian ice cut from freshwater lakes in Oslo Fjord, then storing it in insulated semi-subterranean ice houses until needed. Robert was quite early into this business, importing his first ice for the Hull fishing industry in 1859. The following year he joined with other owners to form the Hull Mutual Ice Company, which supplied the fish trade with ice, and also local businesses and surrounding country residences, many of whom built their own ice houses.

Robert Hellyer's son Charles was born in Brixham in 1846[9] but grew to adulthood in Hull. By the late 1860s he was engaged in the sailmaking trade but he soon entered the trawling trade in his own right. His father provided the £835 mortgage for his first smack, *Index*, built in Hull by W & J McCann and registered in March 1870.[10] During the 1870s several other members of the Hellyer family bought smacks; some went to sea in them, but Charles seems to have been mainly involved in the business side of the catching from the very first.

At the end of that decade the Hellyer family played a prominent part in the formation of the first boxing fleets. Fleeting was a system whereby a group of smacks would work together on the grounds almost in unison, under the command of a senior skipper. They were serviced by fast sailing cutters that collected their catches and ferried them to market. The system had been devised by Hewett's of Barking around 1828 and by 1864 the firm ran two fleets: the Home fleet worked the southern North Sea whilst the Short Blue fished further north.

Fleeting dispensed with the need for ice and meant that smacks spent much more time working on the grounds and less voyaging to ports, but the Hellyers, like many Hull smackowners, had deep reservations about its efficiency. For them, the crux of the problem lay with incentives. Under the Barking system, rowing boats transferred baskets of fish from smack to cutter, where it was stored in bulk and run into London's Billingsgate Market. The proceeds were divided equally between the vessels of the fleet and for the Humber smackowners this was the system's weakness. Bulking, as it was known, provided no individual incentive: hard working and lazy, lucky and unlucky crews, all claimed an equal reward. The crews from both Hull and Grimsby were paid under this system, which created great dissatisfaction with smackowners and crews alike.

What made fleeting much more commercially attractive to Hull smackowners like the Hellyers was the introduction of what became known as 'boxing' in 1878. Under this system the old practice of sending fish to the carrier in bulk baskets was abandoned. Henceforward, smacks sorted their own fish and sent it across to the carrier in boxes with tokens marked with their own name. Individual smacks could now be credited with the fruits of their own labour.

There were other advantages. Cutters could run the fish directly from the grounds into Billingsgate and completely cut out the cost of overland conveyance from the Humber to London. Moreover, the introduction of steam cutters to bring the boxes to market seemed likely to improve profitability still further. They could voyage to Billingsgate much more quickly than sailing cutters, so the fish they carried arrived fresher and fetched a higher average price. Hewett's had introduced steam cutters in the 1860s and Grimsby owners began the large-scale construction of such craft on taking up boxing in the late 1870s. In January 1880 a meeting of Hull smackowners, including the Hellyers, decided to form two boxing fleets. These were named the Red Cross and Great Northern fleets respectively, and four iron-built steam cutters were ordered to service each fleet. Such steam cutters were costly and the smackowners formed limited liability companies to finance their construction.

These cutters were the first steam vessels in the Hull fishing industry and were expensive to build. Hellyer and the other owners were keen to ensure a good return on their investment and wanted them to run fish to market throughout the year, meaning the boxing fleets would have to work during the winter months. This brought Hellyer and the other smackowners into confrontation with their crews. Most trawlermen preferred to go single-boating, as the average smack would stay out for a week or so, whilst fleeting meant spending up to six weeks or more far out in the North Sea, with little vestige of comfort. Until the steam cutters were built, the fleeting system had only operated during the spring and summer. The idea of spending autumn and winter fishing in such a fashion was unpopular with the working fishermen, who tried to resist its introduction.

Not long after the new steam cutters came into service in mid-1881, the Hellyer family played a key role with other smackowners in making the fishermen continue fleeting during the forthcoming winter, and the men were eventually forced back to work after going on strike in the autumn. However, the Great Gale of March 1883 reignited the winter fleeting issue. All told, 43 smacks and 250 fishermen were lost in this tragedy, including 180 Hull trawlermen.[11] When the subsequent combination of strikes and adverse public reaction forced the other Hull smackowners to make substantial concessions on winter fleeting, Charles Hellyer, always a hard-liner, deemed the changes to be uneconomic. Shortly afterwards, he announced he was pulling out of winter fleeting and henceforward dispatched his sailing smacks to the grounds as single boats, working alone.

But Hellyer was far from finished with innovation. During the 1880s a number of trawler owners began to order sailing smacks made with iron, then steel, rather than wooden hulls. A few trawlers were ordered with the latest compound engines and high-tech multi-tubular boilers. A specially designed steam winch—a fundamental part of the new trawling technology—was also developed. Wire cables rather than hemp ropes were increasingly used for the warps that towed the trawl.

But perhaps the major marine technological change of the 1880s was the introduction of the triple expansion steam engine. This had three cylinders and the steam produced in the boiler was used in each of them in turn, increasing both fuel efficiency and the amount of power that could be produced by a given size of engine. According to the firm of Amos and Smith, who built steam engines for the Hull fishing fleet, the early triple expansion steam engine and high pressure boiler gave fifteen percent greater fuel economy than the earlier compound engine. In the merchant shipping sphere, the triple expansion engine finally gave steam ships an advantage over sailing ships in the carriage of high bulk, low value cargoes such as coal or wool. Over the following couple of decades tramp steamers with triple expansion steam engines rapidly replaced sailing ships across the world's long distance trading routes.

Charles Hellyer quickly realized that this combination of steel and triple expansion steam could also revolutionize the economics of trawling; he embraced the new technology with considerable enthusiasm. He was not alone in recognizing the potential of this new technology. All the vessels in the existing Hull boxing fleets were sailing smacks but in 1890 one of the fleeting companies ordered four steam trawlers. They proved so successful in the boxing fleet business that other orders were swiftly placed, and a rapid replacement of sail with steam was soon underway amongst the fleets. The Hull fishing industry was well placed to take advantage of steam. The port already had an established expertise in building steam-powered merchant ships in steel, and possessed substantial marine engineering facilities. It was awash with good-quality coal, for large quantities were brought to Hull by both rail and water for export. Hellyers were to bunker their trawlers with one of the best of these, South Kirtley Smalls, a renowned South Yorkshire steam coal, right down to the outbreak of the Great War.

One marine scientist, speaking in the 1890s, estimated that a steam trawler was four times as efficient as an equivalent sailing smack. It could work when a smack was becalmed or stopped through high winds, and unlike the sailing smack it proved capable of taking advantage of more efficient fishing gear, the so-called otter trawl, introduced in the 1890s. A steel-hulled steam trawler was more profitable than a wooden sailing smack but was much more expensive to build. Those smackowners who wished to start steam trawling needed to restructure their operations in order to attract the capital necessary to purchase and operate the vessels. In short, they needed to adopt modern business practice. Here Hellyer proved to be in his element:[12] in 1891 he formed Charles Hellyer and Company with an authorised capital of £40,000. Many of the shares were held by members of his family but by this time he moved in influential circles and proved adept at encouraging wealthy individuals from outside the fishing industry to take an interest; amongst those who ventured their capital was Sir Tatton Sykes of the famous landed family from Sledmere in East Yorkshire.

His new company built and operated a number of steam trawlers and, as these had a greater range than the old sailing smacks, Hellyer sent some of them to the rich distant water grounds being opened up off Iceland[13], not long after they were first worked by the steam trawler *Aquarius* of Grimsby in 1891. The new venture proved successful. Within a short while Hellyer was fully committed to the development of steam and began selling off his sailing smacks. In 1897 he restructured his interests once more, this time adopting limited liability. Charles Hellyer and Company was wound up and a new firm, the Hellyer Steam Fishing Company Ltd, was formed.[14]

As the new century opened Charles Hellyer was unquestionably Hull's leading trawler owner. Although many of his company's new trawlers sailed

for Iceland and the Faroes, he seems not to have been deterred by his somewhat painful experience with the North Sea boxing fleets. He decided to
return to this branch of business but on his own company's terms, and in
February 1905 he announced his intention of forming a new boxing fleet[15], a
decision confirmed during the following summer.

At the age of sixty he had lost little ambition or drive. This venture was of
massive proportions by the standards of the contemporary fishing industry,
and involved assembling a fleet of around fifty steam trawlers to be serviced
by five new steam cutters. The majority of vessels were to be newly built although a number of existing craft were also refurbished. Speed was of the essence and the fleet was scheduled to be constructed and operational within
nine months. Whilst a number of orders were placed with Mackie & Thom-
son of Govan on the Clyde, most of the trawlers were to be constructed by
the local firm of Cook, Welton and Gemmell, whilst Earle's Shipyard on the
Humber foreshore built the cutters. Hellyer's new enterprise was reported to
have required an investment of £320,000, a sum hitherto unmatched in the
history of the British fishing industry.[16]

In an era of steam and steel, Hull and the Humber were always overshad-
owed as a shipbuilding area by the likes of the Clyde and the Tyne, but the
region's engagement with the development and construction of nautical technology stretched far back beyond recorded history. The remains of numerous
log-boats have been found along the estuary and its tributaries. Amongst the
most impressive of these is the Hasholme Boat, hollowed out of a fifty-foot
oak log. The three Bronze Age Ferriby Boats—amongst the oldest plank vessels ever found anywhere—were unearthed on the Humber foreshore within a few miles of the city at what has been claimed to be the world's oldest
known shipyard.

In the eighteenth century Hull shipyards launched a string of notable ves-
sels including the *Bethia*, better known throughout the world by its later name
HMS *Bounty*. In 1757 HMS *Rose* was launched from Hugh Blaydes' yard.
Built at the beginning of the Seven Years' War, she served on patrol along the
French coast and in the Caribbean. In 1768, the vessel was considered by the

Board of the Admiralty for Captain James Cook's first South Seas expedition, but as she could not be made ready in time, he used the *Endeavour*. The same year, HMS *Rose* sailed for the coast of North America and was active in impressing merchant sailors for the Royal Navy. She subsequently wrought havoc on American shipping during the American War of Independence and in July 1776 she played a major part in the British invasion of New York, shelling the land-based fortifications and making forays far up the Hudson. Her commander, James Wallace, was knighted for his actions in helping to drive Washington and his troops from the city. Some historians have attributed the formation of the Continental Navy—the original US Navy—in part, at least, to the need to combat the depredations of the Hull-built HMS *Rose*. A replica *Rose* was built in Lunenburg, Nova Scotia in 1970 and later used in the film *Master and Commander*. In 1774 HMS *Boreas*, a 28 gun frigate, was also launched from Blaydes' Yard on the same stretch of river, and between 1784 and 1787 was commanded by Nelson in the West Indies. During his time out there he not only met his wife but oversaw substantial harbour works in Antigua and Nelson's Dockyard there survives as an impressive example of 18th century naval architecture.[17]

Just along the Humber foreshore at Hessle Cliff, HMS *Hecla* (the second vessel to carry the name) was launched by the yard of Barkworth and Hawkes on 15 July 1815, the day Napoleon Bonaparte surrendered to Captain Maitland on the *Bellerophon*. Built as a bomb vessel (i.e., to carry mortars, not cannon), she took part in the bombardment of Algiers, a refuge for the Corsairs, by Edward Pellew, Lord Exmouth, in August 1816. Her heavy construction made her ideal for voyages of polar exploration and *Hecla* was adapted for this work in 1819. Captain Matthew Parry used her for his three voyages to Canada's far northern coasts and she became his favourite ship. Indeed Hecla and Griper Bay and Fury and Hecla Strait are named in honour of the Humber-built vessel and the ships which accompanied her on different voyages of exploration. In 1820 *Hecla* with *Griper* set a record for the distance traversed through the North West Passage in one season. The record stood for almost 150 years. (The next ship to make it so far west in one season was the 940-foot icebreaker tanker *Manhattan* in 1969.) Such early voyages, which required a winter locked in the ice off Canada's far northern coasts, stretched human endurance to the limits. On the last voyage, *Hecla* and *Fury* were driven ashore by the ice and the *Fury* was wrecked leaving *Hecla* to bring Parry and his men back to Britain. *Hecla* was a very famous ship and a celebrity in her day. More than 6,000 people visited her when she was opened to the public at Deptford in May 1824 prior to her departure on the third voyage. Parry used *Hecla* again in 1827 for his attempt on the North Pole. Since then a series of Royal Navy ships involved in hydrography and the like have been named *Hecla*. This scientific tradition was continued into the twentieth century by the Royal Research Ship *William Scoresby,* which was built at Beverley and fitted out in Hull in the 1920s. With Hull men in her crew she made a major contribution to our knowledge of the marine biology of the southern oceans until the late 1940s.[18]

William Scoresby was built by the firm of Cook, Welton and Gemmell at their Grovehill shipyard on the banks of the River Hull in the 1920s, some twenty years after the same yard had won the bulk of the Hellyer order. This shipbuilding firm had been founded in 1884 by three self-made men, William Cook, Charles Welton and William Gemmell. Cook and Welton had been born in Deptford on the Thames whilst Gemmell had hailed from Port Glasgow. All had served apprenticeships within the shipbuilding trade and worked at one time or another for the large Hull shipbuilding firm of Earle's. In 1884 they joined forces to lease premises by a patent slipway close to the mouth of the River Hull.

Cook, Welton and Gemmell went into business on their own account just as the trawl fishing trade was on the cusp of the momentous change from sail to steam, and from wooden to iron and steel hulls. Although the first half dozen vessels they launched in 1885 were iron-hulled sailing trawlers, from then on they concentrated on building the new steam trawlers. They opened for business in the right place and at the right time. By the mid-1880s Hull and its neighbour Grimsby had established themselves as the largest trawling ports in the world. More than 1,000 wooden sailing smacks worked from the Humber ports. By 1903 they had all been sold and replaced by fleets of the new steel-hulled steam trawlers. The old skills associated with building in wood fell out of favour and many of the yards which specialised in building sailing trawlers went to the wall. New companies such as Cook, Welton and Gemmell, firms that epitomized the modern age of steam and steel, went from strength to strength. By 1900 their first yard was unable to cope with the orders they received and they took over a larger yard at Grovehill nine miles further up the River Hull on the outskirts of the ancient town of Beverley.[19]

The iron smacks *Precursor* and *Bassano* were the first two vessels built by Cook, Welton and Gemmell in 1885. Both had been ordered by Robert Hellyer, and afterwards his son Charles regularly placed orders with the firm as he built up his fleet of steam trawlers during the 1890s and early 1900s. When he embarked upon the new boxing fleet venture, no less than thirty builds were placed with the company. The first at Grovehill was *Rosalind* and she was launched in October 1905. *Viola* was the eighth vessel; her keel was laid in the autumn of 1905 and, like all ships built at the yard, she was constructed with her bows facing south and side-launched into the River Hull.[20]

Necessity rather than custom required this spectacular means of meeting the water. The River Hull is a minor waterway draining the East Riding of Yorkshire and at Beverley is little more than forty feet wide. After launching in January 1906 *Viola*, like most other vessels built at the yard, did not linger long in the vicinity of Grovehill but was coaxed by tugs down nine miles of the tightly meandering river, through open green fields set below great skies, and into the environs of the city of Hull. There, the vessel was towed past the old Greenland Yards, once used for processing whale blubber; and onwards by Lime Street, the birthplace of John Bacchus Dykes, the son of a shipbuilder and the composer of the haunting music of the maritime hymn *Eternal Father Strong to Save*; and by old shipyards which had turned out scores of Hull vessels that covered the world's seaways during the sailing ship era. This voyage down the River Hull could be difficult and it sometimes took three tides or more to float such half-finished vessels down it and into the Humber. One tugman involved in this operation recalled that when the tide fell the vessels were often staked to the bank and most of the men moving them downriver adjourned to the nearest pub until the waters returned. Yet, despite all the difficulties these movements entailed, bigger and bigger steam and then finally diesel trawlers were turned out at Beverley and eased down the river over the ensuing decades. Such operations only ceased in the early 1960s when the advent of the great factory freezer trawlers finally brought an end to the construction of fishing vessels at Grovehill.

Once she was securely tied up in dock at Hull, work on the next stage of construction began. It was here that *Viola*'s motive power—her triple expansion steam engine and boiler—was installed. Cook, Welton and Gemmell concentrated on fabricating the hulls and superstructure, and always subcontracted the construction of the steam engines and boilers to other companies in the port. *Viola*'s power plant was built by Amos and Smith, one of Hull's leading engineering firms. Amos and Smith were another product of the new era of steam and steel and had started building marine steam engines in the 1870s. They were part of a whole host of new firms: iron shipwrights, boiler makers, ship's insulation manufacturers, wire warp manufacturers, and traders, that grew up as part of every British port's transition from sail to steam.

In the later nineteenth century, Amos and Smith had come into the ownership of the Wilson family. Two brothers, Charles and Arthur Wilson, controlled Thomas Wilson, Sons and Company of Hull, then the largest privately owned shipping company in the world. The firm had been founded by their father in the 1840s as Britain was emerging as the workshop of the world. They subsequently made a fortune by exploiting opportunities offered by Britain's vastly expanding overseas trade. They also made substantial amounts of money by shipping emigrants bound for the New World from Eastern Europe through Hull. More than 2.2 million people, many carried by Wilson's ships, passed through the port, then by railway to Liverpool, and on to the New World. Many of those who passed through the portals of Ellis Island in New York had trans-shipped through Hull. As the firm prospered Charles Wilson became an an MP, married a descendant of the Duke of Wellington, and was eventually elevated to the peerage as Lord Nunburnholme. Like many other

Victorian businessmen the Wilsons bought their way into the establishment. They purchased country estates and forged strong connections with royalty and aristocracy. Arthur had built a brand new mansion, Tranby Croft, on the outskirts of Hull: an opulent edifice, a means of displaying his wealth, well-suited for entertaining those in high places.

Unfortunately for Arthur, his lavish hospitality hit the headlines for all the wrong reasons when he entertained the Prince of Wales and his entourage in 1897. A member of the Prince's party was accused of cheating at Baccarat and the ensuing Tranby Croft Affair, as it was known, led to a court case for libel that scandalized late Victorian Britain. Yet any embarrassment Arthur Wilson may have felt did little to dent his business reputation, and by the time his firm, Amos and Smith, were building *Viola*'s steam engines and boilers in 1905 he was one of the richest men in Hull. Today, Arthur Wilson's family having left the great house many years ago, Tranby Croft is now a private school but the Baccarat Room remains, a reminder of the long-gone era of the Prince of Wales, of leisure, opulence and questionable morality.

Although never as rich as the Wilsons, Charles Hellyer had also become a very wealthy man by the standards of the port. In the era of sailing smacks he had lived in a fine house in the well-to-do Coltman Street on the periphery of the Hessle Road district, but his involvement in steam trawling companies seems to have made him much larger sums of money. By the early 1900s he had purchased a grand, twelve bedroom house, Lambwath Hall, set amongst fields in the parish of Sutton, then a leafy, rural village on the northeastern outskirts of Hull. Here he too could entertain the great and the good of Edwardian Society. He also indulged his individual passion for the sea and for yachting, that most opulent of Edwardian leisure pursuits. In 1904 he had a large oak-framed yacht, *Rosalind*, built by Stow and Sons at Shoreham on the south coast of England. She was designed by the eminent naval architect, H.T. Stow, and Hellyer had her gaff rigged with three foresails and a spinnaker; at 86.5 feet she was almost as long as a contemporary North Sea steam trawler but far more elegant; she was built to hold her own amongst the most wealthy of vessels during an era of luxury and leisured style for a few. Her quarters were lavishly fitted out with woodwork, fittings and fixtures of the finest quality. She was a beautiful vessel: on *Rosalind* Hellyer could undoubtedly mix in rich and influential circles. Later, he sold *Rosalind* and had a second vessel, *Betty*—known under later ownership as *Tally Ho,* when she won the 1927 Fastnet Race—built to a design by Albert Strange. Both yachts survive to this day, though in far different corners of the world.

Leisure and opulence were far from high priorities when it came to fitting out *Viola* in the January of 1906. Her cost—fully fitted—was about £5,400 and, as with many of the other vessels, Hellyer seems to have raised a mortgage with the Union of London & Smith's Bank to pay off the construction bills.[21] Although perhaps a sophisticated fishing vessel by the standards of her time she would now be regarded as extremely basic. She was built on the flush deck principle with stiffened bulwarks of two foot six inches in height. Her hull was just over 108 feet in length and at her widest she was just over 21 feet. In the maritime vernacular she was described as being built with her bridge aft-side. In landsmen's terms this means she was built with her bridge behind her funnel, a rarity today but a common enough arrangement on early steam trawlers. Another feature of her bridge that differed from modern trawlers is that it was open to the elements. Her skipper and helmsman enjoyed no wheelhouse to protect them from the weather, they were almost as exposed as the old smacksmen. Vertical canvas sheets, known as dodgers, were the only additional protection provided on the bridge. It is often said that Charles Hellyer and other trawler owners who adopted this arrangement did so because they felt that an enclosed bridge may make the skipper too snug and not sufficiently focused on the job in hand—perhaps it was thought too opulent for the likes of working fishermen. Another explanation may have been the need to keep down costs; open bridges were cheaper to construct than closed ones. Moreover, open bridges probably provided the best all-round view which was important when working amongst the comparative congestion of a boxing fleet. Whatever the case, such open bridges were to prove exposed and sometimes dangerous places to be in winter storms. Apart from the helm for the hand steering gear, the bridge carried two compasses which were generally adjusted at least once each year. Hellyer boxing fleet trawlers also carried a *Cherub* taffrail log and, of course, leads and lines for checking the depth and the nature of the seabed.

Below decks, space was at a premium. Later trawlers had substantial superstructure and the crew's quarters tended to be more centrally situated, a more comfortable place to be in a heavy sea. But *Viola* and other early trawlers had little superstructure other than the small bridge and raised engine-room casing. Her compact hull was crammed with engine, boilers, bunkers and fish room so the tight crew's quarters were installed fore and aft in what space was left. Over the aft crew space was a steel watertight skylight with fixed lights of five feet in length and two foot six in width. Here, the mate and third hand had their quarters—replete with bunks and a table—from which abutted tiny cupboard-like cabins for the skipper and chief engineer. The fact that both had separate cabins reflects the importance of the engineer in the new set up. In the old sailing smacks, skippers had the skills to carry out almost every one of the jobs on the trawler, but running the engine-room required engineering skills they did not possess. Yet, the concessions to skipper and chief's status were minimal, their individual spaces were tiny and as the propeller shaft passed below the aft quarters, the vibration in heavy weather must have been tremendous. But even this situation was probably preferable to the quarters for the remaining six of the crew. They were crowded into the bows in the claustrophobic fo'c'sle, quarters which were subject to considerable movement in heavy seas. They were entered by a small companionway fitted with two folding doors on hinges, and what natural illumination there was came from a steel skylight three foot six inches long and two feet wide, with four lights; the height of the coaming being fifteen inches above the deck. The small galley—sometimes described as a small steel house—occupied the superstructure beneath the bridge. The galley was compact to say the least, being six feet long, seven feet wide and just six feet high. Meals were eaten in the cabin below.

The engine and boiler casing was raised above the deck by some three foot six inches; a large hinged steel skylight was situated above the engine-room whilst small hatches over that and the stokehold were there to provide additional light and also ventilation. There were also two distinctive fifteen-inch diameter cowl ventilators that extended to seven feet over the top of the stokehold section of the casing. The entrances to both the engine room and the aft crews quarters were by way of companionways through the hold.

These 'fleeters' carried little if anything in the way of washing facilities, and the toilet or heads, for want of a better name, was no more than a curved shelter on the starboard foreside of the ship. This shelter did apparently have one less obvious use for these type of fleeting trawlers. When navigating back up the Humber and approaching the village of Paull on the East Riding bank, skippers were reputed to be able to find the channel by taking a lining up from the bridge of the curved shelter of the heads with the navigation lights on shore, which as a result acquired the soubriquet amongst the fleet as the Shithouse Lights, a name that somehow never made it to the official estuary charts.

Viola's bunker space was substantial but, as in many steam trawlers, was increased by stowing coal in the forward hold during the early stages of the trip. This greatly extended the time the vessel could spend at sea, but the coal stored there had to be dragged in baskets through a low dark tunnel in the bowels of the ship—usually by the younger deckhands. Should this hold be required at any time as an additional fish room, then it had to be thoroughly cleaned; coal dust mixed with fish added nothing to its value.

Deck facilities continued the basic theme. The deck for'd of the long stove-pipe funnel was dominated by the great steam winch, a fundamental part of the steam trawler's equipment, used primarily for hauling the fishing gear from the depths of the sea but also for shipping and unshipping the trawler's boat, which was stowed for'd on the starboard side. Unlike many other vessels, the steering chains and other steering gear which linked the helm on the bridge with the rudder were open to the elements, and added to the mechanical clutter found around the deck. Much of the work of fishing was carried out on the deck for'd of the winch and the area was fitted with pounds—wooden dividers used for storing the fish—but otherwise was as open as possible given the constraints of space on such a compact vessel. As new, she was also fitted with two bower anchors of more than 4cwt, and ninety fathoms of cable.[22]

Almost as soon as her fitting out was completed in Hull's Humber Dock, *Viola* ventured out for the first time under her own steam, and sailed down the river and into the North Sea to undergo trials which included a run down a measured mile. These proved successful; she was handed over to Hellyers by mid-February 1906 and readied for her career in the boxing fleet.

III

NORTH SEA FLEETING

Viola's working life began on 20 February 1906. Family and friends waved goodbye to the crew as the trawler slipped out of St Andrew's Dock lock pit and sailed down a chilly Humber estuary with the rest of the Hellyer fleet. Like all boxing fleet trawlers she left port with scuppers awash—water almost on her decks—crammed to the gunnels with stores and more than 150 tons of bunker coal: sufficient to sustain a fishing trip of five weeks or more. Such heavy cargo could compromise stability; Samuel Plimsoll had successfully campaigned to have a load line painted on the side of British merchant ships: once a vessel had settled to this line in the water no more goods could be loaded. But trawlers were a law unto themselves: they had no Plimsoll Line—as it was known—on their hulls. They were not covered by these Board of Trade regulations because, it was argued, they consumed their cargo whilst fishing, even though it could take six or seven days of hard work in heavy seas to appreciably lighten their load.

Ten men signed on for the first trip, settling into their cramped berths as the ship sailed towards the North Sea. The old sailing smacks had typically shipped a crew of only five—skipper, mate and three deckhands—but the new steam trawlers carried more men with a wider range of specialist skills, and *Viola* was no exception. Her crew included a skipper, mate, third hand (bosun), two other deckhands and a spare hand, first and second engineers, fireman/trimmer and, last but not least, a cook. All found berths in the claustrophobic fore and aft cabins. Her first skipper was William Alexander, at thirty-nine already a widower with dependent children, as well as the oldest man on board, and a native of Great Yarmouth. He was probably a relative of the bosun, also an Alexander, who hailed from the same East Anglian town. The spare hand, twenty-three year old Edward Brocklesby, was the youngest man on board.[1]

It was not unusual to find a sprinkling of Yarmouth men amongst the Hull boxing fleet crews. Most had previously worked in Hewett's famous Short Blue boxing fleet, once the pride of the ancient East Anglian port. Hewett and Company were part of the old order, their name synonymous with generations of North Sea fishing fleets. In 1882 they had owned eighty-two trawling smacks but Hewetts eschewed steam, continued to expand, sticking almost solely to sail, and finally paid the price. As late as 1898 they still ran the largest fishing fleet in the world but within a few months Hewett and Company shut most of their operations, brought low by the unprofitability of their sailing smacks and finally finished by a catastrophic boiler explosion which destroyed much of their substantial maintenance workshops at Barking Creek on the Thames, in January 1899.[2] The firm did reconstitute and continue but on a vastly reduced scale.

William Alexander had probably moved to Hull in the mid 1890s, drawn by the prospect of better earnings, but many others must have followed in his wake during the last months of the old century, after Hewett's boxing fleet went down and they were thrown out of work as the once-proud sailing trawlers were laid up at Gorleston Quay. The demise of Hewett and Company's large fleet was the end of an era. Few people wanted these sailing trawlers: some of the redundant smacks were sold abroad at a knock-down price, others were converted into coastal trading ketches or else broken up, whilst many former Hewett sail fishermen moved on to the Humber where they shipped once more for the North Sea grounds, but this time on the new steam trawlers.

But now there was no time for nostalgia, and no standing on ceremony, when Hellyer's new steam fleet reached the grounds after a day or more's voyage from Hull. The sole purpose of each and every vessel was to catch fish and to catch them as efficiently, effectively and frequently as possible. Once on the grounds, life for *Viola* and her crew was governed by the shooting, towing and hauling of the trawling gear, the gutting and packing of fish and the transporting of fish boxes to and from the steam cutters. Theirs was a rigorous and seemingly unremitting regime that took scant account of time or weather.

Boxing fleet operations were directed by a man known as the admiral. He was always an experienced and successful skipper: an individual with a life-long knowledge of the sea and the haunts of the fish the fleet sought. Boxing fleet admirals in the steam trawling era often stood apart physically from the other skippers and their crews. A typical admiral was what was called a fine man—what today we would describe as fat. Few men in these fleets were overweight thanks to the sheer hard labour of their physically demanding work. Putting on weight in their society was an indication of having escaped such direct toil, a mark of affluence in much the same way as having a well-honed and constantly tanned body today might suggest that an individual has the time and money to work out at the gym or indulge in expensive foreign holidays. Certainly boxing fleet admirals owed their position to hard-won knowledge and experience and these, not physical labour, were the essential components of their profession. They had risen from deckhands at the very bottom of a crew to the top of their game, and psychologically were the hardest of the hard men who made up the workforce of the fleets, possessing the presence and force of personality needed to direct these iron and steam armadas and cope with whatever the North Sea threw at them. An admiral's trawler had a crosstree of lights affixed to the mast so it could be easily picked out by the rest of the fleet.

In that last pre-wireless era the admiral relied on visual signals to direct operations. During the day flags were used to signal when and where to fish, and after dusk rockets were deployed. Various colours and quantities of rocket were fired into the night sky to indicate different manoeuvres, but basically one green rocket was the signal for the fishing gear to be shot on the starboard tack whilst two white rockets signified it was time to haul the trawl. When steam trawlers worked on their own they used a large float known as a dan buoy which they set in the sea to track the stretch of ground they were working over, but these large boxing fleets used a mark-boat instead, generally an old sailing smack—later a redundant steam vessel—manned by older fishermen. This mark boat was moved from place to place in line with the admiral's thinking on the best grounds to trawl. By 1908, Hellyers were using one of the firm's oldest steam trawlers, *Eudocia*, built in 1890, for this purpose and she was expected to stay at sea with the fleet for between ten and twelve weeks at a time. The general rule was that all trawling operations were carried out within ten miles of the mark boat, which also acted as a rendezvous for the steam carriers. The fleet's pursuit of the best fishing grounds was known as skirmishing, and the admiral took daily account of the working position of the trawlers making the best yields when determining the overall direction to take.[3] His knowledge was seen as crucial to the fleet and this showed in the time he spent with it. The surviving log kept by Robert Glanville, a post-Great War admiral, shows that he spent an annual average of little more than nine weeks ashore during the years 1923 and 1924, and there is little reason to suppose this differed much from his Edwardian predecessors.[4] When the admiral's trawler ran low on fuel and sailed back to port, a deputy or vice-admiral took over until he returned.

The trawling operations generally spanned a six-hour period. *Viola* and her sisters usually shot their fishing gear around midday and then towed for around five or six hours, at a general speed of two and a half miles an hour. About five in the evening the signal to haul would come from the admiral's vessel, the engines were eased to 'dead slow', crew hurried up from below and, amidst a cacophony of clanging from the wheezing steam winch, the warps were gradually hauled from the depths until the net reappeared. Even with the aid of the winch, those on deck had to grapple with heavy sodden gear in the gathering gloom, dragging and tugging it aboard. Finally, the bulk of the cod end was reached and swung over the ship's side, its knot unleashed and a silvery mass of fish slipped and splashed into the pounds on the open deck. The knot was retied, the trawl hoisted back over the side and another tow began. Meanwhile the deck crew set to work with their knives, gutting, sorting and boxing the fish. A couple of moon boxes—paraffin lamps set in square metal containers with a glass on each vertical side—fixed to stan-

chions amongst the pound boards provided some sort of illumination for the
mate and bosun as they gutted and sorted the fish but, as former boxing fleet
skipper Herbert Johnson later recalled, the spare hand and anyone else working further forward of these lights could scarcely see to sort their fish on a
dark night.[5] Once each fish box was filled, metal tokens were affixed to its side
indicating the vessel and the species of fish, before it was either stowed below
in the fish room or, more often, stacked on the starboard deck to await transfer to the carrier.

Viola's trawl net was about 100 feet in length and when towed through
the water its mouth was between eighty and ninety feet wide. Steam trawlers deployed the otter trawl and in those days the so-called otter boards—a
form of vane—were directly attached to the net. When the net was brought
in, each otter board was clipped to one of two arch-shaped frames known as
gallows, respectively situated fore and aft on the port side. The boards were
quickly released and dropped into the seas when the gear was deployed once
more. The force of water passing between the otter boards as the trawl was
towed along the bottom of the sea pushed them apart and stretched open the
mouth of the net. The otter boards were connected to the trawler by wire
warps, and the length of the warps paid out was usually about three times
the depth of the water being trawled. One possible advantage of *Viola*'s open
bridge 'aftside'—behind the funnel—was that it made it easier for the skipper to observe the warps: he would judge the depth of the water he was towing in by the angle of the warps to the water and by the amount of spread,
that is the opening, of the wires.

Viola carried many hundreds of feet of heavy wire warps and, to the un-
initiated, their arrangement on deck looked complicated. The winch was the
key to the complex operations of setting, towing and hauling the trawl. A warp
from one of the winch's barrels passed round a centre fairlead (vertical roller),
thence round another midships fairlead before running over the after gallows.
The warp from the other barrel also passed over the centre fairlead then directly over the fore gallows and into the sea. On shore, Factories Act legisla-
tion required moving machinery to be guarded but such rules did not cover

trawlers at sea. Constant work amongst the open machinery of steam winch and rollers, amidst moving, heavy warp wires in the sea-washed half light of an exposed and rolling deck led to many accidents amongst fishermen, especially when fatigue set in.

Whilst much use was made of the accreted wisdom and experience of the admiral who directed the overall hunt, boxing fleets were not subject to Royal Naval style discipline. Working in relatively close proximity, most though not all of the vessels followed the admiral's broad directives; fishing on the tack indicated by his signals minimized the chance of collision. When trawling, each vessel set its mizzen, and sometimes mainsail, and the whole Hellyer fleet might cover an area of seven or eight square miles. Whilst the fishing gear was down every craft hoisted a ball in its rigging which was replaced at night by a white globular light, carried in addition to the ordinary mast-head and side lights.

Viola and her sisters were among that first generation of mechanized fish-catchers, and in some ways there was something typically industrial about the relationship between men and machine. The pace of life was usually dictated by the winch and the trawl. The faster the men were able to deal with the catch, the more rest they could hope to snatch below before the winch brought them on deck once more. A spate of full cod ends meant the crew made a good living, but brought on an endemic exhaustion: a deep fatigue unassuaged by all-too-brief respites between gutting and packing multitudes of fish. During a typical twenty-four hour period when fishing was good and weather permitted, trawling would commence around noon, with the gear hauled then reset between five and six pm. This procedure was repeated in the black of midnight: all deckhands out gutting and packing the catch once more. All were on deck yet again when the gear was hauled at 6am.

This seemed almost a continuous production process, yet it was not conventional industrial activity, the pitching deck was no factory. This was not mere mechanistic processing of raw material. There was something far more ancient, more elemental about these salt-stained configurations of seafarers, steam and steel. These steam trawler crews were still hunters at heart and their toil took place against the myriad moods of an ever changing maritime canvas: a backdrop of drab green-grey skies giving way to shimmering silver seascapes; pitching waves to flat calm; claustrophobic foghorn-filled evenings to clear, coal-black or radiant moon-gold nights. This hunting ground was a harsh, uncertain, windblown wilderness, incessantly reworked by weather and waves, and set beneath an enormous star-filled universe that dwarfed even the vastness of the sea. But fishermen had little time to dwell on such perceptions of natural beauty. Together, the skippers, ships and crews of the boxing fleet pursued their prey in all sorts of weather through all four seasons: a pack of ever-hungry vessels, relentlessly scouring the watery wastes, far out in the North Sea, far from the gas-lit streets, from the industry, factories, furnaces and welcoming home hearths of Edwardian England.

Life for the deckhands was not all fishing. Each hand had to stand a watch, take his turn spelling at the helm for the skipper or mate and play his part in the running of the ship. Fish boxes had to be washed, and repaired with hammer and nails if necessary then stowed below, whilst the ashes from the boiler fires needed pulling up for the fireman in heavy weather. This was a particularly awkward job, with as many as twenty or more buckets of ash being hauled up from below on one watch. *Viola* had no ash chutes: the ash was pitched bodily over the side or let go on the deck to be washed through the scuppers. Even the task of lighting the vessel each night could prove an arduous one. The paraffin lights were first lit—difficult enough on an open windy deck—then hauled aloft, but in rough weather they were often dashed against the mast whilst being raised, went out, and the whole procedure had to be repeated.

The fireman trimmer needed deep resources of strength. His work in the pitching, dark interior of the vessel involved the shifting of around one hundred and fifty tons of coal from bunkers to stokehold every trip. *Viola*'s furnace consumed an average of four to four and a half tons of coal a day, which meant she had sufficient fuel for about 35 or so days at sea. All of it was moved by hand. On either side of *Viola*'s stokehold there were wing coalbunkers whilst a thwartship bunker ran right across midships. Foreside of the thwartship bunker was the hold where the bulk of the coal was stored on boxing fleet voyages. A dark sloping tunnel around eight feet long led through to the stokehold. As each voyage progressed and the coal in the fore part of the hold was consumed, the trimmer had first to shovel and throw an amount of coal into the tunnel then crawl in and throw it on into the stokehold. The coal had to be kept evenly spread or trimmed—hence the name trimmer—to prevent the ship developing a list. Towards the end of the voyage, as coal supplies depleted, the trimmer sometimes had to make several throws to get coal into the stokehold.

After the trawl was hauled and the catch dropped on to the deck around five or six in the morning, the gear was generally stowed for a few hours. The main task most mornings was to transfer fish boxes to the steam cutter, and in any weather this was some feat. There were clear rules for this procedure that all concerned were expected to follow, for with more than forty craft converging on the cutter on a busy day, the danger of collision was all too evident. As the vessels assembled, the admiral's trawler stood off from the cutter to oversee proceedings and the other trawlers started to circle in an anti-clockwise direction. Once signal flags were hoisted from the carrier's mainmast, the proceedings began. As each steam trawler bore down on the cutter in turn, the boxes of fish were stacked ready amidships on the starboard side. Then the rowing boat was launched, and once the mate and bosun climbed in, the deckhands hauled each box in turn on to the rail, they pushed them over the side to the mate who threw them across the pitching boat to the bosun who stacked them as best he could. The cook was also on the job: he had to take the stern rope and every time the trawler rolled and the boat went off he had to pull her close in again. The boats were clinker built and beamy, specially constructed for the job being about seventeen feet long, three feet in depth and seven feet wide. Three crew members usually went in the boat, although they were designed to be rowed by two men. The oarsmen were widely spaced and in an unusual formation, one faced the bow and the other the stern. All-round visibility was essential in such operations to protect a load of up to thirty substantial fish boxes.

The daily process of transfer was the most perilous part of the whole fleeting business and extremely difficult in any wind. Boats often overturned in the heavy swells and fractious cross currents. The cutter was always boarded on the starboard side and trawler laid on the port tack. If there was any wind the skipper brought his vessel as close as he dared to the cutter's weather bow. He tried to stay there, providing some vestige of shelter, until the boat was able to round the cutter's weather bow. Rowing the heavily laden little craft from trawler to cutter was first and foremost an act of sheer physical labour. A transfer in rough seas stretched the strength and skills of the oarsmen to their limits, and as the rowing boats came alongside the cutter in a pitching sea, they ran the danger of being dashed against its sides. The third member of the boat's crew, poised on the bow thwart, waited for a moment when a wave lifted the small craft to the level of the steamer's rail then, gripping the end of the long painter in his teeth, he leapt for the deck. In an instant he was on board, made the rope fast then grabbed at the fish boxes as they were lugged rather than thrown towards him by his shipmates as the waves brought the boat to his level once more. In a heavy sea the practicalities of heaving and grabbing such heavily laden boxes were formidable. There were hand holes at either end of the box but these could not always be grasped. Gloves were rarely worn, fingers could be trapped, boxes might slip, but once grasped they were pulled, shoved, dragged, almost anyway or anyhow, on to the rolling deck. Although at least a couple of life-jackets and a lifebelt were carried in the boat, they seem rarely to have been worn. Yet the boat's crew regarded the sharp knives they carried in their pockets as essential for survival and they certainly saved lives for, in the chaos by the carriers, a rowing boat's line sometimes caught round the larger vessel's propeller and unless the errant rope could be quickly cut the little craft was dragged under.

Each rowing boat also carried a bag containing spare wooden thawl pins, two or three sheets of lead, a block of tallow, copper nails and corks. Thawls were often used instead of rowlocks whilst the tallow, lead and nails were to make emergency repairs to the boat should it be thrown against cutter or trawler and damaged. Once the boat came under the lee of the cutter, the skipper headed straight out, away from the centre of the melee, so the next trawler could approach. The skipper then took his vessel round in a wide sweep to the port then closed in once more, this time, to the cutter's starboard quarter trying to protect the little boat on its return. Not surprisingly, given the harsh treatment they endured, these rowing boats had a short working life and were usually worn out and replaced within eighteen months. The trawlers themselves were worked remarkably hard. An analysis of *Viola*'s running logs for the years 1907 to 1909 inclusive shows the vessel spent an average of little more than six weeks in port each year, including her annual refit.

Many people who witnessed the boarding process were truly overawed by this raw struggle of strength and skill on the open sea. E.J. Mather, founder of the Royal National Mission for Deep Sea Fishermen, first saw the process of ferrying back in the 1880s and was amazed:

> For more than twenty years I have been accustomed to boating, had pulled my 33 miles a day against the stream, had taken an oar in a rough sea in quest of a capsized boat but never had I seen rowing like this.[6]

A few snatches of grainy film taken in the 1920s are all that survives to show us the boarding process but these old flickering images convey something of this awesome task, a black and white, albeit silent testimony to the incredible everyday skills and seamanship of boxing fleet fishermen.

The Hellyer fleet initially built five steam cutters to carry the fleet's boxes to market and, like the trawlers, they also had Shakespearian names: *Cleopatra*, *Hamlet*, *King Lear*, *Caesar* and *Brutus*.[7] Earle's Shipbuilding Company of Hull had been building such craft since at least 1879, and many contemporaries regarded them as amongst the finest seagoing craft of the early twentieth century, capable of weathering the heaviest seas. They needed to be: theirs was the unrelenting task of running, heavily laden, between fleet and port, of finding the catchers, collecting up the catch and then driving through the seas with the telegraph at full speed.[8] Despite everything the elements could throw at them, more often than not they would make the morning market. Charles Hellyer built the fleet with an original intention of running most of his fish into the Hull market, but from January 1907 he was directing all of his cutters to Billingsgate.[9]

On reaching Billingsgate's wharves on the Thames, the turn-around time of these cutters was close to modern standards. They were usually in port just long enough to unload the fish, take on board fresh boxes and replenish supplies. The Hellyer trawling fleet was constantly at sea from 1906 to 1914 and the task of running its catches into Hull or Billingsgate never ceased. The cutters were celebrated for the scant account they took of the weather. Whether heading to or from the fleet, their decks were often awash with water when driven hard through the worst of conditions. Their standing order was to make the morning market and thus obtain the best prices, so the pressures on cutter's skipper and crew were considerable. On reaching the grounds they first faced the task of finding the fleet, which—in the pre-radio era—could be an exasperating experience even in fine weather and in poor visibility seems almost impossible to the layman. The fleet's trawlers were following the best fishing and the admiral may have steamed them up to fifty or a hundred miles from their previous position.

In an attempt to ensure continuity, one cutter often reached the fleet before a sister vessel left and then remained on station until the following morning and the next transfer. On station, but not idle: all the cutters were rigged for trawling and if they had time to spare they tried a haul or two of their own for the benefit of their owners and crew, but their primary purpose was to carry fish and as soon as the loading was completed they drove hard for the Humber or Thames, not steadying until they took on a pilot at Gravesend. The ultimate aim remained to make Billingsgate before the market opened at 5am.

The cutters passed under Tower Bridge and into the Pool of London before coming alongside the busy wharves in the heart of the City. Billingsgate was an ancient market, a centuries-old centre of the food trade, a site literally steeped in the business of provisioning London. Since the late 1600s it had increasingly specialised in fish. And fish of all sorts, shapes and sizes came through its portals: fresh water species from rivers and lakes, salmon from Scotland, Ireland and Norway, salt water fish of almost every variety found round Britain's coasts and beyond, shell fish, round fish, flat fish and eels packed variously in hampers, baskets, trunks or boxes. So much fish: fish to feed the myriad mouths of the metropolis, rich and poor, young and old alike. The scale of Billingsgate's transactions had grown with the city. A new market building had been constructed in the Italianate style between 1847 and 1851 but by the 1870s this was stretched beyond capacity and re-built once more. But the new edifice crowded onto much the same old site and the trade continued to grow. Approaching visitors could smell the fish and hear the bustle before reaching the market. On the landward or city side, the surrounding streets were jammed with horse-drawn fish vans and carts carrying consignments from Paddington, Shoreditch, Camden Town, Kings Cross and other railway stations across the capital. Fish was forward-ed by train from every quarter of Britain but Billingsgate's medieval site was tucked away from the Victorian railway terminals. It was built hard against that older thoroughfare, the river, and much fish still arrived by water by way of the ancient quays.

As soon as a cutter from the boxing fleets tied up at Billingsgate, anoth-er order of activity enveloped the vessel. Before daybreak, under the bright glare of new electric lights, an army of men—the fish porters—clad in white smocks, black hard hats and clogs, streamed aboard up one of two hurriedly laid gang planks then hastened ashore by way of the other, carrying boxes of fish on their heads. A clamour of clogs, cries and curses carried across the cold quayside air as the ship's dark hold was rapidly emptied, its boxes rushed into the market and mixed amongst a teeming mass of fish and men converg-ing from every direction. By 5am the fish salesmen were ready at their stands, the market bell was rung and Billingsgate opened for frenetic trading. A vast amount of trade was done in the first hour or so of business through auctions and the like: first to the capital's fishmongers—they catered for the more af-fluent—then afterwards the costermongers, London's street traders, took their share. The task of forwarding the wares of this ancient fish factory con-tinued through much of the morning. Meanwhile, outside on the Thames, the cutter was reloading with ice and boxes and preparing for sea to search once more for the boxing fleet.

Out on the grounds the boxing fleets continued their unrelenting hunt but the fish they took, although common property, were far from free. Like all fishermen, before and since, they paid a cruel price, a tithe seemingly counted in terms of men and boats, ships and souls. No groups of fishermen, no ports or fishing villages, however large or small, ancient or modern, escaped these dreadful dues. All working the North Sea were at risk and the later nineteenth century had witnessed a string of disasters that struck at the very core of many fishing communities. Just north of the border with England, the little Scottish town of Eyemouth still marks Black Friday, 14 October 1881. That day 189 local Berwickshire fishermen lost their lives: they had put to sea on an apparently calm morning after weeks of bad weather and had just set their lines when a sudden, savage storm descended on the fishing grounds. Many of the 129 Eyemouth men who were subsequently drowned lost their lives as their small boats were smashed onto the rocks when they attempted to make harbour. Two years later a large number of east coast trawlermen, many from the boxing fleets, were drowned in the Great Gale of 1883 whilst in December 1894 Hull alone lost eight smacks and six steam trawlers in a gale of hurricane-like proportions.[10] Although such large-scale disasters were not regularly repeated after steam trawling was established, the sea continued to take individual fishermen, occasionally one or more vessels and sometimes whole crews: a steady attrition, a toll that continued without fail, throughout the Edwardian period, every single year down to 1914, and on throughout most of the twentieth century.

The Hellyer fleet's baptism came quickly, on its first voyage. After about three weeks at sea the trawlers were caught by violent storms which raged across the North Sea grounds on and around 12 March. *Viola*'s sister ship *Antonio*, built alongside her on the stocks at Beverley and launched just a few weeks earlier, was last seen on that day then disappeared from the surface of the sea. None of her crew were seen or heard of again and to this day no one knows for sure what happened to either them or to their ship.[11] Yet this was not the first such disappearance and certainly not the last as the more than forty-year controversy that surrounded the disappearance of the stern trawler *Gaul* in 1974 so graphically illustrates.

Antonio may well have succumbed to a similar accident to that which almost overwhelmed another member of the Hellyer fleet during the same gales. The extreme weather seems to have disrupted fishing and dispersed the fleet; after dodging head to wind, the trawler *Honoria* lay to for a couple of hours. At midnight the mate William Windsor and deckhand John Townend relieved the skipper on watch on the bridge with orders to keep eyes open for the rest of the fleet. The gale did not abate and around 2am the skipper awoke to the sound of a great sea being shipped and on rushing up the companion-way he met a wall of water that swamped the cabin. He struggled upward, onto the deck, jumped for the bridge but mate and deckhand were nowhere to be seen, the telegraph was on full speed ahead just where it had been when the missing men went on watch. A huge sea had overwhelmed the open bridge, sweeping mate and deckhand away, the ship's boats and the lifebelts had also been washed overboard. The trawler's situation was now perilous: the force of the sea had shifted the bunker coal and she lay on her beam-ends with one side under the water. The skipper quickly called the rest of the crew from the forward accommodation and they began a desperate fight for survival. Unless they could right the vessel, they were lost. They worked frantically, shifting the coal to trim the vessel and pumping water out of the hull. Eventually, after a long struggle, the vessel was righted and a vain attempt was made to find mate and deckhand in the patchy darkness. The forlorn search was eventually abandoned and the vessel headed back to the Humber. On the same day as she returned, the steam cutter *Ariadne* also arrived back in St Andrews Dock with damage from the storm.[12]

Viola did not entirely avoid the hazards of the profession in the early months of her career. On 29 September 1906, less than six months after entering service, she was involved in a collision on the grounds some 130 miles east by north of Spurn Point, not long after returning to the fleet. The steam cutter *Caesar*, which was taking the opportunity to trawl whilst waiting to load

boxes of fish for Billingsgate, towed into *Viola* causing slight damage to her
port beam. Collisions were a hazard of such close working and she was able
to stay out on the grounds for her full trip but on returning to port, William
Alexander, her skipper, was discharged by Hellyers and replaced by William
Casson, a native of Hull who also lived off Hessle Road.[13] Less than three
months later, the trawler had just embarked on her seventh voyage to the fleet
and was making her way out to sea from St Andrew's Dock when gathering mist and deteriorating light obliged her to anchor in the river a few miles
downstream of Hull near the remote Paull Holm Buoy. Here, in thick fog, the
steam trawler *Terrier* ran into her at about 5.30 in the afternoon. Such collisions in the Humber amidst its fast flowing tides and sandbanks could prove
fatal but *Viola* limped back to St Andrew's Dock with a damaged stern.[14] The
next day she was sent for repairs and her entire crew was discharged: in the
owner's eyes you didn't keep a crew on pay when they couldn't earn. Repairs
were completed within two weeks and she sailed once more for the fleet on
the morning of 1 January 1907.

The combination of rough weather, fatigue and relentless work was a constant cause of injuries and all too often loss of life. On 4 February 1907, *Viola*'s
third skipper. John McCue, reportedly turned dizzy and fell whilst ascend-
ing the cabin companionway steps, sustaining two severe scalp wounds. The
fifty-three year old was sent back to port by way of a returning trawler the next
day and taken to his home in one of the terraces of St George's Road in the
heart of the Hessle Road district. He never recovered and died there a few
days later on 10 February leaving a wife, Clara, and two grown up daughters.
There would be no pension or compensation for the widowed spouse, just a
settling up of what was owed. Yet even before John had passed away, there
was already a new master at *Viola*'s helm. A replacement skipper, Edward
Lodge, had travelled down to London then shipped out by way of the cutter as
the trawler and fleet continued their work.

Salt water boils, trapped fingers and influenza took their toll of crew members over the ensuing years and in August 1907, one B. Petty was discharged
from service at sea by the skipper and sent in with the steam cutter *Lorenzo*

after a week on the grounds because he was considered to be incompetent as a cook.[15] In a life lived on cold grey seas and governed by the monotony of constant fishing, eating was one of the few immediate pleasures to look forward to. Mealtimes on these trawlers assumed an especially important significance, and poorly prepared food was a source of unwanted aggravation and unrest amongst the crew.

As on other vessels, the task of ferrying fish from trawler to cutter was the most arduous of the daily jobs and a common cause of injury. In October 1911, for example, *Viola*'s third hand, William Dawson, badly injured his hand whilst apparently lugging the boxes between boat and cutter, and in the following December the second hand, N.C. Hess, a Norwegian born in Bergen, injured his back after jumping on to the cutter *King Lear* and pulling boxes on board. A few weeks later, another crew member smashed his little finger between the boat and ship's side as they came alongside in heavy seas after transferring fish, a common occurrence when fleeting and an accident that happened more than once to *Viola*'s crew members. Ferrying fish in bad weather was particularly daunting and in December 1911 the log recalls that the skipper, George Richards, threatened the third hand C. Harmer with 'punishment according to the law' after he refused to go in the boat. In the event, all seem to have thought better of it for the log also records that no proceedings or action were actually taken.[16]

In the early days of fleeting few knew much of the hazardous life it represented and there was little done for those who were injured other than to put them on a trawler returning to port, but by *Viola*'s time things had changed. Thanks to the efforts of Ebenezer Mather, who founded what became the Royal National Mission for Deep Sea Fishermen, the Edwardian boxing fleets were supported by Mission Vessels, financed by public subscription, which provided fishermen with medical aid, warm clothing, tobacco and bibles: spiritual support but no spirituous liquors. The Royal National Mission continues its invaluable work supporting fishing communities to this day.[17]

Most boxing trips on *Viola* lasted between five and six weeks. Individual trawlers left the fleet when coal and provisions were close to exhaustion and

then ran for the Humber. The latter part of the trip and on the voyage home
was also a time when the skipper needed to be particularly skilled in his seamanship, for by this time most of the coal had been consumed and virtually
all the fish had been sent by carrier to London. The vessel was returning light
and its stability had changed drastically from the outward bound voyage when
it was laden with coal, feedwater and stores. Such empty vessels probably ran
a real danger of capsizing in heavy seas. In those days, issues of vessel stability were much more a question of a shipbuilder's judgement than of exact
calculation. It would be a further half-century before the fishing industry took
stability issues seriously enough to include them in the examinations for skippers and mates' proficiency certificates—tickets, as they were known down
the dock. It was not until after the notorious loss of *Gaul*, a modern factory
freezer ship, that we came to fully understand the full process of capsize in a
fishing vessel.

As *Viola* came up the estuary and approached the dock, souwesters and
the like were discarded as the crew changed into civvies, anxious to make the
most of four or five days of rest and recuperation at home. At that time virtually every trawlerman lived within at most a couple of miles of St Andrew's
Dock. The Hessle Road district from which they were drawn was built on the
business of the sea. The crowded streets and terraces of the area—Brighton
Street, Manchester Street, Eastbourne Street, Strickland Street, Eton Street
and many more—were home to fishermen, merchant seamen and those who
found their livelihood repairing and maintaining ships, working on the docks
or handling, processing and forwarding fish. This was a vibrant, energetic
place. A teeming mass of churches, chapels, factories and fish-curing houses,
pubs and drinking clubs and, of course, shops: shops of every description
from provision merchants to pawnbrokers, pork butchers to pie sellers, tailors
to tripe dressers. Immediately to the south, running parallel with all this, were
the docks and the broad brown mud estuary, the very vitals that sustained
Hessle Road's life and light.

In earlier decades, in the days of sail, when the trawling trade had been
establishing itself, the trawlers and smackowners dwelt quite close together.

Many of the latter had risen from the ranks of the deckhands. Although the owners of the trawling smacks were always more affluent than those they employed, the social divide had not at first been particularly wide. Yet by the time *Viola* worked the North Sea fleets, the catching sector of the industry was in the hands of rich men. The owners who had successfully adapted to the shift from sail to steam had mostly become substantial, wealthy and well-connected capitalists. A few still lived amongst the more prosperous fish merchants and the like down the well-to-do Hessle Road thoroughfares such as The Boulevard or Coltman Street, but the big players had followed many of the merchant shipowners and moved out to the leafy, attractive villages which surrounded Hull. Charles Hellyer was a case in point. In the 1880s he had lived in a residence off Coltman Street, within a mile of the Fish Dock, but by the 1900s owned Lambwath Hall, a substantial residence on the outskirts of the rural village of Sutton, some five or six miles away.

Back on Hessle Road, the crews made the most of the short time their trawler was in port: a few days of frenetic activity after weeks of hard, uncertain work on grey unforgiving seas far from home. Their livelihood did little to encourage a long term view of life, and for many there was an almost insatiable immediacy about the short time ashore. It was a time to live life to the full. Home to greet wives, parents or children, a wash in the scullery or in the tin bath set on the clip mat in front of the kitchen range, perhaps another change of clothes, then out, out into the smoke, lights and noise of the district's pubs and clubs. Some ventured a little further, heading for the pubs, theatres and music halls of Hull's Old Town, still a magnet today for Hull folk seeking to escape the working week's grind. Compared with the rest of the twentieth century, licensing laws in Edwardian England were remarkably liberal. Members of the crew, young and old, could drink late into the evening. Parties back home for family and friends sometimes followed. Many trawlermen were notorious for being profligate with money when they had it, thought little of giving a backhander to others out of a ship: children, parents and pals were lavishly treated whilst earnings lasted. Trawling and trawling terminology permeated the very vernacular of Hessle Road language. A woman down one of the local streets who was thought to know everyone's business—when her neighbours' husbands were sailing and in what ship—acquired the soubriquet of 'Mrs Mark-Boat' after the mark-boat of the boxing fleet which knew where each vessel was working.

Yet such apparent prosperity could easily yield to poverty as fishermen and their families—like the whalers before them—understood all too well. Trawlermen were classed as casual labour, hired for the single trip with no guarantee of being taken on again. With total wages substantially dependent on their share of the proceeds of the trawler's catch, a few poor trips could spell penury, as would a spell out of a ship. Even a skipper was not immune. His earnings might be high for a while but a few poor performances, or a collision causing damage amongst the crowded boxing fleet, could see him sacked and out of a ship. The owners, with a keen eye on the bottom line, were not slow to try someone else on the bridge.

Trawlermen's wives usually bore the practical brunt of such uncertainty, for they had to run every aspect of family life during the long weeks their husbands were at sea. They had to make ends meet between the brief bouts of extravagant living that often followed the end of a good trip. Mothers were left to deal with the situation on the all-too-frequent occasions that husbands—the main breadwinners—were lost at sea. The loss of the breadwinner was a catastrophic occurrence at all levels. In 1893, for example, Skipper John Johnson was lost with all hands on a trawler in the North Sea. He left a wife, Charlotte, in her thirties, and eight young children. She had little to fall back on but was determined to keep the family together—to keep them out of the orphans' home—even though she received no more than five loaves and 3/6d from the parish each week. After paying 2/6d rent for a modest house in Manchester Street, she was left with 1/- a week to keep the family. To make ends meet she took work washing and ironing. Without modern appliances this was a long and hard drudge, starting each load around 7am and often continuing washing and drying until 6 or 7 in the evening, sometimes not completing ironing until 9 or 10 at night. Charlotte's income was very low: she might earn 1/6d for the washing and 3d extra for the ironing. Her aim was to survive, keep all together, until the older children could start contributing, although eventually, when things became so tight that she could not make ends meet, she had to take a heartbreaking decision and put one of the boys in the orphanage until he was old enough to work.[18]

The absence of any long term security and the struggle to keep at bay the all-too-close spectre of poverty was the lot of many working people in Edwardian England, particularly those whose lives were bound up in one way or another with the uncertain business of fishing. Billy Wells, a fisherman in the boxing fleets from 1910, later a mate and a skipper, recalled how his father, a boilermaker for one of the engineering firms serving the fishing industry, died not long before he was born. His widowed mother had six children to sustain and managed on a seasonal income of 3/9d a day in the fish trade. Her work, smoking herrings, often involved twelve hour days and more, but being seasonal it sometimes took her to other ports as the trade followed the herring shoals, and she was forced to make arrangements to have her children looked after when she was away. She supplemented her income providing lodgings for visiting women during the winter, when Norwegian herring were imported into Hull in large quantities to satisfy the kipper trade, but outside of these seasons there was little call for her labour; with no money coming in she had no choice but to fall back on the parish. To obtain sustenance she was required to labour in the workhouse laundry and young Billy was sent along to Hull's Anlaby Road workhouse to pick up the supplies of bread and provisions made available by the parish. He never forgot the workhouse, describing it many decades later as a fearful place, with iron grills at the windows of the area where those with mental illnesses were lodged, whilst old men chopped cinders for the boilers in dark cellars.[19]

Many families like the Wells and Johnsons had to make agonising decisions about placing one or more of their children in a workhouse or orphanage when times were really hard, so that the rest of the family could be adequately fed. Much was made in the later twentieth century about Victorian values, and whilst there was parish charity available for all in late Victorian and Edwardian Britain, all too often it was a begrudging, mean-spirited affair. Those claiming parish relief were stigmatized, were left in no doubt that they were claiming charity—albeit such meagre fare that it scarcely kept body and soul together. Workhouse Boards of Guardians had one main performance indicator: that was to keep down the cost of the poor rate, and at that many were formidably efficient. It was not unknown in fishing ports for trawler owners to be on a Board of Guardians.

But many of those forced into such strictures proved resilient. The Johnson and Wells families scraped through the worst years. The Johnson girls started in service as soon as they were able but, although earning their keep, their weekly wage of little more than 2/6d meant they were unable to provide much for the family pot. Billy Johnson, the eldest lad, was set to be apprenticed to a whitesmith at the age of fourteen, but after a few months experience in the trade decided that he could serve his family more immediately by going to sea. He took his first trip to the boxing fleets as a cook, was sacked and then went a few trips as trimmer, then a few more as deckhand. He opted for the deck and determined on reaching the bridge. After spells as deckhand, bosun and mate, he took his skipper's ticket at the age of twenty-three. He joined the Hellyer fleet and became one of the most popular figures on St Andrew's Dock in those last years before the Great War until his untimely loss in late 1913.[20]

Indeed, all the boxing fleet skippers had worked their way up through the ranks. Many of those who went on to skipper Hellyer vessels in the following years had begun like Billy Johnson, trying their hand as a deckie or trimmer; a few shipped as cook. Billy's brother Herbert, who was a skipper by 1912, had done a couple of pleasure trips during the summer—to get a feel for the sea— with his uncle when twelve and thirteen. When he left school at fourteen he tried a trip as trimmer between shore jobs and went to sea on the trawlers in earnest from the age of sixteen. By the age of twenty-two he was a skipper with the Great Northern fleet and within a few months joined the Hellyer fleet. As both brothers moved through the ranks they were able to provide support for their widowed mother and siblings. The family moved from a poor terrace house in Manchester Street to a better property on a street further down Hessle Road.

The emotional impact of such bitter-sweet experiences of family warmth
and adversity often resonated through generations of Hessle Road families—
they had long memories—as one surviving story of *Viola*'s early years illustrates. On 7 August 1907 John Hill signed on the trawler as second hand or
Mate. Hill was by then forty-nine and had spent much of the last few years
working for George Beeching and other trawling firms. He completed just
one trip on *Viola* and was classed as very good on his discharge at the end of
the trip.[21] Hill had been born in Rotherham but his father, a painter and decorator, had moved his family to Hull a few years later. He had first gone to sea
on smacks as an apprentice and worked as bosun and mate before making the
transition to working on steam trawlers in the 1890s. Like many other trawlermen from the boxing fleet, he carried a knife everywhere, indeed, Hill slept
with it under his pillow, whether afloat or at home. He married, had seven
children, five girls and two boys and over the years the family moved—flitted
as it was known locally—from house to house in the streets off Hessle Road.

No picture of John Hill seems to have survived but from family stories he
seems to have been a proud man with a fine moustache. He had, in common
with many of his compatriots, a liking for a few pints between trips which
could cause tensions at home. On one occasion his wife, Frances, not best
pleased at finding him sleeping off a session, caused ructions by snipping off
half his prized moustache whilst he slept. His two lads went to sea but entered the merchant navy, sailed on 'bigboats' as they were called in Hull. One
day about this time, so the story goes, these two young men were both home
from sea at the same time and went drinking around Hull's Old Town. After a
few pints they wandered into the Shambles—an area full of butchers and the
like—and at the 'back a market' as it was known locally, bought a couple of
young goslings. Why, no one is sure but on the way back home they continued
their spree, calling in countless pubs. Youths and goslings alike, all drank until incapable. On reaching home they staggered into the scullery and left two
drunken goslings to sway out into the yard. One promptly fell over the back

step and broke its neck but the other not only survived but thrived. It acquired the soubriquet of Micky Dripping, became a close companion of Frances, an unusually tall woman for her time, and usually accompanied her when shopping. Not unnaturally, the goose took a great fancy to the greengrocers' wares. The six foot woman, known locally as the Duchess, and her white goose were a picturesque part of the Edwardian Hessle Road scene.

John Hill's eventual demise was less rosy. Almost a year after he left *Viola* he was remanded on bail at Hull Police Court to await sentence having been found guilty of willful disobedience on board the trawler *Owl*. On 22 July 1908 he had signed on the *Owl*, owned by Kelsall Brothers and Beeching, ordered to report to sea at 12 noon. According to the family, John was taken quite ill, developed bronchitis or the like and was soon running a temperature. He was really unfit to sail and never turned up; *Owl* left St Andrews Dock without him. When found at home, although ill, he was sent out to the trawler waiting in the roadstead by motor boat. Once on board, according to the witness testimony, he told the skipper he wanted to go ashore again. On reaching the mouth of the Humber, off Spurn Point, he turned in and refused to take his watch at midnight. Hill continued to refuse to work and was eventually sent ashore on the steam trawler *Wing*. In October he was sentenced by the Police Court to six weeks in prison.[22] The incident, and the actions of the owners in prosecuting him, still aroused bitterness amongst his children and grandchildren more than sixty years later.[23] His previous record, so far as can be gleaned from the surviving logs, was exemplary both with Kelsalls and other trawling firms. After years of going to sea and never missing the tide something seems finally to have snapped; his treatment was merely one of a catalogue of indictments laid against some of the trawler owners of the period. By the time of his illness or breakdown he was one of the oldest men still sailing to the boxing fleets. Whatever the cause, whether physical or mental, John Hill had clearly had enough. He completed his sentence, never recovered physically, and died the following year.

Whilst the boxing fleet fishermen had from four to five days ashore, those voyaging to places such as Iceland or the Barents Sea generally managed about forty-eight hours between trips. This reflected the different voyage length: the distant water trawlerman was usually away for up to three weeks compared with the boxman's five and a half weeks. Either way, by modern standards both seem all-too-brief periods of rest. Many fishermen might change ships on several occasions during the year and take the opportunity during the summer of having a few weeks ashore. Trawlermen who stuck more or less to one vessel usually had a few weeks' break when their vessel was laid up for its annual summer survey.

The casual nature of trawling meant that the labour force shipped aboard *Viola*, like the other vessels in the boxing fleets, was very mobile. Crews and skippers changed trawlers regularly, *Viola* having at least ten skippers during her eight year trawling career, and although most of the crew lived or lodged close in the Hessle Road district or Old Town, many hailed originally from much further afield, their background still sometimes illustrating links with the pioneers from the south-west. William Blewitt, skipper of *Viola* in 1910, and his wife for example, were a case in point. William was stepfather to three children; his wife Elizabeth, who hailed from Brixham, was a widow and ten years his senior. William himself hailed from Lostwithiel in Cornwall. The Blewitt household had lived in Hull's Old Town in the early 1890s but later lived on West Dock Avenue off Hessle Road. William moved on from *Viola* to skipper other Hellyer vessels, including *Beatrice* and it was on this latter vessel that he and his crew rescued most of the crew of a sinking Swedish barque in February 1912, an action which led to Blewitt and several crew members being awarded medals and a silver cup by the King of Sweden.[24]

Many individually intriguing personalities took charge of *Viola* during the vessel's long working life but one of the most striking of these was Green Willows Tharratt, also known, amongst other names, as George William Tharratt, skipper of the trawler in 1912. To describe his personal history and career as chequered would be something of an understatement.

George, as we will call him, was born in 1868, the son of Willows and Caroline Tharratt in Sunk Island, a remote area of reclaimed land lying downstream of Hull on the banks of the Humber estuary. The family later moved to Hull where his father was a police officer who rose to the rank of sergeant before being dismissed from the force in April 1882 mainly for what was described as 'carrying on an improper intimacy with a prostitute.' But even whilst his father was still in the police force, young George was in trouble with the law, being described as a ringleader of a gang of about fifty boys, when charged with disorderly conduct in February 1881. The caution he received seems to have had little effect, for a few months later he was brought before the magistrates once more, this time charged with stealing from the house of a local baker. Sometime after this he signed up as a fishery apprentice on sailing trawlers but was soon back in court and sentenced to six weeks' hard labour, along with another fisherlad, for cutting the trawl warp of the sailing trawler *Foundling* whilst at sea. His troubles continued and at the age of sixteen he was again sentenced to gaol, this time for three months for stealing two silver watches from the house where he lodged. He was alleged to have pawned one of the watches and given the other to a prostitute.

In the 1880s many trawler apprentices had criminal convictions, though often for desertion as well as criminal damage, and these misdemeanors did not hold back his seagoing career. By 1904 he was already a steam trawler skipper, later sailing mainly on Hellyer Boxing fleet trawlers, including *Cassio*, *Beatrice* and *Rosalind*. Wiry framed, five foot ten inches tall and with a character which seems to have been as unyielding as an ocean, he had reached the top of the steam trawling trade but not before he had been married twice. George was first married when 19 years old, in April 1887, to Rosetta Askwith but when he remarried in August 1893, to Elizabeth Ann Ellis, a widow with several children some years older than himself, at the Congregational Church on Hessle Road he described himself as a bachelor. Rosetta also remarried, describing herself as a widow. Divorce in those days was rare, expensive and carried a stigma and there is no evidence that George and Rossetta obtained one. Like many poorer people in late Victorian Britain, they both committed bigamy, presumably assuming that no one would check up on them. All the rest of his life George kept many personal details to himself.

George, by now a successful skipper and father of at least one child to Elizabeth Ellis, left *Viola* before the end of 1912 and well before the outbreak of the Great War, but his story does not stop there and we will hear more of him in due course.

A few Hellyer skippers took a summer break to visit the seaside or places further afield. Those with some money behind them took their families away to popular resorts such as Scarborough or Bridlington, or more locally Hornsea and Withernsea. It was not unusual on such sojourns for trawlermen to try their hand at catching fish from one of the tourist boats offering fishing trips from Bridlington and Scarborough harbours. More prosperous skippers or mates might extend such holidays to two or three weeks. Some took the opportunity to visit London or other more distant places of interest. Those with less resources or inclination frequented local pubs and clubs. There were always some who shipped out immediately in another ship, in later parlance they were said to 'spend more time at sea than a seagull.'

On leaving port for the grounds once more, the most immediate problem facing the skippers was actually finding the fleet. In that pre-wireless era the details they were given regarding the location and direction of the fleet was already several days old when they left the lock gates, it having been brought into London's Billingsgate Market by the steam cutters and then telegraphed up to Hull. As with other fleet communications, there was a great reliance on rockets. The various rockets used by each fleet for signalling carried a different number of stars and this helped the lone trawler identify its fleet. Even so, valuable fishing time could be lost and coal wasted in trying to find the fleet. Location was made easier for the Hellyer trawlers with the introduction of radio in 1913. That summer Hellyers fitted two new trawlers with the wireless communication and also installed the equipment in an old steam cutter, *Columbia*. She was left on station at the Tail End of the Dogger and kept in daily communication with the two trawlers that were manned by the admiral and vice-admiral of the boxing fleet. All trawlers heading for the fleet knew where *Columbia* was lying and on rendezvousing with her, they received up-to-date information on where the fleet was working.[25]

And the fleet was always out there, somewhere. From that first voyage of *Viola* in February 1906 to the outbreak of the Great War in August 1914 the Hellyer Fleet was always at sea. A constant presence was maintained on the grounds throughout that period, though not without a heavy cost. Out of the fifty or so vessels assembled for the fleet, six craft and all of their crews were lost prior to the outbreak of the War. The first of these, of course, was *Antonio* which disappeared without trace on her second voyage back in March 1906. *Celia*, one of the Govan-built ships, went missing the following February whilst *Lycurgus* succumbed to the ever-present danger of collisions. On 21 December 1908 the mark boat *Eudocia* ran into her as the latter was moving position in thickish weather. Both vessels were damaged but *Lycurgus* was in a particularly serious situation. A six-foot hole had been cut into her stern cabin and her stern plates started. She began making water fast but the skipper and crew were able to stem the flow in the cabin with the help of tarpaulins, bags of flour, fish covers, boxwood and nets. The two stricken craft were some 180 miles from the Humber and left the fleet together but the following day *Lycurgus* was abandoned and sank when about 110 miles from Hull on the dangerous NW edge of the Dogger Bank.[26]

In March 1913 *Oberon* also vanished and before the year was out *Desdemona* and *Angus* also disappeared without trace. The lack of a load in heavy weather on the return voyage may well have compromised their stability but, as with many trawler losses, it is difficult to know for certain. Billy Johnson's successful career as skipper ended when he was lost with *Angus* during November 1913; her loss, like that of many other trawlers over the years, will perhaps always remain shrouded in mystery. On 17 November 1913 Billy and Herbert, the two brothers, brought their trawlers alongside each other out on the fishing grounds. They exchanged greetings and Billy asked his brother to take his fish and transfer it to the cutter the next day as his engineer had told him that coal was running low. Billy and his crew were never seen again.[27] That evening, after *Angus* had left the fleet, it came on to blow almost a hurricane. The fleet trawlers had to lash up their gear and dodge out the storm. *Angus* never reached port and some months later the steam trawler *Emily* trawled up a crane and lantern-cage believed to have come from the vessel. It seems possible that the homeward bound *Angus* may have succumbed to the weather. However, a bottle which later washed ashore on the Norwegian coast contained a message believed to have been written by the mate saying the vessel had been run down by a foreign barque. The official report put this down as the reason for the loss but perhaps we will never know for certain.[28]

Despite such vicissitudes, Hull's Hessle Road district was one of the most vital and vibrant urban communities in Edwardian England. Although most of its streets and houses had only been built since the beginning of Queen Victoria's reign, and had drawn people in from far and wide, it had developed a strong identity. Its inhabitants relied for their livelihood on the docks and the business of the sea, particularly fishing and 'big boats', as the merchant service was colloquially known in the district. Britain was then the world's leading maritime nation, Hull was its third port and Hessle Road was then at the heart of its maritime activities. The skills and experience of its shipping companies and the level of seamanship found amongst the peoples from its crowded street were world class. When Shackleton set off in 1914 on his famous, if ill-fated, expedition to Antarctica, more members of his team were either born or based in Hull than in any other place, and mainly connected with the Hessle Road district.

The dangers of trawling were all too evident to everyone in the Hessle Road community as the steady toll of trawler losses over the Edwardian years and beyond amply illustrates. At least five Hull trawlers, and often many more, were lost in each year of the new century down to 1914 and the Hellyer fleet did not escape, losing six of the vessels Charles had ordered for his fleet back in 1905/6.[29] Often, though not always, whole crews were lost and these bald statistics say little of those individual crew members who were lost over the side, or like *Viola*'s skipper John McCue, died as a result of their injuries. Such losses seem unacceptable today but as August 1914 loomed they were set to worsen. During the impending war, Hull trawlers and trawlermen were to play a major role in the conflict at sea and the grim struggle to keep the country's sea-lanes open.

By these last months before the outbreak of war it seems likely that *Viola* and some of her sister vessels were being fitted with covered bridges, proper wheelhouses for the first time. By now Charles Hellyer, having largely retired, seems to have left the day to day running of the firm to his son who perhaps looked more favourably on enclosed bridges for fishermen.

IV

TO WAR AND SHETLAND

IN FEBRUARY 1906, some three weeks after *Viola* had slipped almost unceremoniously into the River Hull, HMS *Dreadnought* was launched to almost universal acclaim by Portsmouth Dockyard. *Dreadnought* too was destined for a fleet, albeit one of somewhat more formidable proportions. She was the first of a line of super-battleships; a new marque that would always bear her name.

The dreadnoughts possessed formidable firepower, an expensive accretion of almost everything that was new in capital ship technology; more than 18,000 tons of armour plate, steam turbines and massive twelve inch guns. They were said to render all earlier battleships obsolete.

These great ships were seen as Great Britain's riposte to the naval ambitions of the German Empire, to the Kaiser's audacious challenge to the Royal Navy's supremacy, but they did little to ease the growing arms race. Henceforward, it was thought no modern navy was worth its salt without a fleet of dreadnoughts. France, the United States and, above all, Germany embarked upon the construction of such craft. The British government, spurred on by the Royal Navy and public opinion, ordered more. In terms of capital ships, a lead over Germany was maintained. By 1914 Britain's Grand Fleet could boast twenty-one dreadnoughts—many much larger, faster and more heavily armed than the original: the German High Seas fleet could muster fourteen.

Yet although dreadnought fleets were clearly a product of the modern military-industrial complex, a case can surely be argued, with the benefit of hindsight, to support the view that the strategic thinking behind their construction was rooted in an earlier age. Britain's glorious naval successes during the Napoleonic Wars, above all the example of Nelson, cast long shadows. In any future conflict between European powers the Royal Navy intended to resurrect both blockades and commerce warfare as means of sapping an enemy's strength. Moreover, there appears to have been a common assumption that the ultimate control of the North Sea, of all seas, would be decided by a major battle between fleets of capital ships, and for more than a decade Britain's naval strategists seem to have planned for a huge battle—envisaged a second, perhaps greater, Trafalgar—an armour-plated back-to-basics lesson delivered by big guns, a decisive re-assertion of the nation's naval dominance.

Indeed, Britain had risen to industrial and maritime pre-eminence during the eighteenth and early nineteenth centuries thanks in no small measure to its powerful navy and vast web of overseas trading links. By the middle of the nineteenth century, by the time of the Great Exhibition at the Crystal Palace of 1851, Britain was described as the 'Workshop of the World' importing vast quantities of food and raw materials to feed its growing urban workforce, their families and the insatiable factories whilst exporting manufactured goods all over the world. Britain's ultimate strength was her position at the centre of the growing world economy but her reliance on seaborne commerce was also a potential strategic weakness.

The full implications of technological change on the nature of any future war at sea were far from clear and much less appreciated by all sides. Though there was a great emphasis during the Edwardian era on the construction of the dreadnoughts, there was a growing uneasiness, in some circles at least, that the development of the torpedo, U-boat and sea mine might have changed the equations of warfare at sea in a way that was not clearly understood, but might threaten Britain's traditional supremacy and thus the protection of the country's very vitals, her overseas arteries of trade.

The efficiency and potential future threat posed by sea mines was perhaps the most immediately obvious worry. Their value had become apparent during the Russian-Japanese conflict in the Far East in 1904 and prompted an interest in mine clearance. Various experiments had taken place during the following years, particularly at the request of Vice-Admiral Lord Charles Beresford. It became clear from trials that conventional wire sweeps offered the best way forward. Such sweeps, dragged through the sea by vessels such as trawlers could cut through the cable which secured the mine to the bottom. The mine then bobbed up to the surface and could be detonated from a safe distance with gunfire. That at least was the theory.

After some generally successful trials with two Grimsby trawlers were carried out off Portland in February 1908, the Government eventually accepted Beresford's recommendation that in any future war these vessels and their crews should be used for minesweeping duties. By the close of 1910 the Admiralty had purchased six trawlers and following discussions with leading trawler owners the next year, a Trawler Section of the Royal Naval Reserve was formed. Arrangements were made with a number of leading trawler owners for a range of their vessels to be hired into service when requested. It was agreed that the hull and outfit of these vessels was to be initially valued at £18 per ton of gross tonnage and £40 per unit of nominal tonnage. In return, the Admiralty was entitled to make periodic inspections. Training of trawlermen in minesweeping techniques was extended and by the outbreak of war 146 vessels were covered by the arrangement.

When war was declared on 4 August 1914 North Sea fishing operations were in full swing. The North-east coast summer herring fishery was reaching its height, the seas teemed with fish, the waters there awash with steam drifters seeking the vast silvery shoals, each vessel and crew intent on taking as many fish as could be quickly and safely carried to ports such as North Shields and Scarborough. Further south, old sailing smacks, still based at Lowestoft, were out trawling between the Dowsing and the Gab whilst Hull's four boxing fleets and hundreds of other steam trawlers toiled on their traditional fishing grounds further to the north and east. Early that morning the Hellyer steam carrier *Brutus* had arrived at Billingsgate with the usual cargo of fish it had brought from *Viola* and thirty-six of her Shakespearian sisters, a fleet which included *Ariel, Angelo, Bianca, Jessica, Juliet, Miranda, Rosalind* and *Sebastian*.[1] No-one out at sea, amongst the Hellyer fleet, realised that this was probably the last time a steam cutter would race for Billingsgate with their catch of fish from the North Sea grounds. Even though it had been apparent for some time that the European situation had been deteriorating, the actual declaration of war took most people, including the fish trade, by surprise. That evening, at 8.15, the Admiralty relayed orders to every east coast harbourmaster prohibiting future sailings for the North Sea grounds, and decreed that all fishing vessels at sea be instructed to return to port.

In an era when the wireless was still somewhat of a novelty, this latter order took some time to execute. Instructions were transmitted to the Hellyer wireless vessel, *Columbia*, lying at the tail of the Dogger; then relayed on to *Bardolf* and *Caliban*, still almost the only vessels in the boxing fleet with radios. The orders were unprecedented, as the fleet had been continuously at sea since February 1906, but put into immediate execution by the admiral. He signalled all trawlers and the whole fleet turned for the British coast, steaming by day but still trawling by night until they reached Flamborough Head. There *Viola* and her sister ships gathered under the lee of the great chalk headland, close to where some 125 years earlier John Paul Jones had fought his epic sea battle with the British Navy, until arrangements were fixed for their return to port.[2] This was no easy matter, for Hull's port facilities were not designed to cope with all the fishing vessels being in dock at the same time. The Hellyer and Red Cross fleets were the first to head back up the River Humber as the Great Northern and Gamecock fleets had been working further from home. Soon more than 400 steam trawlers, distant water vessels as well as the fleeters, converged on Hull. Despite the congestion, berths were allocated quickly; the Great Northern fleet was moored in the old Queen's Dock in the centre of the city[3] whilst the Hellyer fleet was sent into the brand new deep water King George Dock on the city's eastern outskirts. Many other vessels were crammed in St Andrew's Dock which was filled to overflowing. Torpedo nets were drawn across the lockpits and sentries patrolled the docks to guard against possible saboteurs and spies.[4]

Charles Hellyer was by this time more or less retired and living in the West Country, but he hurriedly returned to Hull for a briefing on the situation from his son Owen, who was by now running the firm. Owen Hellyer was keen to resume fishing and concerned about the dispersal of the labour force. The firm could not afford to keep all their skippers, mates and crews in employment with the trawlers laid up, but provided work in the net lofts for those skippers and mates who were in the direst need. The pay was basic—twenty-five shillings a week—but kept poverty at bay until the future became clearer.[5] Meantime, some outlines of the subsequent war at sea began to emerge.

The trawlers and their crews already covered by Admiralty minesweeping arrangements were quickly taken up and dispatched, as planned, to their allotted ports as soon as they were fitted out with their gear. The first five Hull trawlers left St Andrew's Dock on 10 August bound for Portsmouth and minesweeping duties. A number of crews who were members of the Royal Navy Trawler Reserve had already left by train for Portsmouth to man other vessels being requisitioned. A couple of days later a further five trawlers followed them down the River Humber; as they left a large number of fishermen and Hessle Road residents gathered at the St Andrew's Dock lock pit to wish them good luck and cheer them on their way.[6]

Yet from the onset of the war there were immediate indications that many more minesweepers would be required. At 7.30pm on 4 August, not long after the boxing fleets had turned for home, *Konigen Luise*, a Hamburg-American Line steamer that normally ran tourists to German seaside resorts, readied for sea, her captain apparently ordered to proceed at full-speed for England and mine the Thames Approaches. Three hours later she left the River Ems with a deadly cargo, the first of many mines destined for British sea-lanes. The vessel's yellow funnels were hurriedly coated with black paint to make her look, at first glance, like one of the continental steamers running in to Harwich. She never reached her intended destination: her master, Commander Bierman hugged the Dutch coast until off the Maas Lightship and then struck out for East Anglia steaming at a full sixteen knots. *Konigen Luise* got to within about thirty miles east of Orfordness where an English trawler reported her as a suspicious vessel, apparently throwing objects over the side. As the scout-cruiser HMS *Amphion* and a flotilla of destroyers bore down on her, the German vessel made a vain attempt to flee southwards at full speed. The flotilla opened fire; *Konigen*

Luise was hit and soon sank but not before getting a wireless message off to the High Seas Fleet saying the mines were laid.

Amphion picked up the survivors from *Konigen Luise* before midday but next morning struck one of the mines and went down, taking some of the German prisoners with her. The British Grand Fleet had sailed through these waters en route for Scapa Flow just a few days before. Half a dozen Admiralty trawlers from Dover soon swept a path through the minefield but the implications were clear: the Germans were likely to commence an aggressive mining policy. By 21 August another hundred trawlers had been requisitioned by the Admiralty and dispatched to Lowestoft, the chief fitting out depot. *Dorcas*, *Jessica* and *Nerissa* from the Hellyer fleet trawlers were taken up by the Royal Navy at this time. Many more fishing vessels, excursion steamers as well as a myriad of other small craft were to follow in their wake.

Combating mines and large minefields was just one painful aspect of the changing realities of the armed struggle at sea that were brought home to the naval authorities in the first frenetic weeks of the conflict. Whilst it is fair to say that the danger of the sea mine had been anticipated to some degree by both sides before 1914, the potential of the submarine, of an underwater dimension to naval warfare, had been greatly underestimated. Most key players in both the British and German military camps saw the submarine's role as primarily for undersea coastal defence, they viewed it a little more than a marginal player in any future surface conflict.[7] After six or seven weeks of war such attitudes had to be radically reassessed.

On 21 August, Commander Hersing of U-21 made history by being the first U-boat to sink a Royal Navy warship, when he sent the scout *Pathfinder* and 259 of her crew to the bottom off St Abbs Head. The seas at the time were extremely rough and there was some doubt at first on the British side about the actual cause of this catastrophe but there was to be no doubting the dramatic implications of the next encounter. Early on the morning of 22 September, three old British cruisers, *Aboukir*, *Cressy* and *Hogue*—known as the Live Bait Squadron—were steaming on a northerly course in an area known as the Broad Fourteens, south of the Dogger Bank. The weather was bad and they maintained their patrol without destroyer protection. About 6.30 in the morning *Aboukir* was shaken by a violent explosion and within twenty five minutes the warship capsized, leaving most of her crew in the water. The *Hogue* thought the stricken vessel had been mined; she closed in to offer assistance and was hit by two torpedoes, sinking in less than ten minutes. Two more torpedoes sank the *Cressy* when she hove-to in the midst of the carnage. Although 837 men were saved, thanks to two Dutch steamers and a couple of Lowestoft trawlers, 1105 men were lost.[8] The scale of this catastrophe brought home to all naval authorities on both sides the power of the submarine, and the vulnerability of large capital ships despite all their weaponry and armour plate. At first, the Admiralty and the British press thought that several U-boats must have been involved in the attack but the stark truth soon emerged: three 12,000 ton cruisers had been sent to the bottom within an hour by one small U-boat. The U-9 and her commander, Otto Weddigen, had actually been ordered to sea to molest transports crossing to Belgium and only encountered the three cruisers after being forced off course by the stress of the weather. Weddigen never reached his intended targets, having used up his torpedoes but he and his crew received a tremendous national ovation on their safe return to the River Ems.

These sinkings brought home the horror of modern maritime warfare to participants on both sides. Johannes Spieß, Weddigen's then First Watch Office on the U-9, later recalled the horrific aftermath:

"In the periscope, a horrifying scene unfolded... We present in the conning tower, tried to suppress the terrible impression of drowning men, fighting for their lives in the wreckage, clinging on to capsized lifeboats..."[9]

Within the year, Johannes Spieß and the U-9 were to turn their attention to Hellyer's and other Hull trawlers in the ever changing course of this brutal war.

Much earlier, before war had broken out, the Grand Fleet had sailed from Portsmouth on 29 July 1914. This immense, seemingly impregnable armour-plated array of Armageddon-like proportions, almost eighteen miles of great warships, had swept through the Straits of Dover and up the North Sea to reach the new base at Scapa Flow a couple of days before the actual outbreak of war. The strategic aims of the British naval authorities were to block German naval and mercantile activity by tying up both the northern and southern routes around Britain. The twenty-one battleships and four battle cruisers stationed at Scapa were intended to control the northern exit whilst nineteen older pre-dreadnoughts were based at Portland to block the southern route.

In terms of the northern exit in particular, the aim of the battle fleet was not to maintain daily close patrols off the enemy coast but to make sweeps over the area and be ready for sea to combat any German threat. The work of stopping and seizing German-bound commerce was to be left to smaller vessels. However, the early impact of the U-boat and the minefields cast a cloud across this previously clear strategic vision. What was soon all too obvious was that these large ships were far from impregnable, that they were actually acutely vulnerable both at anchor and out on the high seas to these new and unseen threats. Again, using the benefit of hindsight, it seems somewhat staggering that such little prior attention had been paid to planning the protection of this expensive fleet of warships when away from their home anchorage in the English Channel. Indeed, almost as soon as war was declared, even before the loss of the *Aboukir*, *Hogue* and *Cressy*, the naval top brass expressed fears for the safety of their capital ships; Admiral Jellicoe, Commander of the Grand Fleet, became so concerned about the absence of adequate protection that in the first months of the conflict his dreadnoughts used Loch Ewe on the north-west coast of Scotland as an anchorage whilst the defences at Scapa were improved. When Loch Ewe was also considered too exposed, the Grand Fleet moved for a time to Loch Ma Keal further down the Scottish west coast and Jellicoe even ventured to Lough Swilly on Ireland's northern coast.[10] Although this was thought to be beyond the range of existing U-boats, it was too far from the North Sea. The German High Seas Fleet commanders could have capitalized on the Grand Fleet's absence had they but realised. Perhaps the problems surrounding protection should have cast doubt on the whole concept of capital ships and on the real value of the vast amounts of capital expended upon them by both sides during the pre-war arms race. Perhaps it should have highlighted the lack of both thought and investment put into what proved to be some crucial aspects of the actual war at sea: the struggles to keep the sea-lanes open in the face of the mining and U-boat campaigns.

One immediate way of attempting to counter these threats was to call up more small vessels—trawlers, drifters and the like—and fit them out for anti-submarine patrols. Requisitioned steam trawlers were hastily armed with three-pounder guns and often sent into service with their fishermen crews. An early priority was Scapa Flow and under the superintendence of the steam yacht, *Venetia*, a score of trawlers were soon guarding the approaches to the Orkney base. Their main underwater armament was then an explosive sweep, a line of gun cotton charges towed by an electric cable and kept at the right depth by a small kite. Yet Scapa was just one base and similar arrangements and patrols were clearly required up and down the British coast, for there was no obvious reason why the Germans should confine mine laying U-boats to Scapa or other naval bases. By the beginning of September more than two hundred and fifty trawlers and drifters had been taken for minesweeping but it was clear that many more such craft were going to be required for the war against U-boats and minelayers. A structure emerged: a series of operational patrol units were to be created, each was to consist of a steam yacht, four trawlers and four motorboats. During September the requisite vessels were hurriedly called up. Amongst the trawlers taken for this service was *Viola* along with several more of her Hellyer fleet sisters.

The first patrol units were soon operational. Several such units were allocated to Scapa Flow, others sent to Loch Ewe, Rosyth, the Humber and Cromarty. Shortly afterwards further units were established for Dover, the Tyne and Shetland. Whilst this was in hand, *Viola* was requisitioned and sailed from Hull on 15 September 1914. Her trawling gear was removed and she was fitted for out for patrol duties, armed with a three-pounder gun, and eventually sent north, much further north than the trawler had previously ventured. Like others of her marque, although she retained her fishing markings she was now regarded as a weapon of war. We have only sketchy details of her early wartime crew but most seem to have been Hull trawlermen, their homes no more than a few minutes' walk from each other. Her skipper was Charles Allum from Rosamond Street off Hessle Road. Allum had been born in London the son of a waiter, but seems to have begun fishing out of the Humber in his teens; by the age of twenty-three he was married to Mary Avis from Grimsby and living down Brighton Street in the Hull's Hessle Road district. Five foot ten in height and of stocky build, he was evidently already a skipper before the outbreak of war and joined the Royal Naval Reserve on 4 September 1914.[11] The mate was Henry Calvert, born in Dewsbury but at 42 years old a seasoned member of the Hull trawling fraternity who hailed from Haltemprice Street off Hawthorn Avenue on the edge of the Hessle Road district. The youngest member of the crew who sailed with *Viola* to Shetland was probably the fireman-trimmer, Charles Turner of St Andrew's Street, also along Hessle Road. Turner was still only sixteen and too young to officially join the army but this had not stopped him signing on and sailing north to participate in the hostilities. We know a little about another member of *Viola*'s first wartime crew. Thomas Craven aged 42, signed on as deckhand. Although a native of Cleckheaton where his parents still lived, Craven had lodgings down Eastbourne Street, also in the heart of the Hessle Road district. The first war-time steward, E. Callis, was also from Hull, living in De La Pole Avenue off the city's Anlaby Road.

Large numbers of fishermen were drawn into the war at sea in similar ways and, indeed, no less than five of *Viola*'s former skippers, William Blewitt, Edward Lodge, Tom Gordon, George Tharratt and George Richards, were soon on Royal Naval Reserve duty.[12]

Viola commenced patrolling almost a soon as she arrived in Shetland and was joined there by at least one new member. Thirty-three year old John Campbell from Stornoway came aboard as Leading Seaman. By the end of November there were eight Hull sailors and three Scotsmen in *Viola*'s crew. The routine of war service was swiftly established. For much of the following two years *Viola* and the rest of her unit worked out of Lerwick or Scalloway, engaged in anti-submarine work or searching for minefields as well as sometimes supporting the work of larger armed vessels further out in the Northern

Patrol who were beginning to tighten the trade blockade on the deep sea routes to Germany, a most crucial dimension of the war at sea. Armed trawlers like *Viola* were engaged in incessantly patrolling the sometimes sullen and often savage seas around Shetland, participants in a deadly game of cat-and-mouse set against a beautiful backdrop of crofts and small settlements, a seemingly peaceful world of solemn sea lochs, gull-stained rock stacks and skerries set amidst a mosaic of sea-washed, green-grey islands.

Tedium interspersed with tension was the reality of this war at sea. Whilst much of the day to day work was monotonous, consisting of endless patrols between islands and across empty seas, the crew lived with the ever present threat of an underwater attack, their vessel usually following a zigzag course to avoid the attentions of torpedoes whilst a constant watch had to be kept for mines. Days, even weeks of routine patrols might pass without encountering any trace of the enemy then suddenly, without warning, armed trawlers such as *Viola* might be engulfed by the war, by hostile encounters, real or suspected. Then there was the weather which at its worst appeared almost to belittle such bitter human struggles: throughout their relentless patrols *Viola*'s crew, like the enemy they pursued, had to contend with the endemically hostile elements, not least the stormy seas that surrounded the Shetlands. Sheer survival, when working in waters where conditions could deteriorate rapidly, required seamanship of the highest order.

The creation of this Auxiliary Patrol and the recruitment of so many fishermen and their vessels for patrol and minesweeping work proved a culture shock for all concerned. Naval officers, schooled in the traditions of Osborne and Dartmouth found it difficult, if not impossible, to enforce traditional standards of discipline, and there was little about most fishermen's experience that made them likely to respond to what they often saw as a rigid, sometimes condescending, Senior Service approach, especially when they saw themselves very much on the front line of the day to day conflict at sea against U-boats and mines. It was sometimes quite difficult to get fishermen and indeed their families to appreciate the naval wish to adhere strictly to orders and timetables. In short, it often proved almost impossible; many trawlermen simply wouldn't have it. One not too untypical anecdote will suffice. On one occasion, the authorities were sent round to the house of a Hull trawlerman. After months of minesweeping service, the trawlerman had overstayed his brief period of leave. His wife answered the door. When asked if her husband lived there and was he at home, she replied that he only lodged at this address but lived in Manchester Street Club. This was the bar where he had spent much of his time since coming on leave, much to the chagrin of his spouse who didn't drink. Despite the disparity of their approaches to the sea war, it became clear to many Naval officers that most fishermen, especially the trawlermen and those who had manned the drifters, were extremely skilled seafarers and capable of acts of considerable courage. There was much friction in the early stages of the conflict but the relationship apparently worked best where the naval authorities adopted more unorthodox, less formal and direct levels of discipline.

In November 1914 a member of *Viola*'s crew was amongst the earliest casualties of the conflict around Shetland, though not through enemy action. Shortly after midday on Thursday 12 November, a boy gathering firewood from the beach below the Widow's Homes in Lerwick came across the partially submerged body of a sailor amongst the rocks. The dead man was Thomas Craven, *Viola*'s deckhand, who had been missing for over a day. His trawler had been lying at Lerwick since returning from patrol on 5 November, the unusually long break brought about by extremely bad weather. Indeed, the weather was exceptionally awful, even by Shetland standards, as three days of tremendous storms — later described by Rear Admiral Dudley De Chair, flag officer of the 10 Cruiser Squadron enforcing the Northern Blockade, as the most appalling gale he ever experienced in all his years at sea.[13] On the evening of the 10th, at the height of the storm, whilst the armed trawler was sheltering in harbour, several members of the crew, having had enough of their close confinement, took their chances with the elements and rowed ashore for a drink. Once in the town, they split up and Craven made for the Albert Bar where he later became, by all accounts, somewhat the worse for wear. The crew rendezvoused around 11pm on the Esplanade and began rowing back in the dark to their ship which was lying some way out in the harbour. The weather was so bad and the wind so strong that after pulling for some time the erstwhile drinkers found they could make little headway towards their ship and took refuge on a steamer, the *Alfred Nobel*, lying nearby. The storm raged on through the night, their rowing boat was swept away, leaving the fugitives with no immediate means of returning to *Viola*. Craven and Leading Seaman Campbell took the chance of a trip back to shore with the helmsman of an Admiralty launch from the yacht *Shamara* and once back in Lerwick all three sought shelter, more drink, and a chance to warm up in the Albert Bar.

Soon afterwards, *Viola*'s skipper, Charles Allum, concerned to know what had happened to his missing crew members, brought the trawler alongside the Alexander Wharf and by the next morning, as the storm began to blow itself out, all except Craven had made it back to the ship. Wet, cold, tired and possibly the worse for drink, he had left his companions in the bar and walked round to the house of Catherine Leslie and her family in Royal Buildings where he had lodged when previously ashore. Here, he was given a change of clothing and fell asleep. He awoke a couple of hours later and on being told by Mrs Leslie's husband that his ship was now lying by the wharf he hurried off. Craven was seen again a short time later, then disappeared. The following morning the crew began looking for him, the young fireman being sent round to Mrs Leslie's but to no avail; a few hours afterwards his body was found on the beach.[14] How he came to be drowned was never adequately resolved. The Coroner's report found that he had been lost overboard from the armed trawler and may well have fallen into the harbour when attempting to get back on board when the vessel was tied up at the quay. A combination of darkness, drink, stormy weather and sheer fatigue may all have played their part in the tragedy. Whatever way, he was dead: his body was interred in the Lerwick New Cemetery overlooking the Bressay Sound.

Back home, Thomas Craven had no wife or children to mourn him but his name was proudly written up on the Roll of Honour in his native town of Cleckheaton and also on the Roll of Honour down Eastbourne Street in Hull where he had lodgings. Such Rolls of Honour were decorated lists, not only of those who had gone to serve their country but also of those who had fallen. By the September of 1916 Eastbourne Street's Roll recorded that 138 men from the street and its terraces had answered the call to arms; that thirteen had already died in service or whilst fishing.[15] Unfortunately, by the time the Armistice was finally signed in November 1918, these Rolls were to record many, many more losses.

The Hellyer Boxing Fleet lost its first vessel on Admiralty service when *Lorenzo* was wrecked in the Hoy Sound on 17 December 1914. Meanwhile, the patrol work stepped up as the U-boat threat progressively increased. In the first months of the war these underwater vessels had sunk several notable warships and evidently curtailed the activities of the world's greatest array of capital ships, the British Grand Fleet. The lessons of such early encounters at sea taught the German Command the value of these weapons for offensive action. U-boat performance in action surpassed all expectations: these vessels also demonstrated greater powers of endurance and an ability to work over longer distances than had hitherto been thought possible. When it came to taking the war to the enemy, these underwater craft clearly had much greater freedom of action than surface ships. They could cruise almost at will under the water, regardless of Britain's pre-eminence on the surface. Although their initial offensive operations had been mainly directed at naval vessels it was clear that if ordered to attack the commercial shipping lanes—Britain's vital arteries of maritime trade and commerce—they might seriously sap her economic strength, potentially degrade her ability to continue the war.

A vigorous debate developed amongst the German leadership about the value of turning U-boats loose on merchant shipping, and this was fuelled to no small degree by the success of the British Northern Blockade in restricting the sea-borne flow of food and raw materials to German ports. Moreover, as both sides entrenched their positions on the Western Front, the prospects of a swift victory on land diminished whilst calls for a ruthless sea war increased. On 15 February 1915 the German High Command announced an unrestricted war on commerce: the waters around the British Isles were declared to be a war zone where all ships, whether British or neutral, were liable to be sunk, although attempts would be made to adhere to many aspects of international law. At the beginning of the campaign, the Germans had no more than twenty-one operational U-boats stationed in the North Sea and ready to attack but as new vessels were delivered they joined the campaign. Some vessels were torpedoed without warning whilst other craft were dispatched by gunfire. Whenever practicable, the U-boats avoided directly torpedoing neutrals and, if possible, preferred to dispatch their victims with guns as this saved on the valuable torpedoes. Around ninety merchant ships, twenty-eight fishing vessels and other small craft were sent to the bottom during the first three months of the campaign.

The British anti-submarine measures during this period relied heavily on the Auxiliary Patrol. Soon, some five hundred trawlers, yachts and assorted small craft had been requisitioned and dispatched to twenty-one different patrol areas. Vessels like *Viola* bore the brunt of this activity. The Naval authorities had the Auxiliary Patrol vessels work like hunters, scouring the sea in a partially ad-hoc fashion searching for the enemy. The surviving logs for April and May 1915 show her on various patrols in all sorts of weather from Lerwick to Scalloway, Fitful Head to Papa Stour or Lerwick to Fair Isle and other places. On 23 May 1915 at 4am, for example, she weighed anchor off Sumburgh Head after being laid-to for some hours in thick fog. *Viola* covered about fifteen miles in a SW direction before being again forced to lay-to by fog from 7am until around 12 noon. She then proceeded to scour the seas in a zigzag fashion before snatching a few hours anchor off Fair Isle at 1am. The patrol was resumed at 4am and, apart from laying to between 7am and 8am, continued until the armed trawler reached her anchorage in Lerwick Harbour around midnight.[16] Nothing untoward was seen. Such was the nature of many patrols; *Viola* searched the seas for day after day, week after week and her crew saw no obvious sign of the enemy. Apart from the fog, the patrols were frequently disrupted by storms which caused the trawler to dodge into the wind for hours on end. The crew's duties regularly seem to have started by first light and continued until midnight while a watch was maintained throughout the hours of darkness.

The Shetland Patrol was watching for U-boats seeking to take their war to distant waters. To move beyond the North Sea the Germans had either try to penetrate the Straights of Dover or make a voyage round the north of Scotland, most likely through the Fair Isle Channel. The southerly part of this Channel was covered by the Orkney Patrol whilst *Viola* and the rest of the Shetland-based vessels were charged with maintaining a watch over the northerly section.[17]

The Fair Isle Channel was just part of the Shetland Patrol's duties. *Viola* and her companions scoured the length and breadth of the archipelago's seaways. In the month of June 1915, for example, her various patrols took her to many of Shetland's islands and bays: from Muckle Flugga with its remote lighthouse in the far north down to Fair Isle which lay mid-way between Orkney and Shetland. Night anchorages, when practicable, were sometimes taken in Scalloway or Lerwick harbours, sometimes off Fair Isle, now and again in the comparative safety of Ronan Voe or Swarback's Minn on the west coast of mainland Shetland.[18] From April 1915 Swarback's Minn became the base for Rear Admiral Dudley De Chair and his Northern Patrol, a fleet of large armed merchant cruisers, which was charged with the job of enforcing the northern blockade on German commerce. This patrol maintained a stranglehold on northern commerce, despite appalling weather and the depredations of enemy vessels, through the crucial years of the war. Busta House, an eighteenth century mansion, was the operational HQ in Swarback's Minn as well as a place of refreshment for officers, whilst a pub in the neighbouring settlement of Brae across the voe was a popular resort for many of the crews when they could get ashore.[19]

The odds were initially stacked against such Auxiliary Patrol vessels as *Viola* in their struggle with U-boats. Before the war the Royal Navy had concentrated on the construction of capital ships; the need for such a large auxiliary patrol had not been fully anticipated, much less financed. Although as we have seen men and ships were hurriedly assembled after the outbreak of war, the armaments immediately available to counteract the U-boat threat were rudimentary. The shortcomings of the main weapons supplied to the auxiliary patrol in the early part of the war, the explosive sweep and small three pounder guns, made it difficult to effectively counter U-boat incursions. The only underwater anti-submarine device available in August 1914 was a contraption known as the single sweep that deployed a solid metal kite containing 100lbs of TNT kept at depth by a skid on the surface and towed by an electric cable. Improved sweeps became available for the armed trawlers and other vessels a few months after *Viola* was requisitioned. They consisting of nine separate ninety-pound charges of TNT towed astern in a loop kept at depth by a kite. The charges, fired by hand on contact with an underwater object, were carried at the bottom of the loop whilst floats were attached to the surface section. Another somewhat crude anti-submarine weapon sometimes deployed from the early stages of the war was the lance bomb, and this device typifies the shortcomings of early anti-submarine warfare. This was a bomb of up to 25lbs fitted to the end of a long handle and was intended to be whirled around above the head and thrown at a submarine if it got close enough. The athleticism of the crew was rarely successful in terms of making the most of such rare close encounters.

In that first year or so of the war Auxiliary Patrol vessels had no means of locating and tracking the U-boats traveling beneath the surface, and the light armament and slow speed of many requisitioned vessels were a disadvantage in surface encounters. These limitations were brought home to *Viola*'s crew when they spotted a U-boat on the surface whilst patrolling the waters from Sumburgh Head to Fair Isle on 2 June 1915. The trawler immediately gave chase and fired one round from her three-pounder, but the U-boat was out of range. *Viola* chased the U-boat as it sped northwards for over two hours but was unable to close on her quarry. At 10.30am the U-boat disappeared below the waves and, despite a search, no further trace was found.[20] As U-boats increasingly extended their range of operations, the Fair Isle Channel became a regular passage for those with orders to create havoc in the Irish Sea and Western Approaches.

Ramming proved an effective tactic if a patrol vessel could close on an unsuspecting U-boat. Indeed, the U-15, the first U-boat lost in the war, was sunk in this fashion off Fair Isle five days after the outbreak in August 1914 when she was caught on the surface, whilst apparently attempting repairs, by the light cruiser HMS *Birmingham* and cut in two as she attempted to dive. In March 1915 HMS *Dreadnought* became the only capital ship to sink a U-boat when she rammed U-29 in the Pentland Firth, sending Otto Weddigen, who had sunk the *Aboukir*, *Cressy* and *Hogue*, to the bottom.[21] *Dreadnought* had, of course, the advantage of speed in such encounters but the armed trawlers and other auxiliary patrol craft found ways to combine ramming and cunning, as later events were to prove.

The Germans had, of course, deployed sea mines with great effect from the very beginning of the war and their activities continually tied up many requisitioned vessels as minesweepers. At first, British mines proved to be far less effective than their German counterparts and in early 1915 the requisitioned Hellyer boxing fleet cutter *Columbia*, under the command of Lieutenant-Commander W. H. Hawthorne, RNR, a Canadian who had paid his own passage to England to volunteer for service[22], was dispatched to sea with orders to recover an intact German sea mine. This was far from an easy assignment but the vessel duly swept a minefield off the east coast and, on getting a mine in the sweep, gingerly towed it to shallow water. The deadly object was then delicately hoisted aboard by derrick, knowing that one slip could send both vessel and crew to the bottom, and the steam cutter then sailed into a remote corner of port, its lethal trophy swinging above deck. Here another officer, Lieutenant Sir James Danville, came on board, duly unscrewed the horns and removed the acid tubes that could trigger detonation. Once made safe, the mine was packed up and forwarded to the Admiralty.[23] The Auxiliary Patrol crew of the yacht *Sagitta* secured a further mine for investigation in a similar fashion. Whatever the outcome of this particular project, British mines began to improve in terms of both effectiveness and reliability in the later stages of the war.

Cargo vessels were not the only merchant craft lost to the U-boat. In April 1915 the U-10 widened the offensive when it sank a number of unarmed fishing boats working off the River Tyne. Such losses were keenly felt: with so many vessels requisitioned, those left fishing were invaluable for the maintenance of precious food supplies, a fact all too evident to the Germans.

Indeed, those steam trawlers not already requisitioned in the early weeks of the war had been allowed to return to sea under strict Admiralty guidelines, but the situation in the North Sea was hardly conducive to a wholesale resumption of orthodox operations. Fishing was restricted to designated areas thought to be clear of mines. Although the hard-pressed Royal Navy maintained patrols, an unarmed boxing fleet, large numbers of trawlers working in close proximity, presented an all too obvious target for enemy vessels. In the early stages of the war German surface vessels had seized a number of unarmed trawlers, including most of the Boston fleet, and taken their crews into captivity. They were held with interned merchant seamen and others in the Ruhleben camp for the remainder of the war. The Hull Seamen's Union was prominent in organizing subscriptions and setting up a war fund to provide presents and essentials such as boots and clothing for both interned seafarers and their families back home. On hearing the call whilst on station in Shetland in 1915, Charles Allum, Henry Calvert and *Viola*'s engineers were amongst the first to send money through to the Hull union's General Secretary, George William McKee, who was organizing the relief campaign.[24]

Meanwhile some of the boxing vessels were quickly adapted for working on their own, but the owners of the four Hull boxing fleets tried to keep the system working by forming a new company and sending a mixed flotilla of trawlers to the west coast of Scotland.[25] Here they resumed working as a fleet but instead of packing fish into boxes, the cutters brought their fish round to Hull in bulk and split the proceeds equally between all vessels in the fleet.

This arrangement worked for a few months but did not really pay its way and by late 1914 the trawlers were recalled to Hull. Hellyers then set about converting the rest of their trawlers for single boating operations in the North Sea. This involved converting much of the hold, which had formerly been used for storing coal, into a big fish room. Fish storage capacity was thus increased but at the expense of coal bunker capacity, meaning a shorter time could be spent at sea, but this was less of a problem as trips by trawlers working on their own in the North Sea rarely lasted for more than ten days. The trawlers were supposed to fish within the designated boundaries, on pain of suspension by the Admiralty if found working outside these areas, but trawlermen remained a law unto themselves and a number of Humber skippers, with an eye to a good catch, were tempted on numerous occasions to ignore such strictures. In the early months of the war one Hellyer skipper, who decided to chance a trip to the Coffee Ground, almost off the Danish coast, was fortunate enough to avoid both suspension and the enemy. Back in port his transgression was spotted: he was warned that the next time the trawler was tempted to visit prohibited waters, the Mate should be ordered to make sure the fish were more thoroughly washed before being stowed. His manager had spotted the distinctive soil of these grounds in the gills of the fish the trawler had landed.

The Hellyer vessels had hardly returned to working from Hull when all fishing operations were suspended again—albeit briefly. Soon after dawn on 16 December 1914 the German First High Seas Fleet Scouting Group, commanded by Admiral Franz von Hipper, began the infamous bombardment of Scarborough, Whitby and Hartlepool. Over 1150 shells were fired in the surprise attack, which left 137 dead in the three towns and 592 injured. The German warships got clean away and in Britain there was outrage that the Royal Navy had failed to bring them to account. The Germans also laid a dense minefield which brought a harvest of shipping casualties in its wake. For a time fishing was prohibited but one Hellyer vessel, unbeknown to the Navy, had unwittingly slipped out of the Humber, spent over a week trawling in what seemed to be empty seas and only heard about the emergency when the crew returned unscathed to port. There was a sequel, however. Hipper tried to repeat the raid on 24 January 1915 but this time his vessels were intercepted and resoundingly defeated in the Battle of the Dogger Bank by Admiral Beatty's ships in an action which saw the sinking of the German battlecruiser *Blucher*.

Although single-boating was considered a safer option than fleeting in the North Sea, the dangers were all too apparent even before the first restricted

U-boat campaign against commerce. The Hull trawler *Imperialist*, one of the distant water vessels that usually sailed to Iceland or the Barents Sea, struck a mine and sank some forty miles ENE of Tynemouth on 6 September and *St Lawrence*, which went missing almost a month later, may well have suffered a similar fate. The first Hellyer civilian casualty of the war was *Celia*, which disappeared without trace on 8 January 1915. The trawler may also have fallen victim to a mine but the actual cause of her loss has never been determined.

During May 1915 the U-boats turned their attentions to the grounds where many of the remaining Humber trawlers were working, and a spate of losses brought the war home in earnest to the Hellyer fleet. Late in the afternoon of 3 May, Herbert Johnson, then skipper of *Hector*, was fishing some 160 miles ENE of Spurn Point in the vicinity of two other trawlers, *Coquet* and *Progress*. His crew had let go of the cod end and were shooting the trawl for the evening tow when they spotted smoke and some unusual activity on the horizon close to the other two trawlers. A strange craft was seen leaving *Coquet* and heading for *Progress*. As they scanned the scene with glasses, they heard gunfire and realised to their dismay that the mysterious vessel was a U-boat. According to later reports, a U-boat surfaced about a mile from where *Coquet* was trawling and brought up quickly on her port beam. The U-boat skipper hailed the trawler from his conning tower and gave the crew five minutes to get their rowing boat over the side and come over. As soon as the nine trawlermen rowed across they were ordered on to the deck whilst five members of the U-boat's crew then pulled over to *Coquet* with explosive charges. Whilst this squad prepared *Coquet* for sinking, the U-boat set off in pursuit of *Progress*, which was trying to get away. *Coquet*'s crew was still on deck and the unwilling passengers were soon up to their waists in water, hanging grimly on to the lifelines to avoid being swept away as the U-boat bore down on its prey. *Progress* finally hove to after four shots were fired, the crew was ordered off before the trawler was sent to the bottom with explosives. The U-boat then returned to *Coquet* to pick up the German boarding party and the explosives placed on board were detonated.[26] Both trawler crews were left in their rowing boats whilst the U-boat turned its attentions on *Hector*.

With her trawl gear newly shot, *Hector* was little more than a sitting duck unable to flee, and the U-boat was soon alongside. Herbert Johnson and his crew were also ordered to row the ship's boat over to the U-boat where they were taken on deck whilst the Germans sent men to inspect their ship. A short while later *Hector*'s crew were ordered back to their rowing boat and told by the German commander to get away to the westward where they would find their fellow fishermen. He was about to send their vessel to the bottom but did not quite leave them empty handed; as they prepared to row away he passed over some loaves, German war bread he said, two-thirds potatoes.

They rowed clear as the U-boat's gun sank *Hector*. The Germans left them alone more than a hundred miles out in the North Sea in an open rowing boat but they had had also left something else. Wrapped up in an oilskin in the bottom of the boat was a scalding hot kettle of tea—from *Hector*'s galley—and the entire contents of the table; the cook had been preparing a meal when they were attacked. Everything off the table had been scooped up into the oilskin: fried fish, cheese, jam, butter and even some mugs. Although *Progress* had already gone to the bottom, *Coquet* was still afloat. Would she provide a refuge? But as fishermen rowed closer to her she finally slipped beneath the waves. After rowing across empty seas for some time they came across the other trawler crews in their boats much where the U-boat had said they would be, food was shared and all looked around for a way out of their predicament. Earlier a vessel had been seen working to the south-east so the three open boats rowed in that direction. A makeshift signal, made from old papers daubed in grease left from the remains of the fried fish meal, was hurriedly lit as they approached the ship. It was the old *Honoria*: she passed so close to the rowing boats that they could read her name but their attempts to make contact with both light and shouting proved in vain; she trawled straight past and on into the gloom. Herbert Johnson then turned his rowing boat to the north-west where they had seen another vessel working and all crews were fortunate enough to be picked up by a Grimsby trawler the next morning.[27] It was probably no consolation to Herbert Johnson and his crew to know they had been sunk by Johannes Spieß and the U-9. Johannes had been first watch officer on that submarine when it has sunk the *Aboukir*, *Cressy* and *Hogue* and later wrote about how the terrible scene of a sea filled with dying men from the cruisers had affected him.[28]

There was a further dimension to this particular story. Some weeks later, the First Sea Lord, Winston Churchill, received a report showing that before *Coquet* was sunk, the German U-boat commander had retrieved her papers which showed the disposition of British North Sea minefields. This was an important coup for the Germans but would have been of even more value had the early British mines been anything like as effective as their enemy counterparts.

The heat was now on the remaining fishing vessels. A further five Hull trawlers working in the same vicinity were sent to the bottom along with *Coquet*, *Progress* and *Hector* on 2 and 3 May; they included the Hellyer vessels *Hero* and *Iolanthe*. Before the month was out, the Germans had sunk fifteen Hull steam trawlers including three more members of the Hellyer boxing fleet: *Angelo*, *Sabrina* and *Sebastian*. During the first week of June four more Hull vessels were eliminated, amongst them another three of *Viola*'s sisters. The culprits in almost every case were U-boats and the trawlers were usually destroyed with either guns or explosives. Most fishermen were set free in their rowing boats although four crews—two from Hull—were taken to Germany when their trawlers were sunk by torpedo boats on the north-west section of the Dogger.

As the North Sea U-boat offensive began to bite, Hellyers and other owners fitted out more and more of their surviving vessels for voyages to the Iceland fishing grounds. The boxing fleets had not been built with the intention of making trips to such distant waters even though they could stay out in the North Sea for weeks. The adaptation was quite straightforward, with the hold being modified to act as a coal bunker on the outward trip and fishroom for the return voyage; in some cases the open bridge was enclosed to provide those at the helm with more protection from the elements.

Herbert Johnson was amongst those boxing fleet skippers who tried his hand when he took *Cassio* northwards in July 1915. Both trawler and skipper had never been to Iceland before and shipped a pilot—an experienced distant water trawlerman—to show them the grounds. The fishing proved successful; they took as much fish as *Cassio* could carry then set off for home. All went well until early on 24 July when the trawler's crew spotted a large steamer afire on the horizon—with a U-boat at either end. Knowing they would be next *Cassio* gathered all steam she could and headed south at full speed in the hope of getting away, but one of the U-boats, the U-36, set off in pursuit. For more than an hour a grim chase ensued until the U-boat had closed sufficiently to fire a shot from the deck gun. Still the trawler kept going: gradually, relentlessly, the U-36, skippered by Ernst Graeff, overhauled the trawler. Within another hour *Cassio*'s crew could see the Germans in the conning tower. The gap between the vessels continued to narrow; they were soon within hailing distance and ordered to leave their vessel. As Johnson later recalled, by this stage they didn't need telling twice. The boat was thrown overboard and the crew had hardly got clear when the trawler was shelled. Within fifteen minutes *Cassio* slipped below the surface and the U-boat submerged without further communication.

Herbert Johnson was adrift with his crew in an open boat for the second time in ten weeks. They spotted a sailing ship, chased after it and scrambled aboard after a six hour pull across the grey seas. The vessel was Norwegian, originally bound for Germany with a cargo of timber, but had been intercepted by the ships of the British Northern Patrol, put under the command of a prize crew, and dispatched to Lerwick. The Germans had been busy, for the crews of two more homeward-bound Hellyer vessels as well as the fishermen from a Grimsby trawler were also picked up on the six-day voyage to Shetland. *Hermione* had been sunk by gunfire a day before her sister ship *Cassio*, whilst the battered old *Honoria* finally met her end in the same fashion, both also victims of the U-36. Undaunted, Johnson returned to sea almost as soon as he got back to Hull, but had at first to sail as mate for Hellyers as the firm had lost so many trawlers. Later in the war he entered Admiralty service and, like others before him, finished the war as skipper of a requisitioned armed drifter in Adriatic waters, a far cry from either the North Sea or Iceland.

There were sound operational reasons, apart from a lingering wish to spare as many lives as possible, which led the U-boats to adopt the strategy of surfacing to finish off fishing boats. Each U-boat could only carry a small number of torpedoes and saved these for use against warships and the larger, faster merchant ships that might outrun them if given the chance. By surfacing to sink smaller and slower vessels through either gunfire or on-board explosives, a U-boat could greatly increase the number of potential kills on each voyage. However, the Royal Navy soon realised that, with a bit of cunning, this tactic offered an opportunity to hit back at U-boats. On 5 June 1915 the armed trawler *Oceanic II*, a member of one of the Peterhead Auxiliary Patrol units, was set as a decoy off the east coast of Scotland. *Oceanic II* was instructed to shoot her trawl whilst the rest of the flotilla—four armed trawlers—kept her in sight at a distance. At 7am the flotilla heard shooting: *Oceanic II* was in action against the U-14. The trap had been sprung; the armed trawler flotilla closed in, pouring rapid fire into the U-boat which was then finished off when rammed between conning tower and bow by the armed trawler *Hawk*[29], built at the same Beverley yard as *Viola*.

Another variant on the decoy trawler approach adopted was to send a trawler to sea with one, sometimes two C class submarines in tow, connected by means of a telephone cable. A few days after the *Oceanic II* incident, the trawler *Taranaki* and the submarine C27 almost sank a U-boat and within weeks the tactic proved successful. On 23 June 1915 the *Taranaki*, this time with C24 in tow, caught the attention of the U-40 whilst steaming in seas to the south east of Aberdeen. Whilst the U-boat was pre-occupied with getting the *Taranaki*'s crew to abandon ship, the British submarine struggled beneath the water to slip the telephone cable. This should have been a straightforward procedure but proved a nerve wracking affair. Finally free, just in time, C24 stalked the unsuspecting U-boat then slammed a torpedo into its hull. Only those on the U-40's deck escaped with their lives. The trawler *Princess Louise* and C27, working in tandem, disposed of the U-28 in similar fashion off Fair Isle on 20 July 1915. The German command then got wind of the practice, the element of surprise was lost and the tactic enjoyed no further successes, but at least German attacks on the fishing fleets eased for some time.

The use of decoy trawlers accompanied the development of the Q ships, yet another means of trapping unsuspecting U-boats. Q ships were relatively small merchant vessels armed to the hilt with a deadly array of concealed weaponry. To all intents and purposes they looked to U-boat commanders like ordinary unarmed merchant vessels, legitimate targets but too small to be worth a torpedo. When a U-boat surfaced nearby, sections of the Q ship's crew started abandoning ship. As the Germans closed in to finish the seemingly stricken ship off with gunfire, their erstwhile prey turned the tables, hidden guns were unshipped and the U-boat was shelled. Ironically the first U boat to fall victim to a Q Ship was the U-36, fresh from sinking the Hellyer's *Honoria*, *Hermione* and *Cassio*. The U boat was sent to the bottom with gunfire from the converted coaster *Prince Charles* on 24 July off the Hebrides, only hours after disposing of Herbert Johnson's *Cassio*.

Germany's first spell of unrestricted commerce warfare lasted from February to September 1915 but the most prominent and controversial event of this campaign was the sinking of *Lusitania* by the U-20 in May 1915. The liner was torpedoed without warning, many American lives were lost, and this action considerably damaged Germany's Atlantic relationship. It was a factor in the USA's later decision to enter the war in 1917.

Indeed, it was the harm sustained by Germany on the diplomatic front, rather than losses in the U-boat war, that brought an end to the first campaign against commerce. The campaign had taken some time to make an impact, thanks mainly to the small numbers of U-boats initially available for action, rather than effectiveness of British anti-submarine measures. But from June to September 1915, when more craft were available, the commerce war proved increasingly painful for Britain and her allies. Whilst some U-boats were sunk, the numbers of merchant vessels sent to the bottom exceeded the tonnage of new British ships launched. Taken as a whole, the Royal Navy's efforts, however individually notable, had done little to stem the summer U-boat tide and the British government must have viewed the ending of the first German submarine war against commerce in September 1915 with considerable relief.

Many fishing boats were destroyed during this campaign and the Hellyer fleet had been particularly hard hit. By early August 1915, apart from the loss of *Lorenzo* on Admiralty service, fifteen unarmed Hellyer trawlers had been sent to the bottom whilst fishing: in other words, more than one-third of the boxing fleet had been lost in the first twelve months of the war. The old Hellyer steam carrier *Columbia* had also been sunk, back on May Day 1915, only a few weeks after recovering the intact German mine, whilst on a distant patrol in the Southern Bight of the North Sea during an action between four armed trawlers and German torpedo boats from Zeebrugge.[30] The armed trawlers had been searching for a U-boat that had tried to torpedo *Columbia* during the morning, when they were attacked by a couple of German torpedo boats around 3pm. Two torpedoes were fired at *Columbia*, the second of which struck her port side abreast the wheelhouse. The stricken vessel immediately broke in half and went down within a minute whilst still under heavy fire from the enemy. The torpedo boats were better armed and possessed greater speed but the remaining armed trawlers put up a strong fight. One of the German boats was damaged and as they made off, two destroyers arrived on the scene. In the subsequent pursuit both torpedo boats were sunk and forty-six German survivors from a combined crew of fifty-one were picked up. The armed trawler *Barbados* searched for *Columbia*'s crew but found just one survivor. It later turned out that three others had been picked up by one of the torpedo boats and confined below: all the others had gone down when the vessel was sunk.[31] The Canadian Lieutenant Commander Hawthorne was amongst those lost. One interesting postscript: *Columbia* had always carried a mascot, a dog called Prince, but, according to a message written in the photograph album of George Gale, the only survivor, the animal had walked off the vessel before the last fateful voyage.

During the winter of 1915/16 *Viola* continued patrolling the length and breadth of the Shetland archipelago. When not on patrol, the armed trawler was allocated to boom duties either at Lerwick or Swarback's Minn. These booms were great curtains of anti-submarine nets that stretched across the harbour approaches. Although a number of vessels rode close to the nets to pick up signs of underwater attempts to penetrate the barrier, *Viola* usually patrolled the waters on either side of the boom. Her task was to keep a close watch on traffic passing through and sometimes to escort vessels through the designated entrance. This in itself could be a tricky business for large vessels—particularly the armed merchantmen and sizeable naval vessels heading out of Swarback's Minn for North Atlantic patrol duties—passed through at speed. This reduced the opportunity for a U-boat to slip through undetected but there was a real danger of colliding with the escorting vessel. The skills of Skipper Charles Allum—honed in the congestion of the pre-war boxing fleets—came into their own at such times.

Before the autumn of 1915 was out however, *Viola* suffered a second loss; Henry Calvert, the mate, Allum's right hand man, who had been with *Viola* from the very beginning, was at last able to take leave from the relentless rigours of the Shetland Patrol. Over the previous twelve months there had been little let up for either vessel or crew. The work during the period of restricted submarine warfare seems to have been particularly intense. There was little opportunity for leave and even *Viola* had missed her annual summer refit because of the pressure to maintain patrols. A presumably exhausted Calvert was no doubt ready for a break and looking forward to seeing his family. He took leave of the crew, in late November, landing in Aberdeen from the steamer *St Rognvald* but whilst rushing across the city to take the train he collapsed and died in Commerce Street, evidently struck down by a heart attack. His body was brought back to Hull where he was buried with full military honours in the Western Cemetery on 29 November. He was just forty-two years old and left a wife and four young children.

The pressure on *Viola*'s crew during such intense and incessant patrols must have been considerable. During the conflict armed trawlers like *Viola* carried a slightly larger crew than when fishing. Additional living space was created on such vessels by converting part of the hold into accommodation, but conditions must have been confined and claustrophobic at the best of times.

Charles Allum was for a time more fortunate. His wife Mary, like a number of trawler skipper's spouses followed her husband to war. They went to many places far from home. Hilda Robinson travelled to Sheerness and Tyneside amongst other places after her husband George, whilst Mary Oliver took her children to Malta when her husband was assigned to minesweeping duties on the island. There were others. Mary settled into lodgings in Commercial Buildings, Lerwick, her presence allowing the maintenance of some vestiges of domestic life for the Allum family when Charles was able to get ashore.

Calvert's replacement as mate was T. Christie and by this time there was a change in the nature of the patrol work. The patrol areas were by now divided into squares and worked by one or more vessels. *Viola*'s sea patrols now regularly meant the endless scouring of a square of open sea, searching for signs of U-boats. By the onset of winter the lack of maintenance showed and the trawler's engines were causing occasional trouble; on at least one occasion in December 1915 she had to lay-to when out on patrol whilst the engineers carried out repairs. Problems persisted and on 4 and 5 February 1916 she was forced to stay anchored in Mid Yell for about fifteen hours whilst the engineers tried to remedy cylinder defects. Such stoppages were dangerous, leaving the armed trawler little more than a sitting duck in the water. She resumed her patrol but within the week was laid up in Lerwick for three more days of engine repairs. Back on patrol, the trawler stopped and searched a sailing ship en route from Trondheim to Guernsey with a cargo of wool on 10 March. As the vessel's papers were in order she was allowed to proceed. A few weeks later *Viola* sailed down to Aberdeen for a two-and-a-half-week refit. When she returned to Shetland in April 1916 a more substantial six-pounder gun had replaced her original armament. Her engines seem to have given little further problem.

The end of the first official U-boat campaign against commerce did not mean that attacks on merchant and fishing vessels ceased. Far from it. U-boat commanders took their opportunities and chances against enemy craft of all persuasions as and when they could. It did, however, provoke a fierce debate amongst the German High Command which split into two main camps: those who wanted another, more or less unrestricted U-boat war on commerce and those who feared such a resort would finally bring the hitherto neutral United States of America in on the side of the British and French. The campaign was resumed—albeit briefly—for a short period in March and April 1916 but when the sinking of more neutral shipping, including some large Dutch liners and further losses of American lives, provoked a strong reaction from across the Atlantic, such actions were abruptly curtailed once more.

When the German underwater campaign against commerce was in quiescence, U-boats were increasingly available to support surface ship actions and the High Seas fleet took a more provocative or aggressive stance after Admiral Scheer assumed command early in 1916. His strategy was to try to goad sections of the British Grand Fleet into taking more risky, more exposed action. If he could locate and surprise an isolated group of warships with his full battle fleet, he believed he could destroy them and withdraw to safety before the British were able to bring the full weight of their capital ships to bear. During the early months of 1916 he adopted an increasingly provocative stance, planning Grand Fleet sorties across the North Sea to bombard coastal towns whilst attacking British coasts with zeppelins and U-boats. Lowestoft was bombarded as part of this plan in April 1916 but the interception of the High Seas fleet whilst on another such sortie led to the Battle of Jutland, the only really full-scale fleet encounter of capital ships during the war. The story of Jutland is well known. Whilst out on sortie at the end of May 1916, the High Seas fleet encountered Admiral Beatty's fleet of battle cruisers and was able to inflict considerable punishment before Scheer was in turn surprised by the arrival of Beatty and the main British battle fleet. As the British battle fleet bombarded and pursued their German opponents, Scheer's fleet managed to escape through a mixture of tight maneuvering and the desperate deployment of torpedo attacks from his smaller vessels. In the face of torpedoes, Jellicoe signaled his battleships to turn away. The bulk of Scheer's fleet was able to elude a further savaging from British big guns and return to the safety of their bases.

Immediately afterwards the Germans claimed that a great victory had been won, and they had certainly inflicted more damage when it came to vessels and crews lost, but in the longer term it was clear that, in terms of conflict between capital ships, Britain had the strategic victory. The German fleets had not been able to destroy the Grand Fleet and afterwards were increasingly confined to base. Yet this was not the second Trafalgar that had been envisaged; the enemy had not been decisively crushed and the course of the action surely must have confirmed the growing doubts about the weakness of capital ships in encounters, not with enemy capital ships but with the other weapons of modern maritime warfare. Jellicoe had, after all, given his signal to turn away at a decisive point because of the risk that torpedoes might sink several of his capital ships. What was the real value of such expensive armoured juggernauts if they could be eliminated by surface or underwater torpedo attacks?

Jellicoe certainly became increasingly uneasy about the menace posed by U-boats and torpedoes and a further—less well-known—action in the North Sea the following August confirmed his fears. Jellicoe ordered the battle fleet out once more in response to another North Seas sortie by Admiral Scheer. Although the great fleets did not engage each other on this occasion, the outing had a marked effect. A torpedo narrowly missed Jellicoe's flagship, *Iron Duke*, as it went ahead of the fleet to pick him up in the Firth of Forth. Then the whole fleet turned back for a couple of hours after the cruiser *Nottingham* was torpedoed and sunk off the Farne Islands. The delay meant that Scheer had turned for home and was out of reach before the British were able to close. The cruiser *Falmouth* was lost during a series of U-boat alarms and attacks on the return voyage. *Falmouth* was initially torpedoed by U-66 but finished off the following day by U-63 whilst being towed to the Humber.

Afterwards, Jellicoe decided he could not risk his fleet again in such waters without sufficient destroyer protection.[32] In future, he said, without such support, the Grand Fleet was to avoid going further south than the Farne Islands and no further east than longitude 4 degrees east. HMS *Dreadnought* and a number of cruisers and already been sent south to defend the Thames approaches but in essence this decision must surely have implied that Jellicoe's capital ships had to some degree abandoned much of the North Sea to the German's forces, if they wished to take advantage.[33] A combination of U-boats and torpedoes, not surface vessels, had surely curtailed British capital ship activities.

On 31 May 1916, the day of Jutland, *Viola* was out on patrol from Sumburgh Head to Fair Isle in rough weather and driving rain. She had begun the day's work at 3am pursuing a zigzag course in her unrelenting search for U-boats, and laid up off Sumburgh Head for a few hours that afternoon in heavy gales. The bad weather continued and at 8pm she anchored for the evening in Leven Wick.[34] During the remainder of the summer the trawler continued to work around Shetland, sometimes on boom duties, at other times on patrol, occasionally escorting foreign vessels, which had been stopped by the ships of the Northern Patrol into Lerwick. Her surviving logs make no further mention of U-boat encounters.

Viola was by this time part of Unit 6 of Auxiliary Patrol Area II (Shetland) as it was known and the other vessels in the Unit were HM Yacht *Mingaray* and the trawlers *Dentaria*, *Hondo*, *Eider* and *Beatrice*, the latter being a fellow Hellyer boxing fleet trawler. In October, a few weeks after Jellicoe had curtailed the southern North Sea sorties of the Grand Fleet, *Viola* and her entire unit were suddenly transferred south. They left Shetland for the last time and moved to the River Tyne.[35]

Shortly before the move another of the Hellyer sister ships went down on active service, not too far from *Viola*'s erstwhile beat. The armed trawler *Orsino*, named after the heroine *Viola*'s betrothed in Shakespeare's Twelfth Night, was patrolling a little south of Orkney when sunk with gunfire during an exchange with the U-boat U-55, off the north coast of Scotland, close to the Pentland Firth, in September 1916. Six of the crew were lost with her.

There was further grief before the move south, another casualty close to *Viola* but this time not amongst the crew. Mary Allum, still lodging in Lerwick with her children, died suddenly in early September. The Procurator Fiscal's report records the cause of death as corrosive sublimate poisoning, a chemical compound similar to caustic soda and a particularly horrible way to go. How did this happen? There is no mention of suicide in the official papers. Was it accidental? It is difficult now to know the reason.

Corrosive sublimate did have an interesting use at this time which may have brought Mary Allum into close and regular contact. By the summer of 1916 the war in the Western Front trenches had reached new heights. The sheer number of casualties created a dire shortage of field dressings. Firms like Smith and Nephew of Hull responded by opening a new factory on Hessle Road and massively increasing their output—the numbers of people they employed rose from 50 in 1914 to 1200 by the end of the war—but the pressure remained high for some time and an alternative, natural, source of dressing was also developed. Sphagnum moss was found to be a useful alternative and the response was to organize collections from moorlands close to ports all round the coast of the British Isles, including Lerwick. Women gathered the moss and treated it with corrosive sublimate when it was brought into town before it was dispatched to the front line, aid posts and field ambulance stations.

Mary Allum could likely have been involved in this vital work and this would have brought her into contact with corrosive sublimate. If so did she swallow this accidentally? It is difficult now to know but her loss left two children without a mother far from home, and with a father about to be sent south with the rest of his flotilla. The children were fostered at first on the island, well treated before joining their father much later on Tyneside. Mary Allum's body was also left behind. Unlike Tom Craven and Henry Calvert whose graves have Great War headstones, she lies in an unmarked grave in Lerwick. Left there as *Viola* and her crew sailed south the following month.

In their haste to move south whilst contending with the day-to-day dimensions of the war at sea, one tragic coincidence of September 1916's events affecting the trawler and Hellyer fleet possibly went unappreciated by all concerned. Skipper Allum had lost his Mary, *Orsino*, *Viola*'s Twelfth Night love, had been sunk. Skipper and ship had lost their literal and literary partners in life.

There were still more than two years of war to come.

V

NORTH SEA WAR CHANNELS

B Y THE AUTUMN OF 1916 there were thousands of vessels in this new and improvised navy. Steam trawlers like *Viola* had been joined by whalers, drifters, tugs, motor boats, yachts and pleasure steamers. All played their part. They carried out a variety of tasks including boom defence work and anti-submarine patrols across many coastal theatres of war from the British Isles to the Mediterranean and beyond. Not only were large numbers of fishermen and other working seafarers engaged in the Admiralty's war through the Royal Naval Reserve, but many other individuals with seafaring skills, generally those having more than a passing acquaintance with boats and the sea—people such as yachtsman, motor boat owners, watermen and the like—served with distinction in the Royal Naval Volunteer Reserve on front-line duties in much the same waters.

And make no mistake, coastal waters were on the front line in both twentieth century world wars. If the seas ever ran dry then we would see something of the thousands of wrecks and other remains of these maritime or littoral fronts scattered across every seabed: Great War detritus left from what was, for those involved, a new form of maritime struggle, a three dimensional conflict, where action took place not only on the surface but also increasingly in the air as well as in a murky underwater no man's land, a place where belligerents of both sides seemingly roamed almost at will.

Though the Western Front seemed to end in Flanders the front line—the East Coast War Channels—continued up the North Sea offshore, and are now all but forgotten about.[1]

In terms of the surface and underwater dimensions of the maritime war, many hundreds of trawlers, together with other suitable vessels and their crews, were incessantly engaged in the grim task of minesweeping, maintaining swept channels, keeping open the seaways so that vital goods, food, raw materials and necessities of warfare could continue to be moved. Minesweeping was an exceptionally dangerous job, requiring vessels to get in and amongst the mines. An unexpected contact, indeed any mistake, was likely to prove fatal to both ship and crew. On average one minesweeper was lost every other week of the war and generally at least half of the crew were killed on each vessel sunk.

Viola's flotilla was not required to engage in sweeping but to carry out their anti-submarine patrols in the mine- and U-boat-infested North Sea waters off the north-east coast of England. They became Unit 5 of what was known as Area VIII.[2] They were expected to work in seas where Beatty had barred his battle fleet from sailing; when the flotilla arrived U-boats were certainly creating havoc in the area and working fishing vessels as well as merchant shipping were once more at the centre of the conflict. Charles Allum—and indeed his crew—had little opportunity for dealing with personal or domestic issues whether back at home or left behind in Shetland. Family and friends had to wait. They were thrown straight into hunting the enemy in their new theatre of war. For many crew members short periods ashore were spent in local pubs or clubs but in July 1917 a Patrol Service Institute was opened at Northumberland Dock by the Missions to Seamen Tyne Section on land lent by the Tyne Improvement Commissioners. These temporary buildings acted as a club room and contained a room for officers and a coffee bar with a galley for cooking meals, as well as provision for playing billiards and other games. A large room contained seating for up to 200 people.[3]

On 24 September 1916, just a few weeks before *Viola*'s flotilla arrived on the north-east English coast, Carl-Siegfried Ritter, Commander of the U-57, surfaced under cover of darkness alongside the trawler *Fisher Prince* on the Whitby Fine grounds, some twenty or so miles off Scarborough. Grabbed by grappling hooks, the unfortunate *Fisher Prince* was ensnared and fastened to its foe. Ritter and his boarding party quickly took control, the trawlermen being confined under guard in the fishroom. The U-57 then slid across the ink-black waters towards the trawler *Otterhound* which was soon overwhelmed in a similar fashion, the captured crew being sent to the *Fisher Prince*. Over the remainder of that night Ritter systematically closed on then captured a total of thirteen trawlers, most hailing from Scarborough. All crews were imprisoned on the *Fisher Prince* and their trawlers were ransacked for food. Once all were taken and the element of surprise was no longer needed, the U-boat commenced sinking the trawlers. All but one were sunk with gunfire, though a scuttling charge placed in the engine room was used to dispose of the trawler *Nil Desperandum*.[4]

Despite the danger, the U-boat captain stayed with the *Fisher Prince* and watched over the captives until he was able to stop a passing Norwegian cargo ship just after dawn. After the trawlermen were transferred to the merchantman, the U-boat finally sank the *Fisher Prince*. All 126 crew members of the thirteen trawlers lost that night reached the shore and safety at South Shields. Ritter was later awarded the Blue Max for his overall contribution to the U-boat war.

Viola's flotilla patrolled from North Shields, carried out by the coal dark currents of the River Tyne into the uncertainties of the North Sea. Subsequent reports show that their beat at different times covered waters from close to the Scottish border right down to the vicinity of Scarborough on the North Yorkshire coast. The North Shields base ship for their operations there was HMS *Satellite*, a former 12-gun sloop built in the 1880s which had later become a reserve drill ship on the Tyne. The Auxiliary Patrol depot was in Northumberland Dock not far from the great staithes where railway truckloads of coal tumbled into the empty holds of steam colliers before being shipped out. The minesweeper base was on the other side of the river at Milldown, South Shields. The Tyne was far different from the Shetlands. Marine engineering was at the heart of this river, shipyards, foundries, furnaces, mills and manufactories of all kinds lined both banks of the river, and the coal sent from northeastern collieries fuelled UK commerce and industry.

But the war at sea here was equally if not even more grim. The arrival of the flotilla certainly seemed opportune. Britannia may well have ruled the waves in terms of surface ships but it was what went on below that was of increasing importance. Those with business in great waters needed all possible assistance as the U-boat onslaught intensified. *Viola*'s armament was upgraded again and her six-pounder gun was replaced with a much more effective twelve-pounder; this was certainly welcomed but not enough in itself. During the period that followed the ending of the first German underwater campaign against commerce the strength of the U-boat fleets greatly increased. The continuing military stalemate on land strengthened the hand of the naval hawks amongst the German military high command and another campaign against commerce was inaugurated in October, around the time *Viola*'s flotilla moved to the Tyne. This campaign lasted until January 1917. The German North Sea, Flanders and Mediterranean flotillas were all reinforced and at one stage 103 U-boats were operational out of a total fleet of 148. The onslaught seemed all-consuming: more than 516 steamers and large sailing vessels were sunk whilst only a small number of U-boats were destroyed. The exchange rate at this time was sixty-five ships lost for every U-boat sunk.

Although British naval forces had a conspicuous lack of success during this phase of submarine warfare, further weapons were becoming available which were to assist in the struggle. On 6 July 1916 the UC-7 was detected with hydrophones and sunk with depth charges. This sinking ushered in new ways of meeting the U-boat menace. The depth charge was basically a bomb with a pressure fuse designed to go off at a set depth and was a considerable improvement on the explosive sweep, as it would explode whether or not it actually made contact with the U-boat's hull. The hydrophone was an early form of electronic listening device and various versions had been under development for some time. It was basically an underwater microphone, which could pick up the noise of a U-boat's machinery or propellers. The portable version, used by many of the slower Auxiliary Patrol vessels, consisted of a microphone protected by metal discs and connected to earpieces or ordinary telephone receivers by a heavily insulated and armoured cable.[5]

Such electrical technology was still in its infancy and of only limited initial value. In order to detect the U-boat's machinery, all vessels in the area had to stop so the sound could be heard, then the hydrophone was lowered overboard to a depth of about twenty feet. If two or more hydrophone-equipped vessels worked together then the cross bearings helped plot the U-boat's position.[6] But stopping dead in the water left a vessel vulnerable to potential attack from the very U-boat it sought. Soon U-boats were also fitted with hydrophones and some grimly intense games of cat-and-mouse developed as Auxiliary Patrol vessels and the U-boats tracked each other's sounds, alternately stopping and starting. The vessel that stopped engines first detected the other.[7] Once a U-boat was located by hydrophones, the surface vessels would move rapidly towards their target whilst the U-boat would turn on its motors and change course in an attempt to elude the pursuers. When the patrol vessels stopped engines to deploy their hydrophones again, the U-boat would hurriedly shut down once more. Should the pursuers gain the upper hand in this struggle and close in on the U-boat's position then the area would be blasted with depth charges, but stopping in the water could leave a surface vessel open to torpedo attack. Specialist hydrophone hunting flotillas were eventually formed but by the end of 1917 *Viola* and a number of the armed trawlers in her patrol flotilla were also deploying both hydrophones and depth charges. Like most armed trawlers, *Viola* carried D Type depth charges.[8] These were specially designed for slower moving craft and fitted with a charge of 120lbs of TNT or Amatol, exploded by a hydrostatic fuse usually at depths of between forty and eighty feet.

The crews of the little ships had to cope with more than the relentless stress of this marine war, there was also the age-old struggle with the sea. The waters off north-east England, especially along the Yorkshire coast, were particularly unforgiving should a vessel get in to trouble. Over centuries of seaborne trade the dearth of safe harbours during an onshore gale had driven thousands of sailing vessels onto the beach or rocks when caught on a lee shore. In an age of steam this was a reassuringly rarer occurrence but in 1917 *Viola* was involved in one of the last such local losses. On 4 March 1917, the French tug *Robur* sprang a serious leak whilst towing the three-masted barque *Cognac* along the coast. The tug left *Cognac*, carrying a cargo of coal, at anchor a couple of miles off Scarborough then headed for Hartlepool as the weather deteriorated, escorted by the drifter *Rodney*. By the time *Robur* got close to Hartlepool she was sinking in weather so bad that the lifeboat was unable to get out, but the little drifter managed to take the crew off the tug before it went down.

In the meantime *Cognac*'s situation deteriorated as the onshore gale built up. Skipper Lieutenant Charles Wood RNR of the armed trawler *Dentaria*, from the Tyne Flotilla, received radio orders to assist *Cognac* and set off at full speed through the heavy seas. He found the barque in a terrible state, being driven towards the beach whilst beset by heavy seas that swept her from stem to stern. *Dentaria* made several attempts with rocket and line to get a tow rope on board and eventually succeeded. The barque began to haul up her anchors but in the process the windlass was badly damaged. Everything worsened: the barque's master signalled that the pumps had broken down and the vessel was leaking badly. Fifteen minutes later, the tow line was carried away and the masters of the two vessels agreed that *Dentaria* would assist the *Cognac*'s crew to abandon ship. By this time Skipper Charles Allum and *Viola* had arrived and the latter was sent to steam ahead of *Cognac* with oil bags out whilst *Dentaria* approached the stricken vessel and took off the crew. This was a particularly tricky operation all round for by now all three vessels were in comparatively shallow water amid heavy seas and snow squalls. Any mistake might have proved disastrous. Nevertheless, *Dentaria*'s skipper was able to get the schooner's crew onboard. One man was washed into the sea during the rescue but also picked up.

The two trawlers stayed as close as they could to *Cognac* throughout that dark, wild night, hoping to take her in tow should conditions abate. *Viola*'s position was by now somewhat perilous as her steering gear had broken down. Skipper Allum was offered the opportunity to run for shelter but his crew managed to make temporary repairs to the gear whilst lying to. At first light it was seen that the barque was in a terrible state, having settled much deeper in the water. Both trawlers stood by the vessel all day but as darkness returned the gale grew even worse; the raging seas were by now extremely dangerous and the trawlers had no choice but to stand further out from the land. They were joined by a third armed trawler, *Stronsay* and passed a further night on watch in heavy seas. When dawn broke it was evident that the barque had been driven ashore. All three armed trawlers were finally able to run for the Tyne and safety. Although *Cognac* was pounded to pieces in Burniston Bay near Scarborough the entire crew was safe. In his report to the Admiralty the Tyne Senior Naval Officer praised Lieutenant Wood of *Dentaria* for his consummate seamanship as well as the gallantry of *Viola*'s Charles Allum.[9] Residents of Scarborough found an unexpected bounty of coal on the beach.

By the middle of 1916 the combined impact of war losses and Admiralty requisitioning had reduced the active fishing fleet to a shadow of its former self. Owners were reluctant to order new vessels, knowing that the Admiralty would in all likelihood call them up for service, as there was an ever increasing need for small ships to carry out the myriad of war duties. In order to satisfy future demand for small craft the Admiralty began ordering armed trawlers direct from the shipyards. Three standard designs of different size were ordered, known respectively as the Strath, Castle and Mersey classes. All were capable of swift conversion for trawling at the end of the war and named after members of the crew that had fought on the Victory at Trafalgar. Cook, Welton and Gemmell built a substantial number of the Castle Class—medium sized vessels—whilst other Yorkshire shipyards at Selby and Goole turned out some of the larger Mersey class craft. Admiralty standard designs of drifters were also constructed. In addition, large numbers of fast wooden-hulled motor launches were ordered from North American builders and shipped across the Atlantic as deck cargo to swell the ranks of the maritime war effort and replace part of the ad-hoc fleet of motor vessels recruited in the early stages of the war. They were dispersed along the coasts of the British Isles and although these eighty foot craft were formed into separate flotillas they soon became an important part of the Auxiliary Patrol.

In February 1917 the seaborne stakes were raised again when Germany embarked upon an unrestricted U-boat campaign that was to last for the final twenty-one months of the war. Although the decision to dispense with the remaining accords of international law was not reached without considerable misgivings amongst sections of the German hierarchy, the Royal Navy's blockade of German ports was causing acute problems. There was also a widespread belief that Germany needed to end the war before facing another winter. The hawks in the German High Command were convinced that Britain's overseas trade links could be severed by an unrestricted war on maritime commerce. Without trade, Britain's supplies of food and war materials would dry up and the country would be unable to support the armies fighting on the Western Front. In short, so the theory went, Britain would have no choice but to sue for peace and some naval leaders believed this could be brought about within six months. Many civilian politicians were opposed to the step for they did not believe that such a U-boat offensive could achieve the predicted results, and also thought such unrestricted action would eventually bring the USA and other neutrals in on the side of the British and French. To the hawks in the military establishment, however, this was a risk worth taking for the USA had no large army available and would seemingly take many months to raise and train the requisite soldiers. By the time the US army was in a position to make a decisive contribution, so this line of thinking went, Germany and her allies would have won the war. Certainly the hawks finally won this argument and Germany's unrestricted U-boat campaign began.

This final and bitterly-fought U-boat offensive proved a bleak struggle for everyone, belligerents and neutrals alike. This was no Trafalgar, it was very much a twentieth century struggle, a precursor of things to come, a dirty war of attrition, progress gauged by performance indicators and targets. For its advocates amongst the German high command everything seemed to hinge on by how much the tonnage of British shipping sunk each month exceeded the number of new vessels launched. But to misquote Disraeli, there are lies, damned lies, performance indicators and targets. The prediction that Britain would be forced to sue for peace after six months did not materialise even though at its peak—in the late winter and early spring of 1917—an unprecedented tonnage of British vessels was sent to the bottom. Persua-

sion and innovation, creativity and sheer guts, kept the merchant and fishing fleets afloat. The country survived the onslaught thanks in large measure to her ability to keep neutral vessels carrying cargoes into her ports; in
part to the deployment of new weapons and also the arrival of American
destroyers after the USA entered the war in April 1917, as well as the increasing expertise of UK salvage firms in saving war-damaged vessels that
would previously have been lost. It was clear by the summer of 1917 that the
unrestricted U-boat campaign against commerce would, at best, take much
longer than the German hawks had anticipated to yield their desired result.
On the other hand, however, the final withdrawal of Russia from the War,
after the Bolshevik Revolution of October 1917, gave the German High Command a breathing space. They could fight on through yet another winter and
concentrate on the war. They might yet strangle Britain's seaborne supply
routes. The Great War on land and at sea was set to continue for much of the
following year.

The introduction of the convoy system was also to play an important part
in combating the depredations of the U-boats. The Admiralty had steadfastly
refused to introduce convoys until 1917. The system was still largely experi-
mental during the early months of this final German U-boat offensive but after August 1917 many more convoys were set up, though the north-east coast
was one of the last regions to have shipping organised in this way. The system
was successful for several reasons. Firstly, escorts protected the convoys and
if a U-boat attacked there was every chance it would be pursued and depth-
charged. However, perhaps the greatest and most immediate effect of the
convoy system was that it made merchant shipping more difficult to locate.
It has been estimated that a convoy of twenty ships concentrated in one area
was no more likely to be spotted than five separate vessels spread out over a
similar area. The outcome was that many ships in convoy were never spotted
by U-boats. For the Germans the seas suddenly seemed devoid of shipping.
If a convoy was located there was only a momentary opportunity for attack
whilst the likelihood of retaliatory action from the accompanying naval escorts was very high. Losses were dramatically reduced, as statistics for the

north east coast of England show: of the 12,122 vessels sailing through these waters in 1918 just 40 were sent to the bottom by enemy action.[10]

Not all convoys proved successful against surface ships however, and a significant loss during this year involved one of *Viola*'s former skippers. George Richards, skipper of *Viola* in 1912, had joined the RNR shortly before the war started and for a fair part of the conflict he was skipper of the armed Hull trawler *Tokio*. On 12 December 1917, the *Tokio* and three other armed Humber trawlers, the *Commander Fullerton*, *Livingstone* and *Lord Alverton*, as well as the destroyers *Partridge* and *Pellew*, were escorting a convoy of one British and five neutral ships from Scotland. They had got within forty miles of the Norwegian coast when they were attacked by four German destroyers, and in the subsequent action the destroyer *Partridge* was sunk and the *Pellew* badly damaged. With the British destroyers out of action, the German ships then turned on the convoy, which had scattered; all the merchant ships and defending armed trawlers were sunk. George Richards[11] and the rest of the *Tokio*'s crew were amongst those taken prisoners and landed at Kiel, to spend the rest of the war in captivity, whilst John Whelen, the Hull skipper of the *Commander Fullerton* and the trimmer, John Long, from Fraserburgh, lost their lives in the attack.[12] The German destroyers escaped under cover of poor visibility as British surface warships closed in.

Although such attacks by enemy surface vessels in the North Sea made a mark, it was the unleashing of unrestricted submarine warfare that really increased the carnage amongst the cargo ships and intensified the struggle on the high seas. For much of 1917 and the first part of 1918, Britain's ability to survive was continually threatened by untrammeled onslaught on the shipping lanes and the loss of vital supplies of food, munitions and raw materials. Whilst there was an increasing use of convoys, sea mines and destroyers, the armed trawlers and other requisitioned vessels of the auxiliary patrol also remained at the forefront of the anti-submarine war. They made increasing use of their depth charges and hydrophones. The U-boats for their part were often forced by the North Sea minefields to seek their prey on the inshore shipping lanes and this led to regular encounters with armed trawlers like *Viola* and other members of the Tyne flotilla. Early April 1917 was particularly memorable. On the 19th *Viola* and *Dentaria* were on patrol off the Northumberland coast when the latter spotted the conning tower of a submarine. Both armed trawlers immediately bore down at full speed on the vessel which quickly dived. *Dentaria* streamed her sweep, hunting around, and both trawlers spotted oil in the sea close to where the submarine had submerged, so two depth charges were dropped. The trawlers then scoured the area for up to 14 miles from the coast for several hours but spotted little else. The report concluded that the U-boat had escaped.[13]

Two days later, on 21 April, at 3.15 in the afternoon, the two armed trawlers spotted the Norwegian steamer *Peck* torpedoed off Dunstanborough and closed at full speed. Having reported in by radio that a U-boat was active in the vicinity they received orders from the Senior Naval Officer on the Tyne to warn all traffic to keep six or seven miles off the coast when voyaging between the Longstone Rock and Coquet Island. *Dentaria* proceeded to warn northbound traffic off Coquet whilst *Viola* took up station off the Longstone to deal with southbound vessels. At 7.10 that evening *Viola*'s crew heard gunfire to the south-east and ran at full speed towards the reports. Charles Allum and his crew soon came across a U-boat attacking a steamer. The assault continued even as *Viola* closed and at 6,000 feet the armed trawler opened fire on the U-boat which immediately broke off from shelling the steamer and returned fire. Two shots passed over *Viola*'s wheelhouse and a third fell about fifty yards astern but *Viola* was relentless and continued to close, firing rapidly. By the time the armed trawler was about 4,500 feet away its shells were landing near to the U-boat which then turned and ran in a north-easterly direction. *Viola* carried on firing and maintained her dogged pursuit.

Meanwhile *Dentaria*, hearing the heavy firing, also came up at full speed and although out of range those on board could see the duel in front, great flashes from the U-boat gun being plainly visible. *Dentaria* swung outwards to try and get on the seaward side of the U-boat whilst *Viola* continued to come at the enemy craft from the landward side. Shortly afterwards the U-boat submerged and although the trawlers quickly closed on the spot, they lost the scent.[14] Whilst it is doubtful that the U-boat was seriously damaged in the action, *Viola*'s prompt action had saved the Norwegian vessel. Charles Allum was later Mentioned in Dispatches (MID) for this action and for the saving of *Cognac*'s crew during the previous month.[15]

And thus the bleak sea war continued through the summer and beyond for the vessels patrolling off the north-east coast. On 6 November 1917 a torpedo passed across the stern of the armed trawler *John Gilman* whilst she was on patrol off Robin Hood's Bay. *John Gilman*'s crew spotted a periscope 1,000 yards astern and managed to get a round in from their gun before the submarine completely submerged. The armed trawler hurried to the spot, dropping two D Type depth charges in quick succession. Large quantities of oil and some wreckage came to the surface.[16] No kill could be proved but the U-boat was thought to have been damaged.

These events were not untypical of the sort of encounter between the vessels of the Tyne Flotilla and the U-boats over the next few months and over the following winter. Charles Allum was promoted in early January 1918 to Chief Skipper and from then on often commanded *Dentaria*.[17] Even so, *Viola* was rarely far from the action in search of the marauders. On 12 February 1918, in the early afternoon, whilst patrolling off Seahouses, Northumberland, *Viola* and the armed trawler *Lanercost* spotted a U-boat firing at a merchant vessel. Both armed trawlers gave chase as the submarine dived and a deadly game of cat and mouse ensued. *Viola*'s crew spotted a periscope 300 yards off her port bow and the skipper ordered top speed, dropping four depth charges as the trawler sped over the spot. Quantities of oil rose to the surface and towing charges on the explosive sweep were put out by the trawler. Both trawlers then settled down to listen for movement with their hydrophones but nothing further transpired. The U-boat had, it seems, escaped but the event cannot have been comfortable for the underwater crew. Official British navy records classified her as possibly slightly damaged.[18]

Late in the course of this traumatic final year of war, Charles Allum remarried. His new wife was Jane Taylor, a widow some years his senior who lived in Norfolk Street, North Shields.[19] With their father now married and with a secure household at hand, the Allum children appear to have finally been able to rejoin him.

And so the struggle went on, day after day and week after week, throughout the spring of 1918 and into the summer. It is clear from the surviving reports[20] that hydrophones and depth charges were increasingly deployed by the patrols working out of the Tyne, and the number of encounters gradually increased. From the autumn of 1917 the British were finally able to manufacture a reliable mine in large quantities and this also took its toll on the undersea enemy. The U-boats were increasingly forced to hunt inshore, looking for vessels that were joining or leaving the convoys. The armed trawlers and other flotilla vessels were in turn kept busy trying to counter such threats. In March 1918 a merchant vessel outward bound from the Tyne under escort from two of the flotilla's armed trawlers was struck by a torpedo when no more than one and a half miles east of the Tyne Piers. The ship was lucky to survive and limped back to port, whilst the two armed trawlers dropped a string of depth charges on the site of the suspected assailant. HMS *Dee*, on patrol in the same area, steamed swiftly into the fray dropping a further seven depth charges. A considerable amount of oil came to the surface and although a watch was kept for the following twenty-four hours by a hydrophone-hunting flotilla, no further sign of the U-boat was found.[21] The German vessel had escaped, but possibly damaged: it was clear, however, that U-boat encounters were no longer quite so one-sided.

A couple of days after this, hydrophones and depth charges were again deployed in another action by the Tyne Flotilla's vessels. Late that afternoon two armed trawlers, *Sparrow* and *Swallow*, sighted an enemy submarine on the surface firing on fishing vessels. The U-boat kept up the attack as the armed trawlers steamed in at full-speed; when they closed the range to 8,000 yards they opened fire. The shots fell about the U-boat, which at first fired back, then slipped swiftly under the waves. A game of cat-and-mouse then ensued as the two trawlers stopped and set a hydrophone watch whilst the U-boat no doubt tried to creep away. *Sparrow* and *Swallow* were reinforced by two destroyers and a hydrophone-hunting flotilla. A watch was maintained across the area until the next day but again without result.[22]

Encounters between U-boats and Auxiliary Patrol vessels off the north-east coast of England reached a peak during the summer of 1918. At the end of July HMT *Calvia* and other vessels attacked another submerged U-boat off Scarborough. They located the vessel with hydrophones, depth charged the area and maintained a watch. The next morning a headless body was found drifting in the sea.[23] It was later ascertained that UB-107 had been lost and for many years it was believed to have been sunk in this action. But subsequent events have shown its actual demise was much more mysterious. In 1983 a group of divers from Scarborough sub-aqua club, working off the Yorkshire coast not far from Flamborough Head, found the remains of this U-boat amongst the wreckage of the British steamer *Malvina* which had been reported as sunk some six days later and eighteen miles further south. To date it remains unclear just how these vessels became locked together in their watery grave.

Whatever the reasons, there was little let up in the struggle; reports show that the drifter *Rising Sun* was involved in another depth-charging incident during the same period and a couple of weeks later HMT *Calvia* was back in the thick of the action. This time the armed trawler and four motor launches were out on hydrophone patrol in seas off Whitby when the movement of a U-boat was picked up on the listening equipment. The patrol managed to circle the suspected U-boat about 1.40pm and for around fifty minutes they shad-owed its movements in a northeasterly direction. Around half past two the hydrophone bearing seemed to give an accurate position for their prey and the *Calvia* moved in and opened the attack with a couple of depth charges. Another grim game of life and death then ensued: the division bombarded the area in line abreast formation and the enemy could be heard stopping and starting between attacks. Movements stopped and the position was buoyed as oil and bubbles rose to the surface. ML578 dropped a further depth charge some 100 yards SSE of the buoy and about 4.40pm strange noises were heard on the hydrophone. *Calvia* remained on station but the hell being endured by

the U-boat crew incarcerated below in the claustrophobia of a can-like cas-
ket can scarcely be imagined. More strange sounds, similar to high pitched
shrieking, were heard on the hydrophones at 6pm, then again at 6.45pm; the
sub was judged to be close underneath and in all probability signaling. The
Calvia depth charged again and yet more oil erupted on the surface. Nothing
more was heard for some time and about 8pm the hunters launched a further line abreast attack. An hour later the motor launches returned to port but
Calvia was joined by other armed trawlers from the Tyne Flotilla as she maintained an overnight watch on the site. In the morning further depth charges
were dropped and the vessels towed explosive sweeps across the area, one
caught on an obstruction; air bubbles and oil hit the surface but this seemed
to signal the end of the drama. Despite a further watch on the site no further
sign of the vessel was found and the event was not classified as a kill.[24] If so,
the U-boat and her crew seem to have had a harrowing escape.

That same week, *Viola* and her crew saw action in an engagement that
brought about destruction of UB-30. This U-boat had been launched back in
March 1916 and had an eventful war, completing seven Baltic patrols under
her first commander Kurt Scapter before moving base to Flanders. The U-
boat had been interned for five months after being stranded off the the Dutch
shore whilst under the command of Cassius von Montigny. After release the
vessel had carried out eight patrols under the command of Wilhelm Rhein before being bombed and damaged at Zebrugge on 24 March 1918. The U-boat
had been swiftly repaired and by early August 1918 had carried out four more
patrols off the English coast, this time under the command of Rudolf Stier.
During her career UB-30 sank 22 vessels, totaling 36,271 tons.

The normal crew complement for this class of vessel was twenty two but
when she had left base on 6 August 1918 with orders to hunt for allied vessels
off the English North Sea coast she shipped twenty six men. One week later,
shortly after midday on 13 August, the U-boat was shadowing a southward-
bound convoy a few miles off Whitby when the armed trawler *John Gilman*
spotted her periscope. The Beverley-built Admiralty Castle Class armed
trawler *John Gilman* cleared for ramming and bore down at full speed on the

1. The Hull Steam Trawler *Viola*

2. *Viola*'s sister ship *Cassio*

3–6. Boxing fleet crews ...

... at work and rest

7. Boarding: Transferring the catch to the steam cutter for conveying to market

8. Boarding operation instructions issued by the vessel owners & underwriters committee

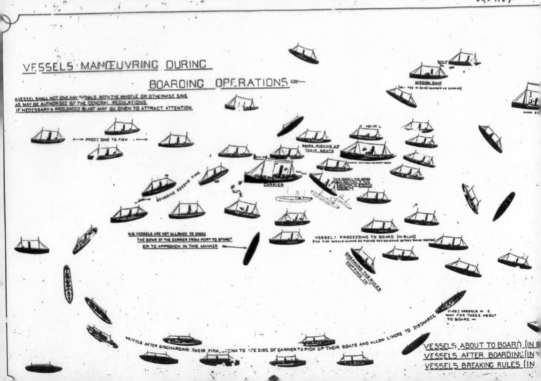

9. G W Tharratt

10. Charles Allum in his later years

11. Charles Allum's Certificate of his Mention in Despatches

The War of 1914-1918.

The Lords Commissioners of the Admiralty hereby certify that

Ch. Skpr. Charles Allum, R.N.R, 260 W.S.A.

was mentioned in Despatches in recognition of distinguished services during the War and that his name was published in the London Gazette dated 20th September 1918. The King has commanded that His high appreciation of the services rendered shall be recorded on this certificate.

By Command of Their Lordships

O. Murray

Admiralty,
Whitehall, S.W.1.

12. The cast & crew of the movie *A Master of Craft*, 1922, Charles Allum 2nd from right

13. Crew of the Admiralty 'Mersey' Class armed trawler *John Appleby* on Auxiliary Patrol duty

14. Harrow Street victory party

15. Harrow Street Roll of Honour

16. Grave of Thomas Craven at Lerwick, Shetland

T. CRAVEN
DECK HAND, R.N.R. 1386/DA
H.M. TRAWLER 'VIOLA'
7TH NOVEMBER 1914

17. *Kapduen* as a whale catcher, taken in Norway mid-1920s, with whale gun platform fitted forward

18. Grytviken Whaling Station at around the time *Dias* arrived at South Georgia, c1927

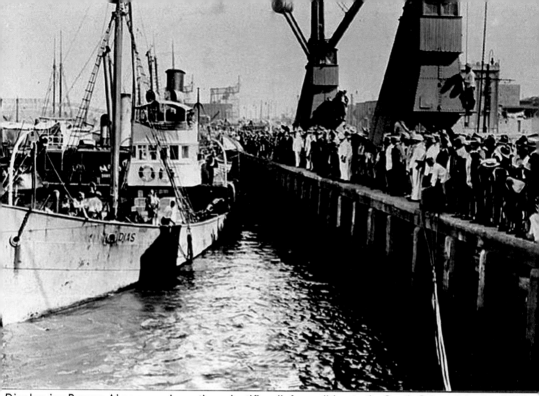

Dias leaving Buenos Aires on an Argentine scientific relief expedition to the South Orkney Islands, c1932

20. Argentine weather station at Laurie Island, South Orkney, 1930s, relieved by *Dias* 1927-42

21. Thorleif Hammerstad, Master, *Dias* 1953-6   22. Duncan Carse, Grytviken, c1957, *Petrel* be

23. Grytviken in the 1950s, *Dias* at Harpon Quay in foreground, floating dry-dock in background

Flenser Pablo Lesbehzk of Buenos Aires, 1961

25. Arne Bogen, Master, *Dias* 1957-9

26. Japanese sealers and *Dias*, 1960s

27. *Dias* at the Catcher Quay, 1965

28. Elephant Sealing at the Bay of Isles, South Georgia, 1958

29. *Dias* at Grytviken, early 1950s, between a whale-catcher, probably *Orca*, and the sealer *Albatros*

30. *Dias* at South Georgia, 1955

31. *Dias* (nearest), *Albatros* and *Petrel* at Grytviken, Dec 1961

32. *Dias*, left, and *Albatros* abandoned and half sunk at Grytviken, May 1976
33. *Viola/Dias* refloated, January 2004

34. Deck aft
35. Deck forward

36. Bell and ship reunited for the first time in over eighty years
37. Model of *Viola* by Alan Richardson of Hull, who saw her at Grytviken while with the Royal Fleet Aux

unsuspecting U-boat. Only as the armed trawler closed did the Germans realise their peril. The periscope dipped beneath the waves, then shot up again
some ten seconds later. All on board *John Gilman* felt a grating as they slid
over the U-boat, scraping the periscope as it passed abreast of the armed
trawler's winch: two depth charges set to detonate at eighty feet went over
the side. Explosions juddered through the trawler, knocking the crew across
the deck, but the effect of the depth charges on the U-boat crew below them
is almost unimaginable. A dan buoy was thrown into the sea to mark the German's last known position; soon afterwards oil and air bubbles rose to the surface. By this time another armed trawler, *Miranda III*, ex-*Miranda* had joined
the affray and more depth charges were pitched into the waves.

Viola and *John Brooker*, another Castle Class armed trawler, then steamed
up and lowered their hydrophones to listen for movement. After more than
two hours on watch both vessels saw the U-boat just below the surface. They
closed, firing two rounds each from their guns, then depth-charged the German vessel as it slipped downward once more. Ten minutes later the armed
trawler *Florio* joined the hunt as the submarine, by now visibly struggling,
and possibly unable to see anything out of the damaged periscope, surfaced
yet again amidst a mess of oil and air bubbles. Then down, down it went
again, seemingly for the last time as another six depth-charges from *John
Gillman* and *Florio* followed it to the bottom. Large quantities of oil and bubbles erupted on the surface then nothing else was seen. Although it appeared
that the submarine had been mortally wounded, the watch was maintained.
The site was depth-charged once more at low water by the armed trawler
Sparrow then the position was swept and an obstruction found on the bottom
near the dan buoy.[25]

Four days later an Admiralty diving team confirmed the kill and the identity of the U-boat. Such dives to stricken U-Boats were about much more than
just confirming sinkings. Some were investigated with a view to possible salvage, others were dived by members of a little-known intelligence-gathering
team. This had been formed back in July 1915 soon after the German mine
laying U-boat UC-2 had sunk after a collision with the small steamer *Cotting-*

ham. The UC-2's site had been marked and the Admiralty decided to send a diver down to see if anything further could be learned from examining the wreckage. The man chosen for the descent was Ernest (Dusty) Miller, an instructor in the Navy Diving School at Whale Island, Portsmouth. The team hurried from Portsmouth to the East Anglian coast and Miller descended to the wreck down the buoyed line and found that one of the UC-2's own mines had torn a gaping hole in its side. Careful not to trap the heavy paraphernalia of pipes and wires that linked his diving suit to the surface, he groped his way through twisted metal and into the pitch black of UC-2's claustrophobic interior. The Admiralty was so pleased with the codebooks and other documentation he brought back to the surface that the covert diving team was created. For the rest of the war they rushed around the country investigating reports of U-boat sinkings off the coast. The work carried out by Miller and his colleagues must have been harrowing in the extreme. Apart from the sheer lack of visibility on many descents, Miller had also to find a way into the wreck. Usually an explosive charge was used to blow open the hatch, and then the diver, clad in his cumbersome gear, squeezed his way into the blackness, searching amidst bodies and the dark internal debris of destruction for the U-boat's vital documents. The sheer hell of the last hours of those who were trapped in the stricken U-boats must have been all too evident to a diver entering a vessel so soon after a sinking. On one occasion Miller found a body with three gunshot wounds, his hands caught up in the handle of the conning tower hatch. It was the commander and he had been shot from below with a revolver whilst trying to either seal the hatch or alternatively open it. Despite the gruesome nature of the work, the intelligence gained from the documents recovered, such as German naval codes, was apparently invaluable.

In 1992 the wreck of the UB-30 was re-discovered by a team of divers off Whitby: its periscope clearly bent from the collision with *John Gillman* on that fateful day seventy-four years earlier and its hatches still open, as blown by the Admiralty diving team. Today the vessel is, of course, a war grave, a solemn underwater memorial to the crew who lost their lives aboard her in that long-ago struggle for supremacy on the seas.

The sinking of the UB-30 was probably not quite the last occasion in the Great War that armed trawlers destroyed a German submarine. There were a number of further encounters, even some sinkings, and the unrestricted U-boat campaign continued until almost the final weeks of the war, and one of these involved *Viola*. On 29 September oil leaking from what turned out to be the UB-115, under the command of Reinhold Thomsen, was spotted by the airship R29 on patrol from East Fortune in Scotland. The vessel was apparently carrying out repairs whilst lying off the Northumberland coast a few miles off the hamlet of Newton by the Sea. The R29's commander, Major G.M. Thomas, dropped two 230lb bombs on the unsuspecting submarine and a calcium flare over the position whilst calling up available help. The destroyers HMS *Ouse* and HMS *Star* soon arrived and dropped seven depth charges. They were followed to the scene by the armed trawlers *Beatrice*, *Bombardier*, *Florio*, *Stronsay* and *Viola,* which then subjected the stricken U-boat to a further sustained attack with ten depth charges. The hydrophone operators on the trawlers heard the U-boat start its engines at 2pm and a further twelve depth charges were sent down. An hour later the U-boat engines were heard again and two more depth charges were dropped. Intermittent sounds continued to be heard until 6.25pm then all fell silent below. Oil welled up to the surface for two more days, which minesweepers reported as coming from a definite obstruction. The thirty-nine crew members were lost with their submarine.[26] This action is believed to have been the first to have involved the use of an airship in the destruction of a submarine, and the UB-115 was probably the last U-boat sunk in conflict in the North Sea during the Great War. In 1920, the crews of the airship R29 and all the vessels involved were awarded prize bounty money.[27] Today the wreck lies in two halves about four and a half nautical miles off Newton by the Sea, a poignant final reminder of the grim North Sea U-boat war.

But even the late sinking of UB-115 was not to be the last submarine lost in the region during the Great War. Just over two weeks later, the British submarine J6 was sunk off the Northumberland coast some 26 or so miles off Beadnell, but her loss was not attributable to enemy action. The crew of the barquentine *Cymric*, a Q ship on a southerly patrol from the Firth of Forth, spotted a submarine on the surface steaming in their direction. Lt Commander Peterson, *Cymric*'s commander, had not been warned to expect allied submarine movements even though his course took his ship close to the port of Blyth, base for the 11th Submarine Flotilla. Although the submarine's gun seemed unmanned and people were evidently on the bridge, Peterson was disturbed about the position of the gun, which did not seem to correspond with the silhouettes they had become familiar with. *Cymric* waited until the submarine was on its beam and then, convinced that this was the U-6, Peterson gave orders for action. His ship raised the White Ensign and, although there seemed to be a pause, no recognition came from the submarine. The lack of recognition convinced Peterson he was dealing with the enemy; a U-boat had indeed been reported in the vicinity some days before. After a brief pause, the Q-ship dropped its bulwarks and exposed its guns. *Cymric*'s first two shots fell short but the third hit home near the aft end of the conning tower. The order was given for independent fire and several more shells hit home.

Lt Commander Warburton, at rest in his bunk in the J6, rushed up to the conning tower, ordering full speed on both engines. Signalman Field, who was trying to fire off recognition signals, went down in the attack, mortally wounded, the recognition grenade rolling across the conning tower deck to explode near Lieutenant Brierly whose jaw was blown off. Warburton quickly fired off six grenades but without effect as the smoke from *Cymric*'s guns obscured the signal and still the J6 ran forward.

The J6 was by now completely stricken; shots had perforated the conning tower and there was a great gash blown in the side of the engine room, whilst the ballast tanks were also holed. Though an ensign streamed astern of the J6 the *Cymric*'s command did not spot this and only ceased fire when a white flag was spotted. The J6's commander was unable to stop engines and as his submarine continued to move forward the *Cymric* opened fire once more. The J6 started to go down but the *Cymric*'s crew did not realise their tragic mistake until they came alongside the debris of the sinking; Lieutenants Peterson and Mutch then dived into the water to try and save the surviving submariners.

That evening the *Cymric* entered Blyth with the J6's survivors and tied up behind the other J class vessels, amid much emotion from the submariners and the crowd of relatives and friends gathered outside the gates by the harbour. Fifteen men were lost in this friendly fire tragedy. The subsequent court of enquiry, classified for seventy-five years, found that the J6 was fired upon because the crew did not get away the recognition signals in time. Following this tragedy the flare pistol was mounted close to the periscope for easier access.[28]

The sinking of the UB-115 the previous month was almost *Viola*'s final belligerent action in the Great War. As the German military situation deteriorated on land at the end of the summer, the Flanders U-boat bases had to be evacuated and on 21 October the U-boat offensive was finally called off and this colossal struggle at sea finally came to an end. The German commitment and cost was considerable, they had deployed more than 370 U-boats and lost 178 of these—almost half—together with almost 5,000 men. During the final restricted and unrestricted campaigns the U-boats had sunk more than 11 million tons—5,078 ships—a quarter of the world's tonnage. Around one-third of the tonnage with which Britain entered the war was eliminated. The struggle had been close.

But the bitter war continued on this coast right until the end. On 10 November 1918 HMS *Ascot*, a Racehorse Class paddlewheel minesweeper, specially built for this purpose in 1916, was torpedoed by UB-67 off the Farne Islands. HMS *Ascot* was the last ship to be sunk before the Armistice and her entire crew were lost just hours before hostilities ceased.

The Armistice of 11 November 1918 was not quite the end of the conflict for the vessels and men of the Auxiliary Patrol. Many were retained for service well into the following year on minesweeping and some patrol work and *Viola*, her skipper, Charles Allum, and his crew did not return to civilian duties for a number of months.[29]

Since the conflict a flood-tide of academic and popular print have been devoted to the history of capital ships such as the dreadnoughts and events such as the Battle of Jutland. Far less has been written about the role of the

Auxiliary Patrol and, one could argue, its role has often been considerably underplayed. There might be some grounds for believing that the pre-war obsession with the capital ships has been echoed in the emphasis in many histories of the war that have followed. This is not the place for a radical and full re-assessment of the role of the smaller ships of the Great War Navy, but perhaps it is long overdue.

What is clear is that pre-war predictions by some naval experts that a second and decisive Trafalgar would decide the maritime dimension of any future conflict simply did not materialise. The actual course of the war exposed shortcomings in many aspects of conventional strategic thinking. It proved to be a war of grim attrition, and vessels such as *Viola* and their crews, rather than the great capital ships, were constantly at sea, day after day and month after month, in the front line of the struggle against the U-boats, torpedoes and sea mines. A high price was certainly paid by the fishing industry for its contribution to the War Effort in terms of both active service and maintaining the food supplies. The actual losses of fishermen from Hull during the conflict never seem to have been quantified but an analysis of Alec Gill's informative book *The Lost Trawlers of Hull*[30] shows that a total of 125 Hull trawlers were lost during the war and of these sixty-six were lost whilst fishing and a further fifty-nine were destroyed whilst on Admiralty Service, mostly whilst on minesweeping and patrol duties around the British Isles, but a few as far away as the Mediterranean. Altogether, some 1,467 steam trawlers and 1,502 drifters were requisitioned and of these 244 and 127, respectively, were lost whilst on service. When one includes vessels lost whilst fishing the total is much higher. Altogether 503, or more than one out of every four, British steam trawlers did not survive the war.[31]

The Hellyer fleet paid a particularly high price, possibly greater than any other entity in terms of numbers and proportions. *Viola* survived more than four years of naval service, but the fleet started the war with forty-seven vessels of which twenty-two—nearly half—never came back to port. Eighteen of these were lost whilst fishing and another four on Admiralty service. British fishermen of all ages were engaged in the front line of the war effort at all levels. Many of those who had joined the army in the early patriotic rush fell with their colleagues in the bloodshed amongst the trenches. Even if not recruited by the Admiralty for minesweeping and patrol duties, fishermen continued to fish in the U-boat infested seas around the British Isles and beyond. The shortage of crews meant men in their seventies, sometimes even their eighties, had returned to war. Few communities can have made a bigger contribution to the war effort than fishermen. More's the pity that their commitment and unflinching service have not received a greater level of recognition.

VI

AFTER THE ARMISTICE

A LTHOUGH THE ARMISTICE of 11 November 1918 marked the official end to hostilities, the casualty list from the maritime conflict in *Viola*'s North Sea patrol area, as indeed elsewhere, continued to mount. Eleven days later, on the night of 22 November 1918, HM Submarine G11 ran aground off Howick in Northumberland whilst on routine patrol from the River Tees. The submarine's situation was soon desperate; a barrage of angry breakers battered the stricken craft against the unyielding rocks, tearing open the hull. As water flooded aboard, two officers scrambled through heavy surf to set up a lifeline to the shore. Sodden submariners then slipped and slid across rocks washed by angry waves, finally reaching the safety of the sands where the exhausted and half frozen survivors found warmth and refuge with local fishermen's families. Two crew members didn't make it from that pitching, pitch black wreck. The body of Pliny Foster, the stoker, was never found but the remains of his crew mate, telegraphist George Philip Back, now lie in a peaceful corner of St Peter's churchyard in Longhoughton.[1] Further out to sea, the lives of many fishermen and sailors continued to be claimed by mines and other paraphernalia of war for many months, even years to come.

After the return of peace, further awards were made to RNR personnel and others for exceptional service. In March 1919 George William—aka Green Willows—Tharratt was awarded the Distinguished Service Cross for his services to minesweeping operations between 1 July and 31 December 1918.[2] True to form, George had had an 'interesting' war in more ways than one. He had joined the RNR in October 1914 at the age of 48 and spent much of the war minesweeping on the requisitioned fishing vessels *White Ear* and *Ocean Queen* whilst based at Newhaven on the south coast.[3]

Back home his second wife and adopted family had paid a high price for his working the seas through peace and war. Back in 1893 George had, as we have seen, apparently bigamously married Elizabeth Ellis, a widow with six sons. One of Elizabeth's sons had died in childhood and another had drowned as a youth whilst sketching ships by Hull's Monument Bridge.[4] The four surviving children had followed their step-father to sea but tragically all had been drowned during four or more years of war; Elizabeth's eldest son, Ben Ellis, lost in March, 1917, was also a former Hellyer skipper. Ben's trawler, *Expedient*, had been stopped then sunk by UC-75 at the height of the U-boat onslaught.[5] Although Ben and his crew had been allowed to sail off in the trawler's open boat they were never seen again.

Whilst Elizabeth was coping with these traumatic events, her 'husband' George was also in trouble, albeit of a different nature. In July 1918 he was named as co-respondent in a divorce case brought before an Admiralty Court by Frank Bailey, a Petty Officer. George had been co-habiting with Ethel, Frank Bailey's wife, and they had had a son.[6] Given the stigma such actions then caused it is perhaps all the more remarkable that a few months later George was awarded the DSC. Elizabeth seems to have become aware of the full situation around the time of the divorce case. Certainly George remained on duty on the south coast throughout 1919.[7]

By the end of the war George seems to have been living with Ethel Bailey, they had already had a couple of children, and he was perhaps not anxious to return to Hull and what awaited him there. His minesweeping expertise led to him being retained by the Mine Clearance Service and staying for some time on the south coast.

During the Great War nearly 236,000 mines were laid across the world, including around 191,000 in the North Sea alone. Clearing these deadly relics of war was a priority after the return of peace; whilst minefields continued to cover the seas they threatened a sudden and indiscriminate death to any vessel and crew which chanced upon them. The process of removal was overseen by an International Mine Clearance Service, whose membership eventually embraced twenty-six countries, including some former enemy powers who were invited to join once peace treaties were ratified. The Admiralty played a leading part in this process and the British Mine Clearance Service, formed in February 1919, was charged with clearing 40,000 square miles. The American Navy dealt with the mines sown in the Northern Barrage. At its peak, in June 1919, the Mine Clearance Service consisted of 700 officers and 14,500 men. Tharratt was one of a substantial number of fishermen and other members of the Royal Naval Reserve kept on with their vessels for this difficult work.[8] By the end of 1919 when the Service was disbanded, its vessels and personnel had removed more than 28,000 British mines from the seas with the loss of six craft. As more and more areas were cleared and the work ran down, officers and crew were demobilised, and their ships paid off.

Tharratt remained with the Mine Clearance Service almost to its end, being granted 27 days final leave on 10 December 1919, after which he officially returning to civilian seafaring[9]—but not to Hull. He took Ethel and their children to Grimsby, from where he sailed on trawlers until about 1925 after which time, in bad health, he brought his new family back to Hull where he died in 1928, leaving them destitute.[10] Cause of death was given as Nephritis and myocardial degeneration. His son Eric recalls he had what was then called a stricture, a narrowing of the urethra, and the family could not afford proper treatment. Less than ten years after being awarded the DSC he was buried in a pauper's grave in Hull's Northern Cemetery.

Ethel, now on her own and unable to support her family of, by now, five children, had reluctantly agreed to place one child in the sailors' home, an orphanage. She originally intended putting the youngest child there, but eleven-year-old Eric persuaded his mother that he should go, as he would only have a few years in there whilst the youngest faced many years away from the family. He considered this his duty as he now regarded himself as 'head of the family.'[11]

Although the minefields were eventually removed by the Mine Clearance Service during the following months, the danger posed by drifting mines which had broken free from their moorings remained. Such stray mines, sphere-like spectres of the seaborne conflict, were a lethal form of flotsam littering the post-war ocean. They continued to reap a bitter harvest of casualties amongst the fishing and merchant fleets for several years to come.

During the initial months of peace at least three Hull trawlers were lost to mines whilst fishing. In February 1919 the ten man crew of *Sapphire* were lucky to escape with their lives when their trawler hit a stray mine off the Humber. Crews were warned to keep an especially sharp lookout for military hazards, but the explosion occurred in darkness at four in the morning. A.W. Hartley, *Sapphire*'s spare hand, was making his first trip back, six days after being demobilized following several years of largely mishap-free minesweeping duties. His brother, also on board and another veteran of naval service, was on watch at the time of the explosion and severely shaken when *Sapphire*'s bridge collapsed in the blast.[12] A few weeks later, two other Hull RNR veterans were less lucky. Joseph Raywell, a trimmer, was lost less than three months after being demobilized when his trawler *Scotland* went down, believed mined, off Flamborough Head. Bernard Carlton Brignall, known as Bricky to family and friends, was lost with all hands aboard the Hull steam trawler *Durban* a week or so later. Bricky was making his first voyage on the trawler after demobilization, having served nearly three years minesweeping in the Royal Naval Reserve Trawler Section.[13]

Both Raywell and Brignall are amongst the many fishermen and merchant mariner casualties of the Great War conflict who have no other grave but the sea. Today, their names are commemorated on the Tower Hill Memorial in London. Others whose bodies were recovered were buried ashore; their graves, marked by Commonwealth War Graves Commission headstones, are scattered across many cemeteries in towns and villages around the coasts of the British Isles.

On the River Tyne the demobilization of Auxiliary Patrol personnel and vessels appears to have proceeded apace during the early months of 1919. The Auxiliary Patrol Base at Northumberland Dock was finally closed on 31 March, a few days after Charles Allum had been officially demobilized,[14] but by this date *Viola* had already left the Tyne. The steam trawler seems to have been released from service by early February. Her stores were discharged at North Shields before she set sail for Milford Haven. *Viola*'s voyage was broken by a short final visit to Hull, where she berthed in Humber Dock on 14 February to sail on again some three days later.[15] Official records tell us *Viola*'s crew was demobilized after reaching Milford and dispersed to their homes in seaports across the country.[16] Although we don't know the skipper for this voyage it appears quite likely that *Viola* was taken to Wales by Charles Allum.

All the Hull boxing fleets suffered substantial losses during the Great War, and afterwards the survivors of the Red Cross, Great Northern and Gamecock fleet trawlers were amalgamated into two fleets, operated by the Hull Steam Fishing and Ice Company and by Kelsall Brothers and Beeching Limited. In the last years before the war it had become apparent to the British trawling trade that sending vessels on voyages to northern fishing grounds—later known as the Northern Trawl—was proving more profitable than North Sea fleeting. The fish-rich distant water grounds off Iceland, in the Barents Sea and elsewhere were more productive than the heavily-fished North Sea. The average catches made by distant water trawlers for each day's absence from port were much higher than those made by North Sea fleeting trawlers, even though about six or seven days of each three week trip was spent not fishing, but voyaging to and from the far-off northern fishing grounds.

The Hellyer Boxing Fleet was not reconstituted after the war. As early as the end of 1916, after facing the main onslaught of the U-boat offensive on their fishing vessels, it was already evident to the Hellyer family that they would have to replace more than a third of their North Sea trawlers if they were to re-form the fleet. A few months afterwards Hellyers decided to change direction. Henceforward, their strategy was to largely abandon their North Sea interests and concentrate on the more profitable opportunities offered by distant water fishing. The likely post-war availability, at knock-down prices, of suitable modern Admiralty-built trawlers provided a further incentive for disposing of their fleeting interests. In the summer of 1917 they began selling off their surviving fleeting trawlers. Some were sold to firms like Curzons of Milford Haven whilst others, including *Viola*, were purchased by W.A. Massey and Sons of Quay Street, Hull. Masseys were shipbrokers and though this change of ownership made no difference at the time to the vessels on war service, it meant they were all put up for sale again after demobilization.

At Hull, *Viola*'s old port, maritime change resulting from the war, and the necessity of adjusting to its aftermath, was not limited to the fishing industry. Thomas Wilson, Sons and Company of Hull, still one of the largest shipping firms in the world, was acquired by locally born Sir John Ellerman—one of the richest men in the world—from the Wilson family, and Ellerman's Wilson Line was to be a dominant force in merchant shipping for several decades to come. On a different level, a number of River Humber tug owners, who had been working closely together as Hull Associated Tug Owners since 1913, decided to rationalize the Humber's towing business to better cope with the post-war situation by forming the United Towing Company in December 1920.[17] More than sixty years later Hull tugs owned by United Towing were to play a significant role in another phase of *Viola*'s story.

Skipper Herbert Johnson was just one of many former Hellyer boxing fleet fishermen who had to change direction after the war. For a number of years in the 1920s he took Hellyer Brothers trawlers to fish off Iceland and other northern grounds but in the 1930s, after disagreements with the firm's owners, he found it ever more difficult to get a ship; he ended his seagoing career taking redundant vessels, including the old fleeters, on their final voyages to the scrapyard. Later he took a job ashore as an engineer's mate with Brigham and Cowan, a well-known engineering firm. He died, aged 85, in the late 1970s but not before making a number of wonderful tape recordings recalling his life and times at sea.

Hull's two surviving boxing fleets continued fishing into the 1930s but their persistently low profitability was reflected in a dearth of new investment. A few second-hand vessels were added to the fleets at various times in the 1920s, but over the long term they were allowed to run down and wear out, and by the mid-1930s the number of trawlers still working was no more than sixty, or less than twenty-five per cent of the pre-war peak. The end finally came in March 1936, after months of heavy financial losses due to poor fishing caused by extraordinary weather conditions, and complaints about the rising price of commodities, especially coal. Continued investment and mechanical innovation in the distant water sector had reduced coal consumption and increased efficiency amongst the new trawlers voyaging north, and further highlighted the shortcomings of the ageing North Sea boxing craft. Even the reduced fleets left fishing were said to consume a total of 100,000 tons annually. The shareholders of the two companies met in Hull and the decision was made to call back the vessels from the grounds and liquidate both concerns. Eight hundred men were thrown out of work and all the fleeters and steam carriers laid up.[18]

Henceforward, no one would witness at first hand the perilous transfer of fish boxes from trawler to steam carrier at sea. A small snatch of film taken in the twenties is all that is left. The bringing back of the boxing fleets marked the end of an era, of a tradition started by Hewett's of Barking back in the 1820s. A large number of the older fleeting vessels were sold off for scrap, but some were transferred to other ports such as Aberdeen, Fleetwood and Milford Haven and converted to work as single-boaters. A few continued fishing until the 1950s.

Many of the younger deckhands soon found work in the vibrant distant water trawling sector, but for older skippers and mates, whose expertise lay in their intimate knowledge of the North Sea grounds, this was a difficult time. At least one veteran boxing fleet mate and former RNR minesweeper, George Robinson, eventually found further employment at sea but in a hardly less hazardous pursuit. He signed up as a deckhand on *Strafford*, a tanker which was running vital fuel supplies from the south coast of France to Spanish Government forces fighting General Franco in the bitter Civil War. Although his vessel was dive-bombed on at least one occasion in Valencia Harbour, Robinson continued to sail on *Strafford* until just a few days before the ending of the Spanish Civil War in 1939.[19] We have no idea how many other boxing fleet fishermen followed in his footsteps but whereas today those who fought on the Government side against Franco for the International Brigades are often commemorated, there seems to be little recognition of the contribution made by British seamen in that conflict.

Although a few of the Hellyer trawlers, including *Ariel* and *Bianca*, had been brought back to Hull to rejoin the surviving boxing fleets during the 1920s, most of their sister ships had already been dispersed to ports far and wide. Some were later found working out of Fleetwood, Lowestoft, Grimsby and Aberdeen, but quite a number also fished from South Wales ports, most notably Swansea and Milford Haven. Many were eventually wrecked or were sunk by enemy action during the Second World War and most of the last survivors were scrapped in the 1950s. Those sold abroad usually lasted a little longer. *Dorcas* and *Falstaff* were the last two of the Beverley-built Hellyer vessels still fishing. Renamed respectively *Donostia* and *Pasaya*, they were still fishing from the Spanish port of San Sebastian in the early 1970s. The old *Falstaff* finally foundered in March 1971 after springing a leak in her engine-room off Pasage, whilst the sixty-seven year old *Dorcas* was sent to a Spanish scrapyard some two years later.[20]

It is worth reflecting that of the thirty-one Hellyer boxing fleet vessels built at Beverley before the Great War only twelve reached the scrapyard. All the others were lost, either to enemy action in one or other of the two world wars, or at sea whilst fishing. Since *Dorcas* was scrapped in 1973 only *Viola* remains. The twentieth century was by any measure a tumultuous time for trawlers and trawlermen.

The old Hellyer Steam Fishing Company which had built the boxing fleet was liquidated in 1919. Charles Hellyer himself, having retired to Devon before the Great War, finally passed away in 1930 aged 80. His descendants continued the family fishing business as Hellyer Brothers, and like much of the port of Hull they increasingly concentrated on the distant water fishing; this strategy brought them into increasing conflict after the Second World War with countries such as Iceland and Norway which claimed sovereignty over the their adjacent fishing grounds. In 1969 Hellyer Brothers became a major part of British United Trawlers and as such were one of Hull's last trawling

firms lasting until the later twentieth century, some years after the last of the
so-called Cod Wars with Iceland ended in the mid-1970s.

But what of Charles Allum, *Viola*'s long serving war-time skipper? Allum was demobilized in early March 1919 and although initially based in
South Shields, he and Jane moved to Swansea where he worked as a skipper
during the 1920s. But in 1922 he had the opportunity to deploy his nautical
skills in a rather different way, playing a part in *A Master of Craft*, a silent
comedy, directed by Thomas Bentley and starring Fred Goves, Mercy Hat-
ton and Judd Green. The movie, made by Ideal Films, was based on a book
written by W. W. Jacobs and published in 1900. *A Master of Craft* is a story
of marital mishap and misadventure, of an East End coaster captain with a
love affair in every port. Although his film career did not continue, Allum
is immortalised amongst the cast in a wonderful publicity photograph taken
back in 1922.

Afterwards, Charles Allum seems to have returned to trawling, though he
had at least one spell on a merchant ship in 1925. In late 1930 he was widowed
once more when Jane died in Swansea aged just sixty. He never remarried
but continued in the Royal Naval Reserve, and at the outbreak of the Second
World War was recalled to service. Although by then more than sixty years
old he took command of the minesweeper *Fintray*, based at Port Edgar on the
Firth of Forth, staying with the vessel for more than a year. Afterwards he returned to the merchant service and family legend has it that he was later on a
ship that was torpedoed, and afterwards suffered poor health. He eventually
gave up the sea and moved to Liverpool to live with his daughter's family. His
last cabin was the front room of their council house and he eventually died,
primarily of bronchial complications, in the local hospital in March 1953.[21]
He was 73 years old and his remains were cremated a few days later. His family's lasting reminder of his remarkable seagoing career is a precious box of
medals and certificates.[22]

By the time he died, Charles Allum had probably long since lost touch
with the movements of his old ship and former Great War shipmates. Indeed, *Viola* was by then many thousands of miles away in the South Atlantic.

But back in 1919, after demobilization, the vessel seems to have been laid up for sale for some months alongside a large number of former Admiralty trawlers in Milford Haven.

In February 1920 the vessel was finally sold by Massey's to L. Thorsen of Sandefjord in Norway for £11,000. Thorsen appears to have been acting on behalf of a consortium A/S Sandefjord Trawlfiskeselskap, managed by whaling manager A. H. Andersen, who were intent on trawling in the waters of the Skagerrak and possibly the North Sea.[23] Her master, according to the Veritas Register, was C. Hansen.[24] *Viola*'s new home port was the famous whaling town of Sandefjord, in Norway's Vestfold County, then regarded as one of the richest places in the country. Sandefjord was situated in an area steeped in maritime history, the world famous, Gokstad Viking ship having been unearthed nearby back in 1880. Whaling in the southern oceans was the source of the port's early twentieth century prosperity, but the old trawler was initially destined for other work. She was probably overhauled on arrival at the famous Framnæs shipyard, and at the time of her Norwegian registration renamed *Kapduen*[25], the Norwegian for 'Cape Pigeon,' or the Cape Petrel, a common seabird in the Southern Ocean.

Only a little is now known of the ship's early Norwegian sojourn. Although purchased by a trawling company it seems unlikely that she was used for this purpose. Trawling was a controversial activity there. Whilst Norway was one of the largest fishing nations in the world, most fish landed there was caught in small motor boats, worked by owner-operators, who sailed out of the mosaic of fjords that made up much of the country's long coastline. Inshore fishing from small vessels was the lifeblood of many Norwegian coastal communities, and steam trawling in particular was regarded with much suspicion by many fishermen's interest groups. It was feared that this practice would not only tend to concentrate the Norwegian population in larger fishing ports, thus depopulating many northern parts of the country, but might also lead to an erosion of the rich fish stocks which teemed off its coast. In the 1920s local inshore fishermen's groups were able to gain sufficient economic support to secure a curtailing of Norwegian trawling activities.

Certainly there is no mention in the local newspapers of *Kapduen* going trawling, indeed for a year or two the ex-trawler seems mainly to have been used as a tug, towing vessels in and out of Sandefjord Harbour and the ten kilometre long fjord which linked the town to the open seas.[26] All connections with fishing were not ended, however; during the winter of 1922-3 at least, she was sent to Haugesund, a town near Stavanger on the west coast, to work as a transport vessel in the winter herring fishery there.[27]

Herring fishing was of crucial economic importance to Norway's southwest coastal communities. The large shoals taken during the winter season by myriads of small vessels provided employment and some degree of prosperity for many people. Large quantities of herring were exported, particularly to England where a dearth of home herring landings during the winter season meant there was a healthy demand for these fish; they were carried to ports such as Hull where they were hung by the thousand in kilns, known as smoke houses, above oak chip fires to be turned into kippers, then one of the UK's most popular breakfast meals.

Fish transport and towing apart, it seems likely that *Kapduen* was underemployed during these early post-war years. But all this was to change in 1923, a few months after Sandefjord Trawlfiskeselskap, the company which owned her, was completely taken over by Nils Torvald Nielsen-Alonso, a highly experienced veteran of the Norwegian whaling industry.[28]

VII

WHALING

WHALING, LIKE SEA FISHING, is a pursuit with primeval origins. Whilst whale carcasses washed ashore are today often perceived as either an ecological calamity or a public health hazard, our ancestors viewed them as a valuable, if occasional and unexpected, bounty of the ocean. In England manorial records show they were usually regarded as the property of the local lord of the manor or even the monarch. When schools of whales and other sea mammals were known to visit accessible inshore waters and inlets then neighbouring inhabitants often organised communal hunting expeditions. The Basques were probably the first people in the Western world to take whaling beyond the littoral zone and develop the basic features of a modern commercial whale fishery. By the fifteenth century they were sailing out to hunt whales breeding in the Bay of Biscay. They probably hunted the now extinct eastern population of the northern right whale. Right whales are so-called because they simply were the right whales to take. They were somewhat inquisitive, quite slow swimmers and, most importantly, floated when killed.

Whales were then hunted primarily for their oil, which was a fuel for lighting, and also a lubricant in an age when mineral oil was not available, as well as a base for soap. Later, other whale products such as whalebone (or baleen) were to prove particularly useful for making a range of manufactured items, from corset stays to walking sticks, brushes to umbrellas.

The Dutch and English, in seeking a north-east passage to China across the top of the world in the sixteenth century, encountered vast numbers of whales in Arctic regions, especially in the waters around the Spitzbergen Archipelago. Soon sailors from both nations began voyaging northwards in order to hunt Greenland right whales and other sea mammals.[1] Rowing boats, catching equipment and crews, indeed all the paraphernalia of whaling, were carried north on sailing ships each year. Manufactories for flensing sea mammals and rendering whale and seal blubber into oil were set up on the shore. Whales frequenting nearby bays were hunted from small boats and killed with hand thrown spears and harpoons, their bodies then towed to the shore for cutting up. This method was known as bay whaling.

At the end of the short summer season, as days shortened, weather conditions worsened and the ice thickened, everything, including the casks of whale oil, was packed on board the sailing ships and the homeward voyage commenced. English interest in Spitzbergen at this time was in theory led by the Muscovy Company of London which had been granted monopoly powers by the Monarch, but in these distant waters the company's vessels and crews enjoyed a fractious relationship with Hull seamen who were also early visitors to these parts and continually asserted what they saw as their right to take whales, seals and walruses there.[2]

Hull and London ships continued to make whaling voyages into the later 1630s, but suffered adversely during the upheavals which accompanied the English Civil War and its aftermath, and eventually this first phase of English involvement completely collapsed, some years after the Restoration in 1660. There were probably other reasons for the decline. The Dutch were more innovative at this time, exploring further northwards and westwards, pursuing whales into and amongst the pack ice.[3] Henceforth, the northern whale fishery was largely left to the Dutch until English interest revived in the later eighteenth century.

Across the Atlantic, the North American colonists began hunting whales in the seventeenth century off the shores of Long Island and elsewhere. Settlers on Nantucket Island soon emulated the practices of the indigenous peoples and early Long Island whalers; by the early 1700s they dominated the North American whaling industry. Initially they hunted from the shore but they soon began voyaging far out to sea. They came to focus on hunting sperm whales, a pursuit which took them further and further from their home waters. These whales were particularly valuable because they also floated when killed, and their oil burned clearly and brightly and made a first class lubricant, whilst the spermaceti found in the head of the sperm whales produced the finest grade of candles. Ambergris, sometimes found in their bowels, was also extremely valuable as a perfume fixative. The ports of Nantucket and New Bedford thus came to specialise in the hunt for sperm whales.

American whalers began pursuing whales across the North and South Atlantic, as far as the coast of Guinea in Africa and Brazil in South America. Later, they ranged much further across the southern oceans. Even before the War of Independence and the creation of the United States, American whaling led the world and was at one time the fifth largest industry in the new nation.

British interest in whaling revived during the eighteenth century and was encouraged by the government, who began offering a range of subsidies known as bounties. In part this was to make the country less reliant both on Dutch imports and supplies from the increasingly recalcitrant American colonies; but it was also because the whaling trade was seen as a nursery for skilled seamen, so important to the Royal Navy in times of war, and this was a particularly war-like century for the British. The eighteenth century also witnessed the onset of the industrial revolution, and whale oil was much in demand to light the nation's growing industrial towns and cities as well as to lubricate the new factory machinery. Many English and Scottish ports participated in this second stage of UK whaling, but by the end of the eighteenth century the port of Hull was once more at the forefront of the industry.

The swift rise of the British whale fishery in the eighteenth century was matched by an almost equally rapid decline in its fortunes after 1820. In part this was due to the withdrawal of government subsidies, but the invention of coal gas in the early 1800s was probably a more important factor. Coal gas rapidly replaced whale oil as a source of street and house lighting, and soon afterwards mineral oil began to offer an alternative form of lubrication, as well as yet another competing source of lighting. Moreover, the sheer numbers of whaling ships that worked in Arctic waters had depleted the huge stocks of right whales once found there. Those British ships that still went whaling had to venture further northwards, many rounding Cape Farewell at the bottom of Greenland, voyaging into the ice-cold uncertainties of Baffin Bay and beyond. Casualty rates increased as many whaling ships were lost, crushed in the ice. The writing was on the wall. The British whaling fleet declined rapidly in the decades down to 1850, Hull's last whaling ship sailed in 1868—by that time the Hellyers were already establishing their fishing interests in the port—and soon Dundee and Peterhead in Scotland were the only ports still sending whaling vessels to sea.

In the United States, after the Civil War in the 1860s and the sinking of the first oil well in 1859, the whaling fleet also diminished rapidly, even though there still seemed to be plenty of sperm whales in the world's oceans. American whaling withered because of the decline in demand for traditional whale products in a country which found it had huge reserves of coal and oil. More lucrative returns on capital investment were increasingly available, as the new nation industrialized and western frontier lands were opened up.

Thus the western whaling industries, assailed as they were both by stock depletion and falling demand for whale products, seemed to be on their last legs. Yet in the later nineteenth century, as traditional whalers pulled out of the pursuit, the trade was to be transformed and revived, not by the USA or the UK, but by Norway. The Norwegian revival was based on the development and utilization of new technology, principally the explosive harpoon and the steam whale catcher. The leading figure in this field was Svend Foyn, born back in 1809 in Foynegården near the town of Tønsberg in Southern Norway.

During the 1860s Foyn introduced new methods of whaling which did away with the need to pursue whales in open rowing boats. He perfected the two essential elements of the modern whaling industry. Guns, or cannons, fitted with a barbed explosive harpoon were mounted on the bows of the steam whale catcher; as the vessel came up alongside its prey, the cannon was fired, the barbed harpoon hooked into the whale and the explosive charge finished it off. The technique, which was perfected by Norwegian harpooners, proved formidably efficient and the new whaling techniques not only increased the harvesting of traditionally hunted stocks but, more importantly, allowed the whaling industry to capture large numbers of faster moving large rorqual species, like the blue whale and fin whale, which had eluded traditional whalers in rowing boats. Once captured, whales could now also be pumped full of compressed air which eliminated the problems associated with those species that tended to sink after death. Norway also proved to have another powerful advantage over traditional whaling nations, particularly the USA: its labour costs were much lower as there were fewer alternative employment opportunities for the Norwegian workforce.

These new steam whale catchers initially worked from bases well placed along the routes of the annual whale migrations on the north-west and northern coasts of Norway, especially in Finnmark and beyond the North Cape, as well as in Iceland. After capture, the carcasses of the whales were towed to these coastal whaling stations where they were processed. The efficiency of modern whaling techniques soon made its mark and by 1900 there was already evidence that all species, not just the right whales, were rapidly decreasing off the Norwegian coast. In response, modern land-based whaling stations were set up in Svalbard (known to the Dutch and English as Spitzbergen), the Faroe Islands and Newfoundland. By 1903 some Norwegian whaling companies were looking at moving further afield, including, as we shall see, even as far as the Southern Ocean. In the course of the next decade, Sandefjord, Tønsberg's neighbour, became the world's leading whaling port, a modern Nantucket or New Bedford, sending expeditions to all corners of the world, to everywhere that whales were to be found. In addition to land stations, floating factory ships were employed which processed the whales in the sheltered bays to which they were taken by their attendant steam catcher vessels.

One Norwegian who made his name during the rise of the modern whaling industry was Nils Thorvald Nielsen-Alonso. Born in 1853, Alonso joined a sealing expedition to the Arctic at the age of fourteen in the ice-ship *Jan Mayn*. In 1881 he obtained his Master's certificate in Norway and two years later his British Master Mariner's certificate in Hull. He became the first officer on a British troop transportship during the Anglo-Egyptian war of 1882, and thereafter the Master of eight British ships including several Hull registered steamships: the *Ganos*, the *Alonso* and *Iris* owned by Edward Leetham, the *Beryl*, the passenger ship *Queen* of Liverpool, *Nerissa* of London and *Cotterstone* of Sunderland.[4] Many years later, after a further period in the Arctic sealing industry, Alonso joined the whale factory ship *Allemania* on a whaling expedition to Svalbard. In 1911, he formed his own whaling company, A/S Bas, using a three masted sailing vessel *Alonso* as a whale factory ship which he commanded in his own right, and two whale catchers. During the period 1911-15 whaling expeditions were dispatched to Bahía do Lobito and Bahía dos Elephantos on the coast of Angola, where the company worked in association with small stations erected on shore.[5]

Using the benefit of his former associations with Hull, one of the catchers that Alonso utilized was an ex-steam trawler, *Flying Fish*, originally the *Pericles* (H735), one of Charles Hellyer's vessels and built, like *Viola*, at Beverley by Cook, Welton and Gemmell in 1903 as Yard No.23. The trawler had been purchased by the Akties Trawling Kompagniet of Christiania, Norway in 1908 and sold to new Norwegian owners as *Flying Fish* a year later. Alonso converted the trawler into a combined whale catcher and auxiliary factory ship with a holding capacity of 800 barrels (133 tons) of oil.[5] In 1912 the Brazilian whaling company Duder & Brother, Bahía, converted the Cook, Welton and Gemmell built *Jamaica* (constructed as Yard No 163 at Cook's first yard on the east bank of the River Hull in the Hull district of Drypool) for humpback whaling off Brazil under the name *Bella*.[7]

The Angola expeditions were initially something of a bonanza for all concerned, with the exception of the whales. The Portuguese authorities seem to have thought that whale stocks were unlimited as they allowed many companies to join in the fishery. The expeditions initially targeted humpback whales which were found in large numbers, and relatively quiet, slow moving converted trawlers were very useful for stalking and catching this species. These whales, sometimes called the songsters of the sea because of their music-like tunes, migrate northward from the Antarctic, passing the South African coasts en route to tropical waters further up both the western and eastern coasts of Africa. The humpbacks migrate along these routes every year.

Both mating and breeding take place in tropical waters, gestation being in the region of eleven and a half months, and it was the whales reaching Angola that were to be targeted by Alonso's expedition between July and November each year. On the first expedition in 1911, 149 were caught, out of which were cooked 3,500 barrels of oil.[8]

Although the whales were relatively lean and provided less oil than in Antarctic waters, quantities of guano were also produced from processing the carcasses. Many firms, including Alonso's, seem to have done well for most of these years, buoyed by the increasing value of whale oil following the onset of the First World War. Alonso certainly prospered. He was able to build a large villa, 'Sunbeam', on Hystadveien in one of the most select areas of the port, and gifted a music pavilion to Sandefjord which was opened amidst great crowds and ceremony in 1918.

Not surprisingly, because of the competition from other whaling companies operating in West and South Africa, within a few years the numbers of humpback whales off Angola declined dramatically, and whereas 290 were caught in 1912, only 29 humpbacks out of a total of 612 whales were caught in the following season. The company had realised quickly that they would have to target other species of whale and in the years that followed blue, fin, sperm and Bryde's whales were caught. Nevertheless, Alonso's company in the period to 1915 caught a recorded 1,693 whales and produced 32,750 barrels of oil. His whaling activities were probably curtailed more by the First World War than a complete collapse of the stocks.

In 1916 Alonso was forced to divert into other business activities, including banking, but in 1922, feeling confident that stocks would have revived, he decided to return to whaling and mount another expedition to the Angolan coast. In 1920 he had been involved in Sandefjord Trawlfiskeselskap, the company which had purchased *Viola* for trawling, and brought the ship to Norway. Part of his new strategy was to acquire this company outright. Given his previous modification of the old trawler *Pericles*, *Kapduen* was, for Alonso, a logical choice. In April 1923 he sent the vessel to Framnæs Mekaniske Værksted, the local Sandefjord shipyard and, following a special survey and refit in dry dock and on slipway she was converted into a whale catcher. This involved altering the bows to take a harpoon platform, fitting a new winch and moving the bridge to a new position forward of the funnel. A crow's nest was also fitted on the main mast. These modifications not only radically altered the old trawler's appearance but also required considerable alteration to the steering gear. Designed for towing fishing gear over the seabed, she was somewhat slower than purpose-built whale catchers, but she was ideal for pursuing the relatively slow-moving humpbacks, the species the expedition was primarily seeking.

At the same time as *Kapduen* was being modified, the expedition's factory ship, *Bas II*, a 3,881 ton three-masted steam ship, built as a tanker by Armstrong, Mitchell & Co. Ltd of Newcastle-upon-Tyne in 1893, was prepared for service in the same yard. In early June, 1923, the expedition, which included two other leased whale catchers[9], sailed from Sandefjord to hunt humpback whales off Angola, under the command of Andreas Nilsen, a former pioneer of whaling in the Antarctic peninsula[10]. The nature of the whaling voyage of the *Bas II* was in many ways a precursor of things to come. This was the first ever whaling trip to operate pelagically in international waters, and dispense with the need for a whaling licence, although the factory ship had to enter the estuary of the Congo river in order to take on board fresh water for the blubber cooking processes. The whales taken were thus processed on the high seas, on board ship, rather than at an onshore station or on a processing ship tied up in a bay or harbour. Such offshore techniques of processing catches made on the high seas became known as pelagic whaling and freed the whalers from national regulations. This did nothing to protect or to encourage a sustainable level of hunting during the years to come, when pelagic whaling by factory ships, particularly in the Southern and Antarctic Oceans, became much more common.

The conditions under which the whaling crew on board *Kapduen* and the other Angolan expedition vessels worked were a far cry from the old trawler's cold North Sea haunts. Whaling could always be a difficult, gory business but the perpetually hot, humid and sticky weather made conditions exceptionally unpleasant, and it was soon evident that the catch offered little prospect of adequate recompense, as whales proved hard to come by. Indeed whilst more than 13,600 whales had been taken off the Angola coast during the peak years of 1909 to 1914[11], the stocks of humpbacks which frequented the area had not recovered from the collapse which followed the earlier on-slaught. In the 1923 season, and those which followed, no more than fifty such whales were taken off the Angolan coast each year. The *Bas II* expedi-tion found the humpbacks particularly difficult to locate and only two were killed on the whole voyage; most of the 213 animals they captured were blue whales, supplemented by a number of fin and sperm whales, yielding a mis-erable total of 4,200 barrels of oil.

Certainly, for Alonso, the results proved a disappointment and in order to try and recoup on poor catches the expedition interrupted its homeward voyage to try hunting for fin whales near the Straits of Gibraltar. During the latter part of the voyage, the *Bas II* expedition spoke with the factory ship *Sir James Clark Ross* which was voyaging south to carry out a first season of whal-ing in the Ross Sea sector of the Antarctic. On board that ship was Captain C. A. Larsen, a pioneer of Norwegian whaling in southern waters and already a Norwegian whaling legend. Larsen was to die on his second expedition to the Ross Sea but his legacy was to have a major impact on the future career of the old Hull trawler.

A hundred and twelve fin whales, yielding a further 3,800 barrels of oil, were taken off Gibraltar and the south coast of Portugal but overall returns were so poor that the whaling company was wound up soon after *Kapduen* and other vessels returned to Sandefjord in January 1924. But the vessels were not idle for long and within a few months both the former trawler and the factory ship were sold to another whaling company, A/S South Atlantic, managed by Lorentz Foyn Bruun from Tønsberg. This company had also operated at the same Angola whaling grounds pre-war, and following re-construction with in-creased share capital secured a licence from the Portuguese authorities.

The old *Viola* was now renamed *Dias*[12], whilst the factory ship *Bas II* was given the name of *Esperança*. In July 1924 the expedition, incorporating three other whale catchers, voyaged back to Angola, once more working the whaling grounds off Elephant Bay, reportedly in conjunction with a land processing station, to which *Dias* was probably seconded. On this occasion 47 humpbacks were taken, as part of a catch of 430 which included 242 sei and 75 blue whales, producing 8,710 barrels of oil and 8,100 sacks of guano. The manager, disappointed with the outcome, decided that the expedition should move north to Cabo Blanco off the French West Africa coast near the border with Spanish Morocco. Between November 1924 and February 1925 another 116 whales were captured yielding a further 3,393 barrels of oil—another disappointing outcome.[13] Cabo Blanco—the White Cape—is a remarkable and remote forty kilometre long peninsula, now known as Ras Nouadhibou. It is divided between Morocco and Mauretania and home to the world's largest surviving colony of monk seals, as well as what is claimed to be the planet's greatest graveyard of abandoned ships. The promontory's main port is Nouadhibou, formerly St Etienne, and a centre for fishing and processing iron ore in modern times. The waters off Ras Nouadhibou are one of the most northerly places reached by the Antarctic humpback whales during their annual migration. The area attracted fishermen soon after the first Portuguese explorers reached the peninsula in the 1440s. Perhaps not surprisingly, early whalers soon followed in their wake.

For *Dias* there was to be one final whaling expedition. In July 1925 the vessel was sent down to Angola once more, yet again to Elephant Bay, where she appears to have been attached with another catcher to the shore station, and her operations extended until the following October. There, 6,077 barrels of oil and 6,150 sacks of guano were produced. The *Esperança* and three catchers, meanwhile, were reported to have worked off the island of Fernando Po. Once more, the results proved disappointing for the whalers—if not the whales—and in June 1926 the company was dissolved.

Dias was by now laid up and the prospects of making a return to humpback whaling off the African coast seemed remote, especially as the slow moving ex-trawler was not really suitable for hunting the fast moving rorqual whale species which were now more commonly taken there than humpbacks. As the vessel was no longer properly equipped for trawling her future seemed uncertain. For the remainder of 1926 *Dias* languished in Sandefjord, reportedly under her former name *Kapduen*[14], but the following year a new opportunity emerged.

In 1927, Lars Klaveness, the Norwegian agent for Compañia Argentina de Pesca Sociedad Anónima[15], a Buenos Aires owned but largely Norwegian-operated whaling company, better known as Pesca, was asked by the company to look out for a vessel suitable for undertaking seal hunting activities from its base on the island of South Georgia. *Dias* seemed eminently suitable and was soon purchased by Klaveness, on Pesca's behalf. It seems that his decision may have been based on the fact that another Sandefjord-based agent, A.C. Olsen, had been asked in 1923 to secure a vessel for a South African whaling and sealing company, Irvin & Johnson of Cape Town, who also undertook sea elephant hunting on the French-administered sub-Antarctic island of Ker-guelen, deep in the South Indian Ocean. And it was perhaps pure coincidence that the vessel that they chose was *Hamlet*, formerly one of the Hellyer boxing fleet carriers built by Earle's of Hull, in the same year as *Viola*. There were further coincidences: *Hamlet* had a Lloyd's Register Official Number 123228, one less than *Viola*'s 123229, and also a Hull fishing registration of H.867, also one less than *Viola*'s H.868. A year previously in 1922 Irvin & Johnson also acquired the former Hull steam trawler *Golden Crown*, 184 tons, to add to their sealing fleet. There was a further coincidence. This vessel, like *Viola*, was also built at Grovehill, Beverley but by Cochrane and Cooper for Layman & Co. Ltd. of Hull, in the days before Cook, Welton and Gemmell took over the shipyard. In 1908, *Golden Crown* was bought by the Indian Government through the shipbrokers Massey and Company and voyaged down to the sub-continent for fishing from Calcutta in the Bay of Bengal. During the Great War she seems to have served as an Admiralty tug.

From 7 to 28 July *Kapduen* was put in the hands of the shipyard Framnæs Mekaniske Værksted where the necessary transformations took place. The vessel was docked between 11 and 13 July for survey and repairs, thereafter her whaling gun and platform were removed and modifications made to the bow. Other modifications to her accomodation may have been made to make her more suitable for carrying a sealing crew, and also to the hold to carry seal blubber. Finally, after alterations were completed on 28 July, she was (once again) renamed *Dias* and her registration was transferred to Buenos Aires by way of the local Argentine consulate. Shortly afterwards, *Dias* finally sailed from Sandefjord for the last time under her new Swedish master, Johan A. Johansson on the long voyage south, arriving at Pesca's Grytviken land station on 6 September 1927.

The ex-trawler was now part of a remarkable and most unusual organisation. Pesca had pioneered the exploitation of the enormous natural resources of the Southern Ocean through the use of modern Antarctic whaling methods from its base at Grytviken. Both company and base were created through the vision of one man, Captain Carl Anton Larsen, who played a pivotal role in their story.

Larsen, the son of a Norwegian sea captain, was born in 1860 and spent most of his formative years in Sandefjord. He could certainly claim that the sea was in his blood as he spent every summer from the age of nine on his father's barque, fishing and trading across the North Sea. At sixteen he enrolled in a navigation school and harboured ambitions to become an officer, but initially had to sign up as a cook. But there was no thwarting his ambition. He rose through the ranks to become a captain in his early twenties, and after buying a share in an old barque he soon turned to whaling. By 1900 he had not only made his name as a successful seaman, sealer and bottlenose whaler in northern latitudes but had carried out a number of exploratory voyages to the Antarctic. In 1892-94, in command of the Norwegian-flagged *Jason*, he undertook two German-financed voyages to the Antarctic Peninsula in search of the southern right whale. Larsen spread his wings: he visited South Georgia, discovered the Larsen Ice Shelf and the Foyn Coast, in addition to King Oscar II Coast and Robertson Island. In December 1892 he met four Dundee whaling vessels, the *Balaena*, *Active*, *Diana* and *Polar Star* in Erebus and Terror Bay and exchanged information with their captains. They were only equipped for traditional whaling from open boats, and in the absence of the right whale they all agreed to fill their ships up with seals.

Although Larsen saw few right whales, he encountered large populations of the faster moving rorqual species. These could only be taken, of course, with modern whale catchers which he lacked on this voyage but he came away filled with a determination to exploit the potential of these largely untouched whaling stocks.

At that time, any attempt to deploy modern whaling techniques and thus exploit the rorqual whales required the creation of supporting land based processing stations in the Southern Ocean, where the requisite steam whale catchers could not only be based but also maintained whilst their catches were processed. After returning to Norway Larsen began to seriously consider the possibilities of establishing a whaling station on South Georgia. He corresponded with Clements Markham, President of The Royal Geographical Society, with a view to combining commercial exploitation with scientific exploration of the Antarctic. The rumour put about was that Larsen had secured from Queen Victoria the necessary permissions to proceed, but his ideas failed to attract sufficient financial backing in Norway. There was concern about the logistics of mounting an expedition to an uninhabited, desolate and distant location. Such an enterprise was likely to incur high costs at a time when the demand for whale products and consequently whale prices were relatively low.

Larsen returned south as skipper of Otto Nordenskjøld's Swedish expedition on board *Antarctic*. The expedition called at South Georgia in May 1902 and, whilst there, Larsen visited a smaller bay, off the larger Cumberland Bay, which had been discovered a couple of weeks earlier by a shore party. This was named Grytviken (Pot Cove) after the nineteenth century sealers' try-pots were found there. Larsen quickly recognised that this deep, sheltered 'bay within a bay' with a stretch of flat ground at its head and plentiful supplies of fresh water was an ideal location for a whaling station.

During the subsequent stages of the expedition *Antarctic* was lost in the ice. Larsen and his crew spent a miserable ten months in makeshift shelters on Paulet Island, surviving mainly on a menu of penguins and seals, before finally being rescued by the Argentine gunboat *Uruguay*.

On arrival in Buenos Aires, after months of enforced solitude, Larsen was fêted as a polar hero. He lost no time in capitalizing on the publicity surrounding his Antarctic endeavours, and was able to sell the idea of a South Georgia whaling station to Argentine financiers, led by the Tornquist banking group. They backed his proposed venture with £40,000-worth of Argentine pesos. Finally armed with the requisite finance, Larsen returned to Norway, where he obtained crews, ships, equipment, materials and stores and ordered a modern whale catcher capable of hunting rorquals. Everything needed to create a whaling station was packed into the *Louise*, an old three-masted barque. Leaving Norway in July 1904 Larsen's expedition called at Buenos Aires en route and eventually reached South Georgia on 16 November 1904. The plant was soon assembled and whaling began shortly afterwards.

And thus Pesca came into being: the pioneer of modern whaling in the Antarctic and one of the most colourful and cosmopolitan of the world's whaling companies. Larsen was the first whaling manager whilst the principal commercial force behind the company was Ernesto Tornquist, who although never a director, played a major part in driving through the initiative. The new company's headquarters and most of the directors were based in Buenos Aires, its ships flew the Argentine flag whilst much of the labour force and most of the operational management were Norwegian. All operational activities were carried out from the British dependency of South Georgia. This arrangement was to cause long-term problems for the directors and management, particularly during periods when the inherent territorial tensions between the United Kingdom and Argentina were at their most acute.

Larsen and Pesca's entry onto South Georgia's soil certainly had great implications, not only for the future of the Southern Ocean and Antarctic whale stocks, but for the politics of the wider region. Although South Georgia was considered to be a British Dependency—indeed James Cook had discovered or re-discovered it in 1775—the island had not been specifically mentioned when Letters Patent were established for the Falkland Islands in 1843 and there was even some doubt in Governmental circles whether Cook's 'Lands doomed by nature to perpetual frigidness: never to feel the warmth of the sun's rays' were worth keeping.

Whaling radically altered British perceptions of the island. When Larsen arrived at South Georgia, the authorities were totally unaware of his presence. Larsen had sailed directly from Buenos Aires to Grytviken and established his station without any interference. From his viewpoint the island was uninhabited and in any event, if rumours were to be believed, he may have considered himself to have received consent from the British Crown.

Ironically, it was not until November 1905, about a year after Pesca's arrival, that visual confirmation of Larsen's South Georgia venture reached Governor William Lamond Allardyce at Government House in Stanley in the Falkland Islands. This was supplied by a Chilean expedition led by Durham-born immigrant Ernest Swinhoe who had obtained a two-year lease from the Falkland Islands Government for a pastoral and sealing enterprise. Swinhoe voyaged to the island from Punta Arenas in *Consort*—yet another former Hull sailing trawler with Hellyer connections to appear in our story—built back in 1879 at Newhaven, Sussex for Charles Hellyer's father, Robert.[16]

There are varying reports of the first meeting between the whalers and would-be farmers in August 1905. Swinhoe was reported to have asked the whalers to leave, as he had a lease for the whole island. Captain Larsen was not on the island at the time, but en route to Norway, having been picked up by an Argentine naval transport delivering coal and supplies. It was his brother Lauritz who had to deal with the encounter.

The immediate crisis was defused when the farmers concluded that the island's combination of sparse pasture and severe climate meant that South Georgia was not suitable for their use. They sold their stock of sheep and horses to the whalers, left a note of protest and sailed back to Chile via the Falklands. On arrival at Stanley they reported the establishment of the station to the Government.

Thereafter, a period of very delicate political wrangling ensued between London, Buenos Aires and Stanley—a situation described in some quarters 'as a crisis of potentially international proportions.' But British influence in Argentina was strong at that time, and as far as the Argentine financial backers were concerned, their primary interest was to protect their investment, continue in business and reap the rewards of this burgeoning industry. Matters of a political nature and the sovereignty of a remote sub-Antarctic island of snow and ice were a secondary consideration.

In this climate of apparent Argentine political indifference, a simple but effective resolution was found. After an 'inspection visit' to South Georgia by a British gun-boat, HMS *Sappho*, the British asserted their authority over the island whilst the Argentine company secured a lease, on very favourable terms, from the Falkland Islands Government. Everyone seemed satisfied, and in Government House, Stanley, the Governor patted his Colonial Secretary on the back for a job well executed. Pesca continued to pay lease and licence fees to the Government until the 1960s, and indeed, for the whole period the company was in operation there, but in retrospect the Government may have preferred to have negotiated a percentage of the profits.

The subsequent history of Pesca and South Georgia echoes the history of whaling elsewhere in the Antarctic and indeed other parts of the world. The adage 'initial success, high hopes, vast profits... and final collapse' follows the commercial exploitation of this vast and unique natural resource. The number of whales killed in South Georgia waters was phenomenal; some 175,250 between 1904 and 1966. In the early years, humpback whales spouted in every bay and one whale catcher which drifted close to a pod in fog is said to have harpooned three animals without moving the engine. In 1911/12—by then six other companies had established whaling stations on the island—some 5,635 humpbacks were killed and one establishment's investors complained that their dividend was only 26.5%. By 1914, when Captain Larsen left the island for good, he had made his fortune.

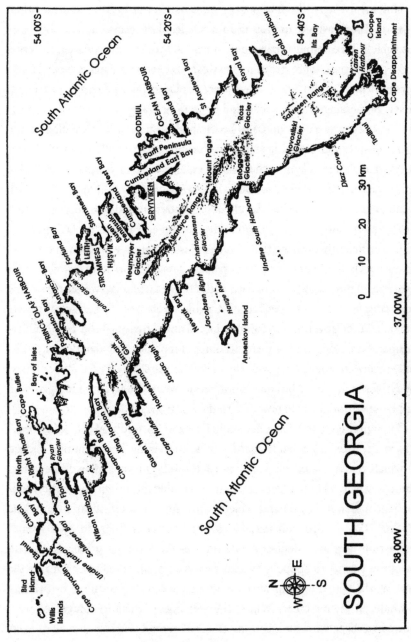

SOUTH GEORGIA

Map from Ian Hart, PESCA, History of the Pioneer Modern Whaling Company in the Antarctic, Aidan Ellis 2001

Not surprisingly, the humpbacks were fished out by 1916 and the whalers turned increasingly to blue and fin whales, larger and more mobile species which were found further out to sea. Although the rewards, in terms of oil production, were greater, the wear and tear on catcher vessels also increased and by the 1920s these were replaced by a generation of larger vessels possessing greater speed and operational range.

The 1920s were considered to be the high-water mark of whaling on the island, despite the post-war slump in Europe: between 1924 and 1927 over 5,000 whales were caught each season, peaking at a total of 7,825 in 1925/26. This cetacean harvest yielded some 404,457 barrels (67,409 tons) of oil, produced by the five established South Georgia stations and one floating factory ship[17] which now boasted the latest processing and reduction facilities, capable of efficiently utilising the whole carcass. Thereafter the catch dropped off substantially. Competition from pelagic whale factory ships, having stern slips and highly efficient on-board reduction machinery, which first came into being in 1925 and operated on the high seas beyond territorial waters and outside of government control, increasingly marginalised South Georgia operations. By 1931/32 many whaling companies had abandoned the island, several of them for good. Between the wars only Pesca at Grytviken and Salvesen at Leith Harbour continued to work from South Georgia, both supplying essential whale products to the United Kingdom.

Though there had been a declining demand for traditional whaling products in the later nineteenth century, new marketing opportunities opened up which reinvigorated the catching sector. The process of hydrogenation, whereby whale oil could be converted into edible fat, provided an enormous alternative source of demand which stimulated an intensification in whale hunting. This in turn led initially to larger catches followed by a greater decimation of global stocks. Whale oil was for a time a principal ingredient of margarine, the popular working class alternative to butter. During the First World War there was also a huge demand for glycerine, a by-product of whale oil manufacture. Whilst the war raged, whaling companies were allowed to dispense with government regulations designed to control over-exploitation in order to boost the quantity of blubber oil and satisfy the needs of the war effort.

By the 1920s the whaling factory at Grytviken was one of the most modern in the world, employing some 300 men and capable of dealing with over one thousand whales in a season lasting from October to May. It was able to produce a range of products from whale and sperm oil, to meat and bone meal and whale guano. The place was practically self-sufficient, with a formidable engineering facility, hydro-electric power station, floating dock and storehouses. The station kept a large piggery—the pigs fed on whale meat—as well as poultry and cows. A church, hospital, even a cinema, were provided for the workforce, who came primarily from Norway but also Argentina. Every austral spring they were shipped to the island by the company's vessels from Sandefjord in Norway and Buenos Aires. Approximately 40 staff remained at Grytviken throughout each southern winter to carry out essential maintenance.

VIII

SEALING

A S WELL AS WHALING, Pesca was the only company permitted to undertake sealing at South Georgia. Seal oil was procured from elephant seals, which had a thick blanket of blubber beneath the skin that could be converted into high grade oil. Commercial sealing from South Georgia had a long history, starting shortly after Captain Cook had landed and claimed the island for Britain in 1775. The first sealers, primarily British and American, found huge numbers of Antarctic fur seals which were valued for their skins. But early hunting was so indiscriminate that by 1822 South Georgia's beaches had been denuded of this species. The hunters then turned to elephant seals, but as this trade was not as remunerative as fur sealing, the species was not overtaxed. British and American sealers plied this trade for many years, some even continued after the commencement of modern whaling in 1904. The last of these old-timers was the New Bedford brig *Daisy* (Capt. B. Cleveland) which visited the island in 1912/13, calling at Grytviken during the trip but mainly using an anchorage in the Bay of Isles to conduct its work.

When Pesca commenced whaling from South Georgia in November 1904, a small number of elephant seals were also taken for oil. But this illegal activity was soon halted by the Falkland Islands Government through the imposition of The Seal Fishery Ordinance of 1881, originally brought out by the Government to protect seals in the Falklands but then extended to South Georgia. In 1909 it was further extended by the Seal Fishery (Consolidation) Ordinance, designed deliberately to regulate the seal fishery in the Dependencies.

But by 1909 the population of elephant seals on the island had increased to such an extent that controlled sealing was again considered a feasible proposition. An application for a sealing licence was made in 1909 to the Colonial

Secretary by Pesca company President, Hermann H. Schlieper. The same application was also forwarded on 13 December that year by Captain Larsen to James Innes Wilson, the newly appointed resident British Magistrate on the island. In the application, Larsen asked to take seals both at South Georgia and the South Sandwich Islands, adding that 'he requested an exclusive right for three years because it would not be profitable to keep a ship for this purpose unless the sole privilege is obtained, as the field is too small here for more than one sealing expedition at one time.'

The following year Pesca was granted a Government licence, permitting the company to take up to 6,000 seals each year. Conservation measures were also introduced. A close season from October to March was created so that the seals were virtually unmolested during the main part of the breeding season, and only bull seals were allowed to be taken. The island was also divided into four divisions, one of which was rested in rotation each season. No more than 2,000 bull seals could be taken from any single division each year and the regulations stipulated that an adequate proportion, approximately ten per cent, should be left on each beach. The first of these sealing divisions stretched from Cape Nuñez on the south-west coast to Cape North, the second from Cape Butler to Cape Saunders, the third from Larsen Point to Cape Disappointment and the fourth from there to Cape Nuñez. Reserves—areas where no seals could be taken—were also created. These were respectively Willis Island and Bird Island as well as the stretches of coast from Cape North to Cape Butler and Cape Saunders to Larsen Point. Sealing was also prohibited in the vicinity of Dartmouth Point in East Cumberland Bay, and the schedule of licences also prohibited sealing in harbours where whaling took place.

At first the Government also permitted Weddell seals to be hunted but these were later given protection as they were confined to a small colony in Larsen Harbour at the southern end of the island. Leopard seals could also be taken but this species never yielded more than a negligible fraction of the oil produced from seal hunting and was ignored soon after the *Dias* arrived in South Georgia.

Elephant seals get their name from their huge size and the male's large proboscis which allows them to roar in a most threatening manner. The bulls are much larger and heavier than the cows, reaching somewhere between fourteen and nineteen feet in length. Early in the austral spring these leviathans of the South Georgia littoral zone start coming ashore after many months at sea, hauling themselves out of the surf onto beaches in coves and bays across every part of the island's long coastline. The males are polygamous and within a short time of coming ashore begin fighting each other for control of females, dominant bulls sometimes possessing harems containing several dozen cows. The cows usually give birth to their calves quite early in the season.

During the breeding season, elephant seal bulls have to continually defend their territory and harem from interloping bulls, and such territorial fixations provided the best opportunity for the sealers to make their main killings The most intensive period of elephant seal hunting took place in September and October during the austral spring, a time when the seals had just arrived on the beach in a fattened condition and ready to give birth and breed, a time when the territorial squabbles between bulls were at their most intense. A secondary period of hunting was carried out in the austral autumn, during March and April, but this was never as productive as the seals were coming to the end of their time ashore and had lost a great deal of body fat. They were somewhat more dispersed by this time in the year, having lost interest in the cows, and some bulls were found as much as a mile inland, making the most of the island's fresh water whilst moulting.

On average, a mature elephant bull carcass in good condition might yield two barrels, or a third of a ton of oil. An analysis of production at Grytviken during the period 1910—1962 shows that seal oil contributed an annual average of about 18% of output in terms of quantity and value. Thus the importance of sealing to Pesca cannot be over-emphasised, particularly at times when operating margins were tight. It has been said that the annual output of seal oil enabled the company to stay in business during the economic slump of the 1930s and also throughout the 1950s when the pressure on whale stocks was becoming acute.

Prior to the arrival of *Dias* at South Georgia in 1927, Pesca's sealing operations had been carried out by a converted naval steam yacht, the aged *Undine*, reputed to have been occasionally used by Queen Victoria in the 1880s, and by the *Carl* (also called *Lille-Carl*) and *Don Ernesto*, both superannuated whale catchers. These vessels were not particularly efficient because their cargo carrying capacity was limited and they had often to store blubber on their decks. Although the ex-Hull trawler had proved somewhat slow as a whale catcher her substantial forward hold—where coal and fish had once been stored—provided excellent cargo carrying capacity.

Dias proved ideal for sealing and was pressed into service soon after arrival at Grytviken in early September and by the end of October the old trawler had delivered sufficient elephant seal blubber to the processing works to produce 3,064 barrels—or 510 tons—of oil. Indeed, *Dias*'s worth soon became apparent because at the termination of the season, the company had caught for the first time over 5,000 seals and produced over 10,000 barrels (1,666 tons) of seal oil, making a valuable contribution of something in the order of 13% to the company's total production of whale and seal oil.

Sealing was carried on in the various bays around South Georgia and involved a range of individual tasks, principally beating, flensing and hauling. As a trawler the vessel had normally carried a crew of ten but as a sealer up to eighteen men had to be accommodated on board. Although there was always an assortment of Norwegians and Argentines, others had been torn from their roots in Russia, Poland, the Baltic republics, Italy, Germany and other places. Indeed, for many years sealing crews were nearly always an interesting if disparate set of characters, drawn to these shores from many corners of the world, often dispersed from their places of nativity by revolution, war or sheer wanderlust, as well as an overriding need to earn their living and accrue capital. South Georgia provided many with an austere sort of haven.

Once *Dias* anchored in a cove frequented by elephant seals, the shore party, typically comprising eight sealers and a gunner, climbed aboard the pram, a small Norwegian dory with little keel, very difficult to manoeuvre in any wind but capable of running well up most beaches. This was then towed as close as possible to the shore by the 'snekke', a motor lifeboat, and on being cast off the pram was rowed rapidly through the often heavy surf and up onto the beach.

Little time was lost. The sealers soon selected and approached their first victim. Poles were used to help them cajole or drive a bull elephant to the edge of the sea. This task was always easier in the spring because the bulls were on the beach and anxious to defend their cows from all comers. An old bull was a formidable creature, his scarred skin carrying the reminders of many battles with his rivals. On being driven to the shoreline and cornered by the sealers, an angry bellowing elephant bull usually reared up, often to a height of eight feet, letting forth an enormous roar. At that moment the gunner ran in as close as he could, extremely close, as near as possible to the animal's open bellowing mouth. The rifle was fired, the bullet aimed at the palate. When the shot was well placed death was instantaneous, the bull immediately collapsed, its carcass crashing to the ground, and suddenly it seemed no more than a bag-like bulk of shivering blubber. Another sealer swiftly ran his knife through the hapless victim's heart, stopping circulation and blood spurting from the cut arteries.

Without wasting any time the flensers set to work. Typically, two men worked each corpse, stripping the skin and blubber from the carcass, using sharp Swedish Eskilstuna steel knives, their crimson coated blades slicing through the blood red gore. The flensers made cuts around the fore flippers, behind the eyes and in front of the hind flippers then down the middle of the back.

Skilled flensers were fast workers and this part of the flensing process took little more than three or four minutes. The material thus stripped was between six and 17cm in thickness, roughly circular in shape with a couple of holes where the flippers had been removed. By this time the gunner had turned his attention to other suitable bulls on the beach and the whole procedure was being repeated.

The shore party was a close knit team, everyone knowing their role and what they had to do. Almost as soon as the flensers finished their gory job, the haulers dealt with the flensed rings of blubber. Strops were tied through one of the flipper holes and when several of these huge seals were killed close together their flensed blubber rings were dragged out into the cold sea and a line threaded through the strop loops. Next, as the pram rowed in as close as possible, the line was thrown aboard and made fast. The pram's crew then rowed hard, bobbing over the crashing waves to close with the hovering motor-boat which then towed the skins to the *Dias*, where they were hoisted aboard and stowed in the hold by the skipper and other seamen using the forward winch. On a good trip, when the hold had been completely filled, blubber was also stored in temporary wooden compartments on the poop or side-decks.

The gunner was the key player ashore. He was responsible for seeing that the work was done efficiently—and elephant sealing was a formidably efficient operation. He also decided which seals were too small to be killed. Gunners on all the sealing ships were usually men of great strength and energy, who could turn their hand to any task. They were always the first men out of the pram on reaching the shore and usually the last to get back aboard. A sealing skipper and gunner invariably worked in tandem and over the years developed their own system of signals for communication between the ship and the shore.

Back on the beach the bones of the long blubberless corpses were left to be picked clean of meat by the seabirds. Only the unskinned head, tail and fore flippers of the unfortunate bull elephant seals provided any indication of their earlier immensity.

During sealing trips, *Dias* and her crew had to deal with everything the merciless South Georgia elements could throw at them. Snow, rain, sleet, fog and incessantly heavy seas came with the territory. They were hunting and like all successful hunters in every age, they needed an intimate knowledge of the territory they stalked and of the haunts and habits of their prey. The *Dias*'s sealing skippers, like the North Sea skippers of the ex-trawler's original incarnation, were no exception. Over time they became familiar with almost every part of South Georgia's rock bound coastline, with its ice-clad mosaic of fjords, bays and coves. A good skipper both respected and understood, but was not overawed by, the hazardous beauty—the spectacular mix of mountains and sea—which surrounded him. He knew where to run for shelter when the weather deteriorated, where best to anchor, and how to navigate safely amongst the numerous rocks and skerries, any one of which could tear the bottom out of his little ship.

Above all he knew the remote beaches where elephant seals liked to congregate, and how best to get in close enough to land a hunting party and then get them safely on shore—a feat in itself. As Ludwig Kohl-Larsen observed, almost every landing on remote stretches of South Georgia's coast represented an achievement of the seamen's art, the little snekke and pram sometimes navigating a narrow seething passage between breakers and reefs on the trip from ship to shore, sealers sometimes leaping hip deep into the chaotic surf to drag their pram onto the beach.[1]

Landing was one side of the equation. Getting off a beach was altogether another. Sub-Antarctic weather can deteriorate rapidly and the ferocity of the surf smashing into the shore at times made it impossible to get back to sea. On such occasions the shore party often tramped about, beset by icy gales, rain or snow, trying to keep warm, often for hours, even all night, whilst their little ship, a storm-lashed but brightly lit refuge of rest and warmth, lay offshore, anchored or dodging into the wind, endlessly waiting, sometimes seemingly in vain, to recover her crew.

Dias, like the other sealing vessels, was seldom out of Grytviken for much more than a week at a time, returning before her bounty of blubber deteriorated. If a sealer had sailed from the whaling station the night before or spent a night at some sheltered anchorage then hunting might begin at about 5.30 in the morning. Had the beaches been worked on the previous day then the anchor would be weighed at first light and the vessel steamed on to another bay. The work continued as long as there were seals to be taken, or until the vessel had received its maximum cargo. An average working day ended as dusk closed in.

Depending on the season and the area being worked, a sealing vessel like *Dias* could typically take on board the blubber of up to 150 large bulls each trip. This worked out at something between 50 and 70 tons in weight. Once flensed, the seal blubber generally remained in good condition for about seven days, primarily because all meat had been cut away, but also because it had cooled rapidly when towed out to the ship through the icy seas. On reaching Grytviken, the blankets of blubber were dumped in the water by the foot of the flensing plan—a wooden platform sloping gently up from the water's edge, where whales were hauled out and cut up—and then drawn up to the blubber cookery area. Here the sections of seal were cut into strips and blocks, then fed into hoggers, machines which minced the material before it was conveyed by elevators to the blubber cookers. There the blubber oil would be 'tried out' under steam pressure for several hours and conveyed to the storage tanks to await future shipment. Seal oil was not mixed with whale oil and was always stored, shipped and sold as a separate product in its own right. It generally had the same quality, value and commercial uses as the best grade of whale oil.

Elephant seal hunting was certainly a gory business, but unlike whaling it had one redeeming quality, at least on South Georgia. Thanks to the pioneering foresight of the Falklands Governor, William Lamond Allardyce, it was subject to effective regulation and has proved perhaps to be the only example of the sustainable hunting of sea mammals anywhere in the world. The original 1909 limit of 6,000 bull elephant seals per year was maintained for many years though in 1948, on the recommendation of the then South Georgia magistrate A. I. Fleuret, the quota was raised first to 7,500 and then, a year later, to 9,000 animals. This proved to be more than the stock could sustain and, following research and analysis by Dr R. M. Laws[2], a government appointed seal inspector, the quota was progressively reduced in the early 1950s, returning to Allardyce's original limit of 6,000 seals in 1952. The management plan proved highly successful over the following decade and, as Nigel Bonner, the government sealing inspector, reported in 1961, this was reflected in a rise in the average age of the bull elephant seals to seven years. Bonner calculated that the South Georgia stock was providing a maximum sustainable yield of about 6% per year, a rare illustration of how a natural resource can be managed on a sustainable basis. Indeed, the stock of elephant seals on the island in the early 1960s was probably much the same as it had been when Pesca began commercial seal hunting in the years preceding the First World War.

Because sealing started in September, before the onset of the whaling season, the sealing crews were generally the first members of Pesca's workforce to arrive back at Grytviken at the end of the austral winter. Before the Second World War they were normally brought across from Buenos Aires in the company supply ship *Harpon*, a last opportunity or excuse for two days of heavy drinking, known as 'the first and second days of the *Harpon*.'

To describe the crews of the *Dias* and the other sealing ships as 'rough and ready' might be something of an understatement. Their behaviour and escapades have become the stuff of legend. Konrad E. 'Pokern' Johanessen, one of the skippers of the sealing ship *Lille-Carl* in the 1920s, for example, was adept at poker. 'Pokern' is said to have won much money off younger crew members, encouraging them to gamble away their hard-earned wages.

When 'Pokern' retired in the early 1930s he was replaced by Karl O Jansen, nicknamed 'Kalle-Sarp' because he hailed from Sarpsborg in Norway. Kalle-Sarp was a large burly man who, after shipping out in 1922, spent five consecutive winters in South Georgia. At the end of the sixth sealing season he was more than ready for a break. He took ship for Buenos Aires and in three months spent six years of accumulated earnings on women, wild living and drink. Other members of the sealing crews also followed a variant of Jansen's practice, spending one or two winters on maintenance duties at South Georgia and then blowing their accumulated savings in a 'glorious bust' in the La Boca district of Buenos Aires.[3]

Jansen, who had a spell as skipper of *Dias*, never washed during a whaling trip, claiming it would bring him bad luck. He also drank heavily when not on the bridge, liked to eat his meat raw and, if on shore when hunting, it was said he drank seal's blood as it poured out of a newly slaughtered animal whenever the opportunity arose. Whether or not this actually revitalised his vigour is not known. 'Kalle-Sarp' retired around 1950 at the age of 56.

Dias's first skipper, Johan A. Johansson, was about 34 years old at the time he brought the ex-trawler from Norway to South Georgia in 1927, and between the sealing seasons he was also skipper of the Pesca company's barque *Tijuca* which carried oil and guano to Buenos Aires, returning with stores and equipment.[4] The place-name Dias Cove or Diaz Cove on the official Crown Agents South Georgia map was named thus by him on rediscovering the cove in 1929. It is located in the south-west coast of the island at 54.45S, 36.18W, sheltered by the Kupriyanov Islands and was a sealing beach in Division IV. Johansson appears to have left the company around 1933 but returned to skipper *Dias* for the 1947 season before spending his last couple of sealing seasons on board the sealer *Carl*.

In 1934 another striking character, Hans Olsen, who had previously acted as relief for Johansson from time to time, became permanent skipper of *Dias*. A veteran of the sailing ship era, Olsen was nicknamed Captain Poison by the Pesca crews, his soubriquet perhaps taken from de Alarcón's popular novelette of the same name published back in 1881. Olsen was 56 when he took permanent command of *Dias*, having previously served on the sealers *Carl* and *Don Ernesto*. He was the ex-trawler's longest serving skipper, spending the next twelve years in charge, by which time, in his late sixties, he was probably one of the oldest men working from Grytviken.

In 1946 Henry O. Hotvedt replaced Olsen for one season. Later, in 1951, another veteran skipper, the sixty year old Hans T. Johannessen, took command of *Dias* for a couple of years, being replaced by Thorleif Hammerstad in 1953. Hammerstad had had a chequered career, having put another sealing vessel, the *Don Samuel*, on uncharted rocks in King Haakon Bay, South Georgia in November 1951 with dire consequences, but he was given another chance.

When Hammerstad took a job ashore as second foreman at the Grytviken whaling plant in 1957, he was replaced as skipper by fifty-one year old Arne Bogen, who was in turn replaced by Ole Hauge in 1960. Sixty-two year old Hauge had first shipped out to South Georgia in 1934, and previously served on the sealers *Carl* and *Don Ernesto*. He was a legend at South Georgia, venturing into all the island's bays, and his collective knowledge of the marine environment was said to be unsurpassed. When Hauge moved to work on the sealer *Petrel* in 1961 he was replaced on *Dias* by another veteran, Gunnar Virik Nilsen. Nilsen had first worked as a 'salonggutt' (messboy) serving the Captain's table on the company's transport ship *Harpon* back in 1935. Progressing to be an able seaman, he transferred onto whale catchers but after the Second World War he moved to the sealing vessels, first working as gunner. By 1957 he had acquired his mandatory Norwegian coastal master's certificate and became a skipper. Before moving to *Dias* he had commanded the *Carl*.

The working conditions on sealing ships were occasionally the subject of much interest and comment, perhaps more so from people in an official capacity but not directly engaged in the industry. It would have been expected that because of the nature of the work, many of the conditions were not equivalent to those normally encountered on merchant ships. The smell was apparently unmistakeable, even amongst those hardened to whaling stations. Ludvig Kohl-Larsen, an explorer with a great deal of experience of Grytviken, recalls clambering over a number of unlit vessels moored at the whaling station in search of his berth on *Dias* during a densely dark evening in March 1929. Unable to see clearly on such a pitch black night, he discovered her only when the stench of old seal blubber assailed his nose.[5]

Overcrowding was endemic on sealing trips. When originally built, the old trawler vessel had to ship ten fishermen but sixteen crew members were usually carried on sealing hunting trips. Only the Captain and Chief engineer had their own cabins whilst the remainder of the crew were accommodated in one crowded paraffin-lamp-lit compartment which they shared with the galley. In February 1959, the Government magistrate on South Georgia wrote a memorandum to the Colonial Secretary in Stanley expressing some concern about compliance with the Merchant Shipping Act, with particular reference to crew health, safety regulations and the Government's responsibility to enforce them. He wrote:

'The living conditions aboard the Pesca seal catchers are, I should hazard a guess, among the very worst to be found at sea anywhere in the world today. I have been out sealing in the *Dias* for a week and the *Albatros* for six days. The crew's quarters are grossly overcrowded and they stink and reek of rotting seal blubber as it accrues in the holds from voyage to voyage and the smell seeps through into the mess. My bunk in the *Albatros*, which was one of the best in the ship, was soaking wet all the time that I was out, so I slept clothed and in an oilskin. Sea water and oily blood dripped almost continuously and occasionally poured through the deck head into the after mess where I was accommodated. Both these sealers have a penthouse on the afterdeck which is unapproachable in rough weather, but in which is housed the ship's lavatory seat. Flush arrangements are not provided. Conditions being what they are, the crews rarely change their clothes or wash. Some do not change their clothes for two months. Food and pay are good.'

Nothing appears to have ensued from this early vestige of health and safety concern, and there is no record of any official complaint on conditions being received from the sealing crews themselves. Nigel Bonner later recalled that *Dias* was far and away the most comfortable of the Grytviken-based ships, especially if there was any kind of heavy sea running. He often took passage on her when he was the whaling inspector, and on various trips to Bird Island where he spent much time.[6]

Rats which had arrived on the island with the first visitors were always a problem, both on South Georgia and on the whaling and sealing vessels. Kohl-Larsen, on one of his trips on *Dias*, recalled settling down to sleep in the crowded crew's quarters to the accompanying melody of the gnawing rats that nested behind wooden panelling in the cabin roof.

Back in February 1930, buoyed by the increasing demand for oil and other products in the market place, Pesca had dispatched Johan A. Johansson and the ex-trawler to the coasts of Patagonia and Tierra del Fuego to make an appraisal of the seal herds and assess other fishing possibilities.[7] During this voyage the vessel visited Staten Island and passed through the Beagle Channel where an attempt at trawling was made but, as she was no longer equipped with a trawl winch and other appropriate equipment, this yielded no useful result. Johansson then took *Dias* along the Argentine coast, voyaging from Gable Island to Spiring Bay thence onwards to Port Parry, Harberton and Picton Island. Sea lions were found but these were generally widely dispersed, only one large colony of about 300 animals being noted. No trace was found of either elephant seals or fur seals, nor did those on board encounter whales, penguins or any sign of Antarctic cod, a species common to the seas around South Georgia. The outcome of the voyage was disappointing from a commercial—if not ecological—perspective and the company accordingly concluded that expansion into the region was not then a viable proposition.

During the Second World War, Pesca was the only South Georgia whaling company to work continuously throughout the hostilities. Supplies of seal and whale oil, deemed essential to the British war effort, were shipped to the UK by way of US ports. Pesca was able to contribute directly to the Royal Navy's more immediate needs as early as December 1939 when it despatched metal plates to Stanley harbour in the Falklands. These were used to effect repairs on the war-torn HMS *Exeter* after her encounter with the German pocket battleship *Admiral Graf Spee* in the Battle of the River Plate, the opening salvo in the struggle for control of the South Atlantic.

HMS *Exeter* was certainly not unfamiliar with the region and had visited Grytviken in 1938 when the warship's two Walrus floatplanes had been used to take the first aerial photographs of South Georgia. Although Argentina was ostensibly a neutral country there is evidence that *Ernesto Tornquist*, Pesca's large transport ship, made voyages to the Antarctic to collect oil from British ships working in the area during the war. Certainly the Germans were keen to curtail allied Antarctic whaling activities and, in January 1941, word was received on the island that the German commerce raider, *Pingvin* (HK33), had surprised the Norwegian whaling fleet amongst the ice floes and captured two factory whaling ships, a supply vessel and eleven of the fourteen accompanying whale catchers. Only one factory ship, *Thorshammer*, and a few of her catchers, escaped to Grytviken, where they berthed alongside *Dias*.

When word was received in the Falkland Islands, the armed merchant cruiser HMS *Queen of Bermuda* was dispatched to South Georgia to gather intelligence, voyaging from there to the South Orkneys, before escorting the Pesca transport ship *Ernesto Tornquist* as it headed to rendezvous with the British whale factory ships *Southern Empress* and *Svend Foyn* in the ice. *Queen of Bermuda* watched over the whalers until the end of February then returned to the Falklands.

During this part of the war there was a considerable fear that the Germans would seek to capture South Georgia and use it as a base for commerce raiding across the Southern Ocean and South Atlantic. To deter an attack several 100mm guns, manned by a Norwegian army detachment and supported by whaling station volunteers, were deployed to cover the approaches to both Cumberland and Stromness Bays whilst the Royal Navy also sent another armed merchant cruiser, HMS *Carnarvon Castle*, to the South Atlantic. Tensions eased when news filtered through that HMS *Cornwall* had eventually caught up with the *Pingvin* in May 1941, when the German vessel was apparently on course for South Georgia, and sent her to the bottom after a fierce battle.

The war continued for a further four years and for many of the station crews, including the sealers on *Dias*, much of this time was spent in an isolated and often ice-cold exile. Norway had been overrun by the Germans and could not be reached. The only respite available for the Grytviken workforce before the return of peace was the occasional off-season opportunity to visit Buenos Aires or Montevideo.

IX

EXPLORATION

Throughout her working life as a sealer at South Georgia, *Dias* was regularly used for other work, especially outside of the sealing season. Because of her cargo carrying capacity, she was called upon to support expeditions both to South Georgia and the Antarctic. Significant among these was the relief of the Argentine 'Orcadus del Sur' meteorological station at Laurie Island in the South Orkney Islands which had been first established by the Scottish National Antarctic Expedition led by William S. Bruce on the *Scotia* in 1902 but then handed over, by invitation, to the Argentine Government in April 1904. This weather station remains the oldest permanently occupied base in Antarctica.

Pesca's association with this outpost seems to date back to 1911 when the company's vessel *Undine* undertook a voyage to Laurie Island from Grytviken carrying a relief team of Argentine scientists, who had recently arrived at the whaling station from Buenos Aires. Over the following years a number of Pesca whale catchers were used on these southern voyages, carrying relief crews and supplies to the island. When the ice conditions were favourable it was possible to complete the round trip to and from the South Orkney Islands, as well as off load stores, in around twelve days.

After arrival at Grytviken, *Dias* became the vessel of choice for these expeditions, as long as they took place outside of periods of seal hunting. In the years between 1928 and 1942 the vessel carried out many relief voyages, taking expedition personnel to Laurie Island, voyaging south from either South Georgia, Buenos Aires or from the southern Argentine port of Ushuaia on Tierra del Fuego. In 1932, for example, under the command of Hans Olsen, *Dias* departed from Buenos Aires on 11 March packed full of personnel and stores. She arrived at Orcadus on 23 March returning to Grytviken on 31 March. The cost to her charterers for this voyage was 5,849 Norwegian kroner (about £400).

Dias was in demand again in 1933 and 1934 when the Argentine Government's own relief ship *Rata* failed to get through the ice to Laurie Island and was diverted to Grytviken. Her last voyage to Orcadus in this capacity appears to have been in season 1941/42 under the command of Hans Olsen, and embroiled the vessel in the region's rising territorial tensions. That year a resurgent Argentina dispatched a large naval force to the Antarctic under the command of Capitán de Fregata Alberto J. Oddera on the naval transport *Primero de Mayo*. The expedition rendezvoused in Ushuaia, where *Dias* collected the relief crews and loaded a cargo of 1,000 tons of coal. The remainder of the fleet headed for the South Shetland Islands and the Antarctic peninsula, where the Argentine flag was hoisted in a number of places and bronze tablets erected announcing that the Argentine Republic had reaffirmed its sovereign rights over all the Antarctic lands and Dependencies south of latitude 60°S between longitudes 25° and 68°W. This claim, of course, overlapped both the British and part of the Chilean claim.

Argentinean government activities apart, various private and scientific expeditions to South Georgia also made good use of *Dias* and the unique expertise of her skippers to access various parts of the island's treacherous coasts. The first was the Kohl-Larsen Expedition of 1928/29, which enjoyed considerable support from Pesca. The company provided passages from Norway and accommodation on South Georgia for the three-person expedition whilst *Dias* and the whale catcher *Tiburon* were used to carry Larsen and his little team to distant parts of the island where they carried out their glaciological, cartographic and biological work.

Ludvig Kohl-Larsen was a veteran of a German South Polar Expedition led by Wilhelm Filchner back 1911. The other members of his team were his wife, Margit, and Albert Benitz. Margit knew South Georgia well as she was the daughter of Captain C. A. Larsen, the founder of Grytviken, and had lived on the island with her father for several years in the whaling manager's first house—the site of the island's present museum. She was one of only a handful of women who ever lived at the operational whaling station. Albert Benitz came equipped to make films and indeed prepared the first commercial cinematographic film of South Georgia.

The Kohl-Larsen expedition used *Dias* for at least two voyages to various parts of the island. The first left Grytviken on 27 February 1929 and headed to the south and south-west coasts. Here *Dias* first investigated the Drygalski Fjord and Larsen Harbour at the southern tip of the island, before voyaging around Cape Disappointment and heading up to Annenkov Island where a first attempt to land proved a failure. Eventually the expedition got ashore and remained there for ten days to explore and film.

Following their return to Grytviken, the expedition made a second voyage on *Dias*, this time a counter-clockwise navigation of South Georgia, and Larsen made detailed notes of the various bays they encountered. It was on this voyage that skipper Johansson discovered, on the inhospitable south-west coast, an old sealing camp and the remains of an old wooden sailing vessel in a long forgotten bay. It looked as if a group of people had been wrecked there many years before and spent some time in the bay, as the *Dias*'s passengers, on digging in the debris, discovered the remains of an old stove and open fireplace. What was the ultimate fate of those marooned there? This is unknown as no graves or skeletal remains were found in the bay, subsequently named Dias Cove after the little ship. An expedition which sailed on 1 April returned to Grytviken a week later having undertaken further detailed biological and geological work on the south and south-eastern coats of the island, and also made visits to Cooper Bay, Wirik Bay, Iris Bay and Gold Harbour.

The Kohl-Larsen expedition departed South Georgia in May 1929, and a full account of the expedition's work was published in Kohl-Larsen's book *An den Toren der Antarktis* (Stuttgart, 1930). A film was also made using Albert Benitz's photography and a version entitled The Bottom of the World was shown at cinemas across the UK in 1930/1[1]. One wonders if any of *Viola*'s old crew saw this and, if so, did they recognise their former ship with its new name and incarnation.

Another scientist to make early use of *Dias* was the Argentine biologist Alberto Carcelles, based at the National Museum of Buenos Aires. He made several visits to the island from 1927 to make a collection of birds, using Grytviken as his base. Carcelles arrived on the factory ship *Ernesto Tornquist* for his last visit in 1929, and made a tour of various bays aboard *Dias*, collecting specimens along the way.

Between 1951 and 1957 a British team under Duncan Carse carried out a major topographical survey of South Georgia, using the Pesca sealing ships *Dias*, *Albatros* and *Carl* to access different parts of the coast. Carse, a former actor, who at one time played Dick Barton in the popular post-war BBC radio series, produced the first accurate depiction of the island. The same support was extended to a privately sponsored British South Georgia Expedition in 1954/55, led by the mountaineer George Sutton, during which an attempt was made at a first ascent of South Georgia's highest peak, Mount Paget (2,934m) from a base near Larvik Cove on the south-west side of the island. This was unsuccessful and the climbers were taken back to Grytviken aboard *Dias*.

Pesca also supported the biological work being undertaken by the Falkland Islands Government. In 1953-54 two British biologists, Nigel Bonner and Bernard Stonehouse, were carried by Pesca sealing vessels to Ample Bay in the Bay of Isles, where they pitched camp and undertook studies. Stonehouse, a native of Hull, was later joined by his fellow townsman, Jim Cowling, for a time when Bonner was laid up by appendicitis. Their work was continued by the Bird Island Expedition of 1958, which made use of both *Dias* and *Petrel*. Further support was given to the Royal Navy Hydrographic Survey Expedition in 1960/61 carried out by HMS *Owen* and HMS *Protector*. *Dias*'s use for such work over so many decades must make her one of the longest serving vessels to be involved in supporting South Atlantic and Antarctic expeditions.

Dias was not the only Beverley-built vessel to be involved in expedition and exploratory work in the southern oceans. The Royal Research Ship *William Scoresby* was built at the same yard and also equipped with steam engines and boiler made by Amos and Smith. Completed in 1926, she was part of the Discovery Investigations, working with Scott's old ship and her later replacement *Discovery II.* The vessel first called in at Grytviken about a year before *Dias* arrived, and she was a regular visitor to South Georgia for much of her working life. The *William Scoresby* and her sister ships spent much time marking and tracking whales, dredging the seabed and investigating all aspects of the oceans. It is fair to say that their investigations played a significant role in extending the frontiers of human knowledge, especially in the fields of oceanography and marine biology.[2]

X

JOURNEY'S END

URING THE 1950S FURTHER ALTERATIONS were made to *Dias*, which was subject to regular survey and overhaul, on Grytviken's floating dock. The little ship's old bridge was replaced by a far less attractive—if functional—whaling bridge and the old Amos and Smith steam engines were converted to burn oil instead of coal in 1956, a modification which also involved alterations to the funnel. Such changes prolonged the active life of the vessel which, as the 1960s opened, had been working in some of the world's roughest seas at both ends of the Atlantic for more than 54 years. She was now valued at a mere £1,950.

In June 1960 Pesca, now wholly owned by Argentine entrepreneur Alfredo Ryan, who formerly had strong connections with the Perón regime, transferred its whaling interests to a British company Albion Star (South Georgia) Ltd. with its registered office at Grytviken. Nevertheless, Lloyd's Register of Shipping continued to register the sealing vessels *Dias*, *Albatros* and *Petrel* in the name of the Compañia Argentina de Pesca S.A. at Buenos Aires, which still existed in its own right as a shipping company with two tramp steamers plying their trade world-wide. This transaction took place at a time when territorial tensions between Britain, the Falkland Islands and Argentina were particularly acute and the whaling station's production was beset by intermittent labour disputes, ostensibly promoted by Argentine government insurgents supposedly intent on disrupting the company's commercial operations. Whatever the causes of the labour disputes, they prompted Ryan, who was apparently tired of working the station with Argentine-flagged transports, to seriously curtail the employment of Argentine labour and rely largely on Norwegian crews for sealing operations. Almost simultaneously, he transferred the remainder of his whaling interests to a raft of wholly-owned companies, operating under Gibraltar and Norwegian flags. It is not known why the sealing fleet of *Dias*, *Albatros* and *Petrel* were not transferred to another flag, but it is probable that the company had no intention of sailing the vessels away from Grytviken, and they therefore remained a remnant and a permanent reminder of the origins of the parent company.

Who was Alfredo R. L. Ryan? The Gibraltar-born Argentine entrepreneur who owned Grytviken between 1944 and 1979 would certainly fit most definitions of a colourful character. Today, he is remembered not only as an astonishingly successful businessman but also for completing, in 1951, the world's then largest whale factory ship, one which holds the unusual record of having never caught or processed a whale.

Ryan was born in Gibraltar on 26 August 1902, the son of an Irishman Ernest A. Ryan and his wife Magdalena Navas. It was said that Ryan's grandfather, who hailed from Cork, had set foot on Gibraltar on his return from the Crimean War and had settled there. Young Ryan had served his apprenticeship as a naval engineer in the Admiralty's Gibraltar Dockyard from 1917 to 1922, qualifying at Christian Brothers College. He then served as a marine engineer and made sea trips with his father, who was likewise a naval engineer and an expert in the salvaging and repairing of ships.

The Ryan family moved to Argentina in 1924 and after a period in the drawing office of the Central Argentine Railways, then British-owned, he became a contractor's representative with a marine engineering company at the Boca, Buenos Aires. In 1931 Ryan and his father purchased the Farina marine workshop and expanded the business by buying additional warehouses and workshops, reportedly financed from the winnings of a lottery in Spain. After the death of his father, Ryan brought his three brothers, Julio, Pedro and Enrique, into the business, renaming the firm Ryan Hermanos.

The company thrived, buying up other businesses in the Buenos Aires district, being contractors to the British-owned railways in Argentina and Uruguay, and providing a comprehensive repair facility for shipping at Buenos Aires and Rosario. Among its clients was Aristotle Onassis, who provided

Ryan with a much needed continuity of work on Greek ships. During the Second World War Ryan's shipyards carried out repair work on more than two hundred allied ships, fitting many of them with gun mountings and degaussing equipment. It was during this period that Ryan diversified his interests, becoming a major share holder in many companies including the Compañia Argentina de Pesca.

When Ryan took overall control of Pesca from the Tornquist group in 1944, he formed a close rapport with Argentina's dictator Juan Perón. Perón's vision was to transform Argentina into a powerful and dynamic state and he saw Ryan, with his interests in South Georgia, as an ally in his declared objective of furthering Argentina's political aspirations in the Antarctic. Perón and Ryan hatched a grandiose project where Ryan would build the world's largest whale factory ship, to be called Juan Perón, and then send it with a fleet of catchers to the Antarctic to hunt whales—the post-war years were a time of acute oil and fat shortage in Europe.

But the project descended into debacle. The £1.625 million contract with Harland and Wolff for the building of the factory ship, and another with Smith's Dock, Middlesbrough for five whale catchers, costing £125,000 each, became embroiled in financial and political controversy. The company was accused of attempting to employ Nazis who had worked on pre-war German whaling expeditions and found refuge in Argentina; but one major problem Ryan faced was a Norwegian law which banned their nationals with whaling expertise from working on foreign factory ships. Ryan also fell foul of local currency regulations. The ship was eventually taken over by the Argentine government, deployed as a tanker operated by the state owned oil company Yacimientos Petroliferos Fiscales (YPF), and after the fall of Perón in 1955 renamed Cruz del Sur. Eventually, because of its running costs, it suffered an ignominious end, being auctioned off by the State and cut in half by an American company, then made into two oil drilling platforms.

After this setback Ryan continued to work the Grytviken whaling station and much investment was poured into the company, to improve both its fleet of whale catchers and the fabric of the station, which by 1958 was considered to be the most modern in the world. Ryan claimed to be very pro-British. He bought much of the materials for his South Georgia whaling station in Britain, used a long established firm of merchant bankers in the City to manage his European business interests, and was a regular visitor, with his Yugoslav born wife Antonia Dorich and two daughters Martha Betty and Mabel Antonia, to Ascot and Epsom racecourses. Ryan doubtless had many opportunities to liaise with British politicians and administrators but there is no record of him ever having visited South Georgia or the Falkland Islands. In Argentina and Uruguay he maintained a wide portfolio of interests covering shipping, engineering, insurance and agriculture as well as a vineyard on the slopes of the Andes near Mendoza.

Whaling continued at Grytviken—as well at Husvik, another South Georgia whaling station, which Ryan had mysteriously bought in 1960—until the end of the 1961/62 season, when Albion Star concluded that poor whale catches and disappointing returns for whale and seal products made operations no longer economically viable. The station was closed down and *Dias* and the other sealing ships *Albatros* and *Petrel* were laid up alongside it; a skeleton crew kept it in working order. In the meantime Ryan made several efforts to sell off the business. One option considered was to enter into a joint venture with the Norwegian firm A/S Thor Dahl, which would combine whaling and sealing at South Georgia with their existing pelagic whaling operations in the Antarctic. When this failed to materialise, negotiations were started with a Japanese consortium, the International Fishery Company of Tokyo. A deal was finally concluded whereby the Japanese company would sub-lease Grytviken for three seasons, at a reported £125,000 per season. Both whaling and sealing were to be carried out, with the Japanese whaling effort concentrating on the production of frozen whale meat for their home market.

Under these arrangements, sealing was also re-started in the austral spring of 1963. *Dias*, together with *Albatros* and *Petrel*, shipped mixed Norwegian and Japanese crews, Ryan having decided that following his troubles with Argentine personnel he would use Norwegian sealers from the Ålesund district of Norway. On *Dias*, the Norwegians included the master, Gunnar

Virik Nilsen, the Chief Engineer, mate and boatman whilst the Japanese filled twelve crew positions in the engine room and galley as well as most of the shore positions other than gunner. This arrangement worked surprisingly well despite certain problems of communication, neither group speaking the other's language.

The crew members might have got on well but the International Fishery Company found the deal a bad bargain. While the returns from sealing were good (in the first season 1963/64 3,998 seals were taken producing 7,156 barrels of oil and in the second season 5,147 seals producing 9,702 barrels), they only caught 391 and 321 whales respectively. This confirmed the now well-established view that the populations of rorqual whales in the Antarctic had collapsed and that whaling from South Georgia, even for the low-cost Japanese, was uneconomic. In December 1964 the Japanese left South Georgia early and did not return for the 1965 season. Although the seal stocks were still strong, without whaling it was not worth keeping the plant and equipment working and *Dias*, *Albatros* and *Petrel* were mothballed and laid up against the whaling station jetties. For only the second time since Grytviken had been founded in 1904, the whaling station was silent throughout the summer season.

XI

WAR AGAIN, AND PEACE

THE DEPARTURE OF THE JAPANESE WHALERS in December 1964 marked the end of whaling and sealing from Grytviken. The station's last products were shipped out over the following months and the final consignment, which included seal oil, left on board the Japanese tankship *Seiyo Maru* in early March 1965 bound for Rotterdam.[1] The ship also carried Carl Thor Thorsen, the last Norwegian whaling manager, and the personal effects of many members of the Norwegian workforce who had left them there expecting to return.[2]

After *Seiyo Maru* sailed out of King Edward Cove, Grytviken fell silent. Not only had the workforce gone for good but so had the steam whale catchers and associated shipping. The quaysides were almost but not quite empty: the little fleet of sealing vessels was still there and for some time seemingly kept ready to return to sea. *Dias* and *Albatros* lay side by side, adjacent to the Harpon Quay whilst *Petrel* idled in the wind against the nearby Catcher Quay.

Despite the closure, a skeleton crew initially kept the three sealers and other equipment in serviceable condition whilst Ryan and his agents made strenuous attempts to sell off the whaling station. Negotiations were held with Soviet and Bulgarian interests apparently interested in combining whaling and sealing with fishing for southern cod, toothfish and krill. The existence of good fishing grounds on coastal shelves just outside and to the east of Cumberland Bay had been verified long ago by Captain C. A. Larsen and also by the Discovery Expedition in the late 1920s, and there was a view that Grytviken and its facilities would have made an ideal re-fuelling and repair depot for a fishing fleet.

Sealing, which could have continued *ad infinitum* under the sustainable management regime then in place, might have added value to the proposals but the plans never materialised, primarily because the British government seemed nervous about sanctioning such deals with the Soviet bloc. The Falkland Islands Government advertised the elephant seal licence with the proviso that whole seal carcass utilisation was undertaken. They wrote to Albion Star's London agents in an attempt to encourage them to return, even stating that the £200 licence fee was 'negotiable.'

The years went by and most of the skeleton crew left in 1967. The windows of the Manager's house were by this time boarded up against the sub-Antarctic elements and the billiard table and the piano moved round the cove to enhance entertainment at the King Edward Point scientific base. Grytviken's last caretaker, Ragnar Thorsen, despite having been advised by Ryan that he would not be paid, stubbornly stayed on there for several more years with the support of a Chilean cook, Luis Vera Aguilar. Thorsen, who lived in the chief electrician's cabin above the hydro-electric plant, did his best to keep everything—including the engines of the three sealers—clean and in working order. Destruction and complete dereliction followed in the wake of his reluctant departure in 1971.

The following year Albion Star were approached by Malcolm Binnie, a Falklander—and great nephew of Edward B. Binnie[3] the South Georgia Magistrate between 1914 and 1927—who wished to purchase the sealing ships, but nothing came of this. Left unprotected and unmaintained, the little flotilla fell prey to forays from the crews of visiting eastern European fishing vessels and the depredations of private yachts.[4] All three sealing vessels were vandalised and then during the winter of 1974 both *Dias* and *Albatros* sank at their moorings under the weight of accumulated snow. The end of sealing also marked the end of an 'important chapter' in maritime history.[5]

There were yet further discussions about reviving Grytviken, including an enquiry from Hull-based British United Trawlers, which considered using the old whaling station as a base for fishing, now that the UK distant water trawling fleet was being progressively excluded from their North Atlantic

fishing grounds by Cod Wars with Iceland and the looming creation of Exclusive Economic Zones; but once again discussions proved inconclusive, as did
somewhat similar proposals and talks with Japanese interests.

Grytviken, left at the mercy of South Georgia's cruel climate, as well as van-
dals on board visiting yachts, acquired all the attributes of a ghost town, its abandoned buildings ravaged by an ice-cold combination of wind, rain, snow and
sleet. On occasion violent whirlwinds—katabatic winds—swept down from
the mountains; at other times, intense sub-Antarctic storms blasted through
the desolate works, scouring almost every vestige of paint from exposed woodwork, ripping through the rusting corrugated iron fabric that covered much of
the plant and machinery, blowing debris from one end of the place to the other.
As the winds rattled around Grytviken, the only regular human presence in the
area—indeed across much of South Georgia—was the British Antarctic Survey station with its main base across the cove at King Edward Point.

In many respects the derelict South Georgia whaling stations remained as
they had been left. Flight Commander Tony Ellerbeck, who visited with HMS
Endurance in the early eighties, recalled seeing their amazing workshops and
stores containing all that was needed to service the whaling fleets. He even
saw a full diving suit with a brass screw-on helmet and attendant hand-driven
air pump. In the hospitals there were still beds made up and drugs in the dis-
pensary; these were removed by the doctor from *Endurance*.

At Grytviken Ellerbeck found it was possible to trace the whole production process from the arrival of the whales on the plan to the storage of the
oil in vast tanks inland from the plant. Lying off the plan on moorings alongside a jetty, he and the rest of the crew were able to visit the three sealing
ships. *Dias* and *Petrel* were upright and it was possible to walk around them,
and numerous sailors had their photograph taken 'manning the harpoon
gun' on *Petrel*. He remembered that *Dias* certainly had a dignity, lacking the
obvious catcher paraphernalia, and it was possible to walk around her wheelhouse—complete with an iron stove! He remembered that Dias certainly
had a dignity about her in her almost upright position, with tall funnel and
mast standing erect.[6]

Whilst the South Georgia whaling stations, together with *Dias* and the other sealing ships, languished in a kind of melancholically idle post-industrial malaise, the time-festered Anglo-Argentine South Atlantic territorial tensions followed anything but a similarly quiescent course.

The long running dispute between the UK and Argentina, initially about the sovereignty of the Falkland Islands, has its roots in eighteenth century international rivalries. The archipelago had been sighted by a number of different European navigators in the sixteenth and seventeenth centuries but the first, relatively short-lived settlements there, involving the French, British and Spanish, were not made until the second half of the eighteenth century. The French were first, establishing a settlement, Port Egmont, on the island of East Falkland in 1764. The British followed a year later when John Byron, grandfather of Lord Byron, set up a fort on Saunders Island, off West Falkland. In 1767 the French turned over their rights to Spain and, although the Spanish subsequently recognised Britain's West Falkland claim, the British departed from Saunders Island in 1774.

The Spanish maintained a garrison until 1811 when it was withdrawn but, after Argentina won its freedom from Spain in 1816, the new nation's government lay claim to what the Argentines call *Las Malvinas*.[7] In the 1820s Argentines began settling on the islands but after the seizure of some United States ships fishing off them, the captain of the USS *Lexington* destroyed much of the settlement there.[8] The British returned in 1833/4, formally establishing themselves as a Crown Colony a few years later. Since then the islands have been permanently inhabited by civilians and after 1834 there has always been at least a token British military presence.[9]

Argentina has never relinquished its claim to the islands and in the early 1900s extended this, first to South Georgia and then to British Antarctic Dependencies. Yet South Georgia's territorial history is somewhat different to that of the Falkland Islands. Some believe the island was first sighted by an Englishman, Antonio de la Roche, in 1675, others by a Spanish treasure ship, the *Leon*, in 1756 after she was blown off course whilst rounding Cape Horn. The first person known to have set foot on the island was Captain Cook, who arrived in 1775 with the *Resolution* and *Adventure*—ships acquired by the Admiralty from William Hammond, one of the Elder Brethren of Hull Trinity House.[10] After the Falkland Islands were granted their Royal Letters Patent in 1843, South Georgia was generally but loosely regarded as under their governmental jurisdiction, provision being made in the document for administration of the Dependencies. Although the island continued to be frequented by fur and elephant seal hunters, the first settlement was Grytviken, set up by Captain Carl Anton Larsen in 1904. Soon afterwards, of course, Pesca was granted and accepted a lease by the Falkland Islands Government to operate from the whaling station. From 1909 a Government administrative centre was established across the cove at King Edward Point and a resident Magistrate was appointed.[11]

South Georgia, the South Shetland Islands, the South Orkney Islands and Graham Land were declared by 1908 Letters Patent to be Dependencies of the Falkland Islands, a position which was not challenged for nearly twenty years. But then in September 1927—little more than a week after *Dias* had arrived at Grytviken from Norway—Argentina notified the International Postal Union that it regarded South Georgia and the South Shetland Islands as part of its territory.

Since then the dispute over sovereignty rumbled on, blowing hot and cold over the intervening years. During the Second World War, after the accession to power of General Perón, the Argentines, embroiled in various territorial disputes with their neighbours, began erecting bronze plaques on the islands of the Dependencies using a vessel called the *Primero de Mayo*—this was an expedition which *Dias* was also chartered to support. The British vessel *Carnarvon Castle* then followed a similar route and removed the plaques.[12]

For some time after the Second World War, Argentina pursued her territorial claims against the United Kingdom primarily through the United Nations, and a war of words interspersed with occasional incidents continued throughout the fifties and sixties. During these decades the people of Argentina endured alternating periods of government instability and repressive authoritarianism, whilst the volatile political environment tended to fuel the resentment felt by many Argentines about British control of the Falklands and Dependencies, and a number of incidents occurred.

From 1976, Argentina descended into one of those dark authoritarian periods. The then president, Isabel Perón, was displaced and followed by succession of military dictators. Eventually General Leopold Galtieri came to power as leader of a military *junta*. During this time inflation, unemployment and falling production ravaged the Argentine economy. Like a number of dictators before and since, Galtieri looked to counter increasing domestic concern over economic collapse and human rights abuses by pursuing external or international ambitions, in this case by invading the Falkland Islands and Dependencies.

Although the wider causes of the Falklands War were rooted in this drawn-out, if increasingly febrile, territorial dispute, the spark that finally, and unexpectedly, ignited the South Atlantic conflagration in 1982 was generated from the seemingly harmless and business-like ambitions of one man, Constantine Davidoff.

Davidoff was an Argentine businessman, apparently of Greek extraction, who had been involved in various business activities around Latin American ports for many years, and was said to have an ever-open eye for the latest opportunity. The situation on South Georgia seemed to offer just such a possibility and in 1978 he approached the firm of Christian Salvesen with a venture that ostensibly offered him the chance to make a tidy profit.

Salvesen's, whose headquarters were at Leith in Scotland, had formerly possessed an extensive range of global whaling interests. They had built Leith Harbour, their main operational base on South Georgia, soon after Grytviken had opened in the early twentieth century but from the 1930's they also leased the Stromness and Prince Olav whaling stations. Leith Harbour was also their last operational station on the island, only closing when Salvesen's finally withdrew from whaling in 1963. Although no longer involved in whaling, the company had retained the leases on Stromness—formerly used for ship repair—and Leith Harbour and by the late 1970s the plant and machinery at these, by now long derelict, whaling stations was deteriorating rapidly.

Davidoff suggested that Salvesen's offer him a contract to salvage scrap metal from their redundant whaling stations. He was prepared to purchase this right and dispose of the old plant and machinery there at his own risk.

For Salvesens, the prospect seemed attractive. They wished to retain a stake for the future in South Georgia but it seemed unlikely that rusting whaling station plant was of any future commercial use and Davidoff's scrap proposal seemed to offer the chance to recoup some money from the old equipment. Coincidentally, Albion Star was also seeking a buyer for the stations at Grytviken and Husvik for which they still held the leases, and in 1979 Salvesen made an offer of £35,000 to Ryan for them 'lock, stock and barrel' through his agents in London, a transaction that included the three sealing vessels, *Dias*, *Albatros* and *Petrel* lying in a forlorn state alongside the derelict station. It was, as their agent described, 'a give away price, but Salvesen are obviously taking a long-term view as undoubtedly there is the possibility of much activity in the future.' Salvesen therefore became leaseholder of all the redundant whaling stations on South Georgia and so gained a commercial interest in many of the island's best anchorages and harbours. They also agreed a contract with Davidoff granting him the right to salvage scrap from the whaling stations.

The deal between Salvesen and Davidoff was finally signed on 30 September 1979. Under the agreement, Davidoff was given the sole right to acquire the whaling equipment and other fixtures at Leith Harbour, Stromness and Husvik but not Grytviken. However, the contract did cover the sealing vessels, including *Dias*, now lying partly submerged in King Edward Cove. It seemed that the old trawler's end was in sight.

Over the next couple of years Davidoff focused his energies on the financial and operational aspects of the project, securing backing from a wealthy Buenos Aires lawyer and the Banco Junta. The contract anticipated paying Salvesen £115,000 in total but Davidoff and the bank rather optimistically anticipated a theoretical profit of about $4.5 million if current world scrap prices were maintained.[13] During this preparatory stage Davidoff maintained close contact with the British Embassy in Buenos Aires but he evidently also talked with friends and acquaintances in the Argentine navy.

Having the right to take scrap was one thing but recovering it from an island as remote as South Georgia was another. For some time it proved difficult for Davidoff to overcome all the logistical and financial problems his project involved, and the prospect of it lapsing through default loomed in the background. In late 1981 he appeared to have found a way forward when the Argentine navy offered to take him to South Georgia to reconnoitre Leith Harbour on board *Almirante Irizar*, an ice-breaker usually engaged in servicing Argentina's Antarctic naval bases much further to the south.

From this time forward, Davidoff's commercial activities began to assume something of a geopolitical dimension. He sailed from Buenos Aires on 16 December 1981 after informing the British Embassy and Salvesen's of his intention to make a visit in accordance with his contract. So far so good but the next steps did not conform to requisite diplomatic procedure.

During the voyage, Captain César Trombetta of *Almirante Irizar* unusually maintained radio silence. All vessels arriving at the island were required to report first to the magistrate at King Edward Point but this protocol was ignored by the Argentine ship which sailed straight to Leith Harbour, where the captain and some of the crew made a brief visit ashore, as did Davidoff who completed an inspection and took photographs of the abandoned whaling stations in Stromness Bay.

The incident hardly enhanced UK-Argentine relations and the war of words, accompanied by occasional incidents, continued over the next couple of months, but it was during March 1982 that the simmering crisis started to escalate. On 19 March a four man party from the British Antarctic Survey, who visited Leith Harbour to replenish the stores at the whaling station's refuge centre, unexpectedly found the Argentine ship *Bahía Buen Suceso* moored in the harbour. The ship had brought men and equipment for the Davidoff scrap salvage expedition and it seemed apparent they had come for a long stay. Around a hundred people seem to have landed and the Argentine flag was seen flying on shore.

The BAS party radioed the news to the Magistrate at King Edward Point who in turn contacted the Governor in Stanley. The subsequent message from the Governor, requiring the *Bahía Buen Suceso*'s party to, amongst other things, return to their ship, lower the Argentine flag and report to the Magistrate at King Edward Point, was passed on to Captain Trombetta. Although the flag was taken down, there seemed little evidence of further compliance.[14] The Argentines looked set to stay.

As the situation on the island became more acute, HMS *Endurance* was sent back from Stanley with a detachment of marines to enforce the Governor's orders. Meanwhile, a British Antarctic Survey group set up a post where they could observe the activities in the Stromness Bay whaling stations and later, after *Endurance* arrived in Cumberland Bay, the Royal Marines took over surveillance. In an effort to ease tensions the original plan to use the Marines to arrest the Argentines was shelved whilst the government sought further negotiations with Buenos Aires.

Soon afterwards *Bahía Buen Suceso* sailed out of Stromness Bay, leaving behind both the disembarked stores and some 39 scrap men, but on the 25th another Argentine ship, *Bahía Paraiso*, arrived with yet further evidence of military intent. She disembarked Argentine special forces who strengthened the occupation of the Stromness Bay whaling stations and surrounding districts. Large quantities of military stores were unloaded and the Argentine flag was reported to be flying once more amidst nationalist chants and anthems.

The final British attempt to resolve the problem peaceably was rebuffed on the 31 March; by now the frigate *Guerrico* had reinforced the Argentine presence at Leith Harbour and at least four other ships, two destroyers, a submarine and tanker were reported to be on the high seas and heading for South Georgia. Only the submarine was to complete the voyage as the tanker, which supplied the destroyers with fuel, had to turn back because of engine trouble.

On the same day *Endurance*, responding to the impending threat of invasion which had by now also enveloped the Falkland Islands, slipped out of Cumberland Bay en route for Stanley, a departure missed by *Bahía Buen Suceso*, now patrolling outside of Cumberland Bay. *Endurance* voyaged round the south-west of the island and set course for Stanley, but left behind at King Edward Point a platoon of Royal Marines under the command of Lt Keith Mills, who set about overseeing preparations for the defence of the area around the scientific station.[15]

Events moved swiftly as *Endurance* headed over the South Atlantic towards Stanley. On 1 April the Falkland Islands Governor, Sir Rex Hunt, broadcast news of an imminent Argentine invasion and the following day Argentine forces made an overwhelming attack on Stanley. After a fine defensive action by the small party of Royal Marines and a firefight around Government House, the Governor surrendered and the Argentine flag flew over Stanley. The Falklands had been occupied.

Back on South Georgia, on the same day as the Falklands fell to the Argentines, *Bahía Paraiso* entered a blustery Cumberland Bay, presumably intent on making military landings, but the weather proved too bad to launch either boats or helicopters and within an hour the ship sailed out again. Ashore, this brief respite allowed further work on defensive positions around King Edward Point whilst many of the civilian British Antarctic Survey staff moved to the church behind Grytviken whaling station, which became a refuge.

After a long night for all concerned, the morning of 3 April dawned clear and still. The Royal Marines at the observation post were brought back to King Edward Point where the air hung heavy with expectation. Around 10am *Bahía Paraiso*, now accompanied by the frigate *Guericco*, sailed back into Cumberland Bay and Argentine helicopters were soon ferrying troops to the shore. The Captain of *Bahía Paraiso* radioed news of the ceasefire to the British Resident Magistrate and invited him to follow suit in order to avoid bloodshed. The Magistrate in turn offered discussions with the captain but, as the dialogue continued, refused the Argentines permission to land. When the Argentines told him they intended to use force he warned them that the place was defended by the British military.

Then the talking ceased. By now the frigate *Guerrico* was lying off King Edward Point, her guns already trained on the radio room. The Magistrate passed his authority over to the Royal Marines commanding officer and defensive plans were activated. On the other side of King Edward Cove, at the church in Grytviken, the civilians who had been listening to the radio communications took shelter on the floor of the library as the fighting commenced.

Across the water from the derelict *Dias* and the other two sealing ships, the Argentine troops jumped out of a helicopter as it landed at King Edward Point jetty and opened fire on the Royal Marines positions. *Guerrico*, sailing close to the scientific station, also opened fire as she passed. But this move exposed her hull to the defenders and at just the right moment the Royal Marines fired a number of anti-tank rockets into the frigate's side. *Guerrico* was caught by the fire, the nearby Hobart Rocks meant the vessel could not change course for some time and had to endure the fusillade but, even when finally able to turn, her port side was hit by yet more rockets. More than a thousand rounds from machine guns also raked the vessel during the action. The frigate was holed below the waterline and the attacks damaged the deadly Exocet missile equipment. During the battle, two Argentine helicopters were also hit, one crashing across King Edward Cove and the other coming down amidst much smoke near Grytviken.

Although the original Argentine King Edward Point landing party was by this time pinned down by Royal Marines fire near the Post Office, the overwhelming fire-power of the Argentine attackers gradually made its mark. The badly damaged *Guerrico* moved offshore and carried out a more distant bombardment of the area around the scientific station using 100mm shells, whilst other Argentine troops who had landed near Grytviken moved around the cove and closed in on King Edward Point. As *Guerrico*'s shells began to find their range, the Royal Marines' Commander finally made the decision to surrender his forces. All told, the battle for Cumberland Bay had lasted nearly two hours and the Argentine forces lost 15 men with a similar number injured. One Royal Marine was injured in the action and the commanding officer was subsequently awarded the DSC.

Later that day the BAS civilians, sheltering in Grytviken church during the action, were taken into custody by the Argentines then marched at gunpoint to King Edward Point. After being allowed to collect some of their personal belongings, they were ferried to *Bahía Paraiso* where they joined most of the Royal Marines. The last of the British to leave King Edward Point were the Magistrate, Bob Headland of the British Antarctic Survey, and the Royal Marines' Commander.[16] Argentine forces now held not only King Edward Point, Grytviken and Leith Harbour but also Schlieper Bay, Lyell Glacier, St Andrews Bay and Bird Island.

Meanwhile, HMS *Endurance*, still voyaging to Stanley when Argentine intentions became evident, had turned back towards South Georgia. Captain Nick Barker brought her in by way of the southern tip of the island and she slipped into Royal Bay. Ordered not to become involved in direct action at this stage, Barker's immediate task was to obtain intelligence on Argentine movements and the vessel used her helicopters to establish an observation post way up on the Barff Peninsula where Cumberland Bay could be overlooked. Indeed, Tony Ellerbeck, Flight Commander on HMS *Endurance*, and Lt David Wells, flew to the Peninsula whilst their ship was still rounding the southern coast, and watched the battle for Grytviken and King Edward Point. From their high observation point they could see where the Argentine troops landed by helicopter opposite Shackleton Point then ran past *Dias*, *Albatros* and *Petrel* on their way to King Edward Point.[17]

After the Argentine invasion HMS *Endurance* slipped quietly away to the south and hid alongside an iceberg about two to three miles long and a couple of hundred feet high. The sides were sheer and required someone to spot the vessel visually rather than as a moving dot on an airborne radar though, as Ellerbeck recalled, the red paint would help.[18] *Endurance* was thus able to avoid the Exocet-armed frigate *Granville* which was hunting her, and remained concealed. One of her helicopters visited a couple of the field stations not occupied by Argentine troops.

Though the Argentine news broadcast reports that she had been sunk, *Endurance* remained very much afloat and elusive. Later she headed back to sea, moving north from the island to rendezvous with a forward section of the Royal Naval task force and there be replenished with much needed food and fuel.

Back in the UK, of course, a task force of vessels, equipment and men was being hastily assembled. Many merchant vessels were requisitioned including the *QE2* and *Canberra*, and not least a number of vessels associated with Hull. The Ro-Ro ferry *Norland* was the largest Hull vessel requisitioned and left from King George Dock—the same dock from which the requisitioned *Viola* had sailed off to war in September 1914. As the *Norland*'s master, Don Ellerby, took the vessel down the Humber he and his crew were seen off by a chorus of cheering crowds and ship's horns.

There were other echoes of 1914. Back then *Viola* had been one of the first trawlers requisitioned and in April 1982, almost sixty-eight years later, five of the port's latest and almost last stern trawlers followed that well-worn path to war. Meanwhile, out at sea, three powerful ocean going tugs, owned by Hull's United Towing Company, were also requisitioned and, after being swiftly refitted for action, headed off to join the Task Force.

In the South Atlantic, the submarine HMS *Conqueror* inspected South Georgia from the westwards and on 21 April HMS *Endurance* returned, now accompanied by the frigates HMS *Plymouth* and *Antrim*. The Royal Navy were back and, although an attempt to reconnoitre enemy positions by way of a patrol landed by helicopter on the Fortuna Glacier had to be abandoned, boat-borne observation parties met with more success though harsh weather continued to impede operations .

News that an enemy submarine was patrolling in the area caused the Royal Navy's surface ships to make a temporary withdrawal but this was of short duration and by 25 April HMS *Brilliant* had joined the force off the island. The British ships then moved to the offensive. Helicopters from HMS *Brilliant*, HMS *Antrim* and HMS *Plymouth* caught the Argentine submarine *Santa Fe* on the surface. The initial attack with depth charges by Lieutenant Chris Parry from HMS *Antrim* caused substantial internal damage to the submarine, rendering it unable to dive. Helicopters from *Brilliant* and *Plymouth* also joined in the attack, as did a Wasp helicopter from HMS *Endurance*, piloted by Flight Commander Tony Ellerbeck. After firing his two missiles, the first of which hit the fin, Tony Ellerbeck turned back to *Endurance* to reload. As the submarine turned back towards Cumberland Bay the other helicopters kept up their fighting forays, coming under fire as they chased her closer to the shore. Tony Ellerbeck also returned to the fray, rearmed with missiles and coming into the bay through the small crowd of helicopters his observer, David Wells, fired the first missile which turned out to be a rogue veering off out of sight. As they closed to two miles, Wells let off the starboard missile which plunged through the submarine's fin. His attack was followed by another, this time from Commander John Dransfield in a Wasp from HMS *Plymouth*. He closed in, steadied his craft and then the missile was fired. Although no direct hit was made *Santa Fe* suffered further damage. The second *Endurance* Wasp, piloted by Lieutenant Tim Harding, then lined up to attack. The Wasp successively fired off its two missiles whilst the enemy returned fire with arcs of tracer, and the second missile caused further damage to the vessel despite failing to explode. Soon afterwards Ellerbeck returned, rearmed with his third set of missiles, one of which hit home soon after *Santa Fe* tied up at King Edward Point Jetty. His helicopter's final AS12 missile penetrated her 'snort' system breaching her watertight integrity. The helicopters had eliminated *Santa Fe* as a fighting force.

Later that morning the frigates *Antrim* and *Plymouth* began bombarding positions at Hesteletten and on the slopes of Brown Mountain across King Edward Cove from the scientific station, in order to neutralise any enemy emplacements there, and shortly afterwards a force of Royal Marines was landed at Heseltetten and advanced through the whaling station, passing *Dias* and the other sealing vessels on the waterfront as they moved towards King Edward Point. The Royal Navy bombardment was terrific and could be heard for many miles around. The combination of bombardment and military landings must have had the desired result for, as the Royal Marines approached King Edward Point, the Argentines surrendered, raising white flags. The surrender was accepted by Major G. Sheridan who sent out a message 'Be pleased to inform Her Majesty that the White Ensign now flies alongside the Union Jack on South Georgia, God Save the Queen.'[19] South Georgia was back in British hands after 22 days of occupation. No lives were lost by either side in the action to retake Grytviken and King Edward Point.

The action against *Santa Fe* was the first time that a helicopter attack had disabled a submarine. The final part of that attack had taken place when the submarine was back in King Edward Cove almost opposite *Dias*, a veteran of another aerial first against a submarine. Back in September 1918 the armed trawler was one of the vessels which, together with the airship *R27*, had sunk the *UB-115*. That was the first time an airship had participated in the destruction of a U-boat. *Viola/Dias* had now 'seen action' in both the Great War and the Falklands War.

The following day the forces at Leith Harbour also surrendered and in total 126 Argentine troops were taken on South Georgia. All the troops, with the exception of Captain Aziz, as well as the 39 civilian scrap metal workers, were taken to Ascension Island on board the RFA *Tidespring* before being flown on to Uruguay and released.

The next step for the British was the re-capture of the Falklands. During this phase of the conflict the harbours of South Georgia, particularly Cumberland Bay and King Edward Cove, proved particularly valuable, providing a sheltered base for transhipping servicemen and supplies.[20] An unprecedented number of vessels called in, including the requisitioned *QE2*, the largest vessel ever to visit the islands, which anchored near Sappho Point. The five Hull requisitioned trawlers *Cordella*, *Farnella*, *Junella*, *Northella* and *Pict* also arrived, and moored not far from *Dias*. These five vessels, the last Hull trawlers ever to be requisitioned from the port's rapidly shrinking fishing fleet, were sharing King Edward Cove with the old *Viola*, one of the first Great War trawlers from their home city to take up the challenge of War back in 1914. In the hustle and bustle of war, no one then appreciated—or perhaps even recognized—that poignant coincidence.

The Ro-Ro *Norland* also came into Cumberland Bay, ahead of its epic role under skipper Don Ellerby in the San Carlos Water landings on East Falkland.

The United Towing tugs *Salvageman* and *Yorkshireman* were other arrivals. In July, the *Salvageman* and *Yorkshireman* played a crucial role in the highly technical and sometimes dangerous work of raising the stricken submarine *Santa Fe* and moving it to a temporary resting place at Hesteletten, across from King Edward Point. *Santa Fe* had war-shot torpedoes in her tubes and there was a danger of these exploding if water leaked into them from extended immersion—known technically as a 'hot run torpedo'. Later *Salvageman* was involved in the difficult and last salvage of *Santa Fe* which was towed out to sink in deeper water beyond the entrance to the Cumberland Bays.

Once *Santa Fe* had been made to Hesteletten, there was much discussion about how to keep *Endurance*'s crew busy whilst the vessel acted as 'Harbour Master' in South Georgia. There was little for the sailors to do whilst in the deserted whaling station and the fighting was by then entirely around the Falkland Islands. Captain Nick Barker looked at the idea of refloating *Dias* and the other sunken whaler, *Petrel*. Tony Ellerbeck recalled that there was great enthusiasm for the idea, and plans were made to include the Royal Marine contingent who had by then made their defensive plans and had lots of time on their hands. But the early end to the conflict meant that *Endurance* was able to return to Stanley and, afterwards, head home. She was the last vessel home, finally docking in Chatham after being away for ten and a half months.[21]

The Falklands Campaign finally ended on 14 June 1982 when the Argentine forces at Stanley surrendered. Cumberland Bay had been a hive of activity but over time operations wound down and Grytviken and the derelict sealing ships slipped back into an almost somnolent obscurity, to remain as neglected and abandoned as ever.

In the later 1990s an outline proposal to return *Dias* to England and to the Grimsby Fishing Heritage Centre was mooted but never came to fruition. By this time concern about the state of the whaling stations and the ecological impact of furnace oil leaking from the vessel was growing.

By the end of the 1980s, initial plans were drawn up to address some of the environmental problems afflicting the South Georgia whaling stations, mainly heavy oil spills. The firm involved in the subsequent work was Marine Salvage Services and this contract brought in Lyle Craigie-Halkett as Operations Manager. Lyle had first seen the old trawler *Dias* when he had arrived at Grytviken as a junior ordinary seaman on board the Falkland Island Company vessel RMS *Darwin* back in 1957. Back then he noticed that the vessel stood out from the other two sealers, the former whale catchers, *Albatros* and *Petrel*, with their distinctive high foc'sle, double panama leads for towing whales and their sweeping decks rising at the stern. *Dias*, with much less rake to her main deck, straight stern and counter type stern told him something of her different, perhaps more remarkable, lineage. Like others, before and since, he became intrigued by the vessel, even before he came to know more of her unique story.

Lyle never saw the vessel again until he returned to the island on board HMS *Endurance* in December 1989 with salvage partner Roy Martin and some senior officials from Christian Salvesen in order to plan the clean-up operations and make estimates of fuel oil in tanks, spills and scrap metal.

By then Lyle, a Southampton based Falkland Islander, was a very experienced salvageman. Born on the Falklands in 1941, the grandson of the local colonial secretary who had signed the papers of memorandum and agreement for Pesca, he had started work when 13 years old at Goose Green Station, also sailing on the motorised ketch *Black Swan*, transporting animals and stores to nearby farms and islands. He then spent a couple of years on RMS *Darwin* running to South America, before spending three years with the British Antarctic Survey on RRS *John Biscoe*. Afterwards he put in a number of years first as able seaman and later as bosun on various merchant navy vessels before joining Risdon Beazley, the British salvage company, in 1966 as bosun on a small diving ship working on wartime shipwreck clearance on the approaches to Le Havre.[22]

Lyle soon graduated to diving and remained with Risdon Beazley until its closure in 1980. Much of the company's work involved cutting up wrecks with explosives to give greater depth for shipping, or else cutting up First and Second World War wrecks to retrieve valuable non-ferrous cargoes. This work took him all over the world and often involved using observation bells when working in exceptionally deep waters.

Because of his local knowledge Lyle was chosen as a Diver/Rigger to be part of Risdon Beazley's team that salvaged Isambard Kingdom Brunel's 1843 built S.S. *Great Britain* from Sparrow Cove in the Falklands in 1970 and returned the vessel to its original dock in Bristol, where it has become one of the UK's finest maritime visitor attractions.[23]

After Risdon Beazley was sold to European interests in 1980 Lyle remained with the firm as Salvage and Barge Master for a number of years, but since then has worked on his own account as Salvage Master for various clients across the world. His knowledge and experience of salvage planning and recovery is perhaps second to none and his expertise is regularly called on to this day.

When Lyle and Roy Martin arrived in Grytviken, South Georgia onboard HMS *Endurance* they moored alongside the Harpon Jetty, very close to the by-now semi-submerged hulls of *Dias* and her running mate *Albatros*. His appreciation of her ancestry grew as he came to realise she was not only an important example, but also the last survivor, from several exceptional chapters in maritime history.

Lyle made another trip to Grytviken a couple of months later with a four-man team to do remedial and preparation work prior to the larger clean-up operation that would follow. They also spent their free time plus periods when operations ceased through bad weather removing human filth, broken glass and other debris from the old whaling manager's house. The team was told the mess there was the legacy of Eastern Bloc fishermen and Argentine military personnel who had practically destroyed every room and used most as a toilet. Later Nigel Bonner and Ian Hart took on the daunting and then somewhat unheralded task of refurbishing the building and really laying the basic foundations of what has now become a remarkable museum.

The final part of these clean-up operations commenced in late 1990 using an ex-MOD ship RMAS *Throsk*, manned with a hand-picked crew, some of whom were ex-whalers. A Uruguayan oil tanker was also chartered.

Though the resources available were limited, all the original aims of this environmental operation were achieved within budget and on time. Over 6000 tons of fuel oil, 50 tons of nitric acid and many other dangerous substances were removed from the whaling stations. Whilst 100 tons of furnace oil was removed from the bunkers of the *Petrel* the remit of those involved did not extend to working on either *Dias* or *Albatros*. But Lyle was keen to go further. During his spare time he worked on a plan to salvage *Dias*, *Albatros* and *Petrel*, not only to remove the fuel oil they still contained but also to give them a more permanent and secure berth.

After the contract was completed, Lyle submitted a report on the Grytviken ships to the Government of South Georgia and the South Sandwich Islands, but this was not acted on and a few years later some Dutch contractors were sent to King Edward Cove to try and remove all the fuel oil left in the three vessels; but this operation was largely unsuccessful.

In June 2003 Lyle went to a meeting with the management of AWG, a civil engineering firm based at Matlock in Derbyshire, who had been contracted to undertake work in the Falklands, South Georgia and Antarctica, including the demolition of unsafe buildings and the removal of oil and asbestos. Lyle's brief was to submit a proposal for the removal of oil, particularly from the three sealing ships, and to make a survey of the sealer *Petrel* with a view to securing her for the future. Excited by the challenge, he referred to the extensive notes he had already made in 1990 regarding the ships, and particularly *Dias*.

On producing his proposal, Lyle was asked to approach some salvage companies and ascertain the cost of the proposed operations. After he travelled to Chile to talk to a couple of salvage companies, a contract was subsequently drawn up with Ultragas/Humbolt, a well-established firm. The remit now included a proposal to refloat both *Albatros* and *Dias*, clean out their fuel tanks and remove any other oils that may be present. The final or worse case scenario was to let them sink again, but if possible the plans were now to beach the two sealers, and ensure it was environmentally safe to do so.

For Lyle, the practical side of the operations began in January 2004 when he arrived at Punta Arenas, Chile, to purchase equipment. Experience of years of salvage in remote regions meant that he knew how important it was to ensure that every single piece of equipment was provided, although he knew how to improvise: many years earlier, during the raising of the *Great Britain*, his team had blocked water flow from an unexpected crack found in the hull by using old mattresses collected from across the Falklands.

Everything from food to the most rudimentary of tools had to be included in the equipment list. Lyle moved on board *Luma*, a Dutch-built anchor-handling vessel, previously operated by Smit-Lloyd of Rotterdam before being bought by Ultragas/Humbolt. The expedition was also taking with them the oil barge *Brecknock*, which was to be towed to South Georgia and could be used for carrying a great deal of the equipment in the hold.

Reaching South Georgia was a trial in itself. On setting sail on 12 January, both ship and barge were forced to anchor in the Magellan Straits as weather conditions worsened to gale force 8, gusting to force 9. The following day conditions were, if anything, even worse with the wind screaming to storm force ten. Finally, on the following day, after some signs of moderation, anchors were weighed and the choppy waters of the Magellan Straits were replaced by a large ocean swell, the aftermath of the storm. Whilst *Luma* handled the sea conditions well, exhibiting just a steady roll, the oil barge bobbed around like a cork in a maelstrom. They were not out of the woods, and over the next few days the Southern Ocean threw more bad weather at the vessels, conditions deteriorating once more to full gale and a six to eight metre swell. Finally, on Sunday the 18th a few large tabular icebergs were spotted, then fur seals, cormorants and occasional glimpses of Gentoo penguins, all signs that land was near.

Early on Monday *Luma* shortened the tow on the barge as the two vessels arrived in Cumberland Bay. They were soon moored alongside the stone jetty at King Edward Point and treated to a magnificent view of the old Pesca whaling station across the cove. Two days were spent unlashing and preparing the salvage equipment whilst the divers began detailed underwater surveys. Most of Wednesday was spent burying anchors on the shore which could be used as anchor points for the work on *Dias* and *Albatros* as well as moorings for *Luma* which would move in close for the next stage of the salvage operation.

By the end of the first week the holes and potential weak spots in *Dias*'s hull were being patched. Each patch had to be fashioned individually and most were made from wooden slabs shaped to fit the contours of the hull. Each slab was covered with a soft base known as a pudding comprising liberal coatings of heavy grease to ensure the best possible seal. A T-shaped bolt was then fitted through a hole in the contrivance and tightened to act as an anchor against the slab. Much time was spent filling very small holes, mainly due to missing rivets, using what was known in the salvage trade as 'Monkey Shit', a plastic type compound that sets as hard as rock underwater. This substance, like putty, is initially softened by hand—though in South Georgia's cold climate this was quite a task in itself—before being quickly passed down to the diver whilst still pliable.

By the end of January the divers had sealed all major openings and pumped out the crew's accommodation in the forepart of the vessel and a fore peak ballast tank, but this made no apparent difference to her trim, though Lyle observed that she felt lighter and even vibrated occasionally when the nearby *Luma* manoeuvred with her twin screw propellers.

The morning of 28 January loomed and this was to be one of the most important days in the whole operation. If *Dias* did not float after being pumped then the team would have to go for the more complicated option of assisting by using *Luma*'s anchor handling/towing winches to lift her stern. All suction hoses and submersible pumps were in place by mid-day. The vessel's forepeak remained dry, an encouraging sign, so pumping began at low water on the cargo hold, forward of the bridge, as well as the engine and boiler rooms.

At this stage there was some unease as the team had only limited means to stabilise *Dias* should the vessel take on a severe list, and this could cause a capsize. Whilst the hulk of *Albatros* might halt any fall to port, restraining tackle was also rigged from the quay and stretched across the other vessel should the old trawler list badly to starboard. Lyle had also hoped to lash *Luma* to the starboard side of the old trawler but her captain was reluctant to do this, having not done this type of salvage before. Time was tight and in the end Lyle decided to go for it and rely on the restraining tackle should the little ship fall over. By the time the hold was emptied *Dias* was definitely showing signs of 'coming alive.' Because of the severe angle caused by the vessel being down by the stern, there was no alternative but to hope she would float with the engine and boiler room only partially pumped out.

Yet the old vessel seemed to instil confidence in everyone, for her hull was sounder than anyone had dared hope and the bulkhead tanks fronting the hull were not leaking. Even so, by this stage Lyle reckoned she should be afloat. The bow had left the seabed giving the deck an even steeper angle. The pumps were making heavy weather of it, some had to be repositioned in through the ventilator openings to the boiler room. The engine room openings, including doors, vents and skylights were hastily sealed as they had not been expected to have stayed submerged by this stage.

The day was closing and it was apparent that pumping would soon have to cease for the day and the vessel be allowed to settle back on the seabed. But, just as plans to bring in *Luma* the next day to exert a lift with her winches were being discussed, bubbles suddenly rushed to the surface near the stern. For the salvors this was a good sign that that the suction of the mud which held the vessel to the seabed was breaking. Then, ever so slowly, but definitely, the old trawler showed she was afloat again for the first time in thirty years, albeit very deep in the water. It was now 1600 hours and there was no time to celebrate as water stilled lapped over her after deck. She needed to be much lighter in the water so the salvors quickly entered the engine room to re-site the suction hoses well under her engine. The pumps did their work. Within an hour *Dias* was securely afloat although still deep in the water. Pumping was stopped for the day and *Luma* was moored close by so that, if necessary, pumping could be started at a moment's notice.

The next three days were spent removing all the water on board. Due to the restricted space, a chain gang with buckets was also set up to remove the contents of the boiler and at least fifty tons of mud. *Dias* floated perfectly, even proudly, and on an even keel at her normal operating draft. Even more rewarding was that she made little water, thanks to both the perfect patching job and the robustness of her original construction. Cook, Welton and Gemmell, her builders, made ships that lasted.

By the last day of January all mud and silt had been removed from the engine and boiler rooms and the vessel had been washed down with a pressure hose. Now all could see the lovely original Amos and Smith triple expansion steam engine, even that the very large pillars supporting the expansion chamber had been made in the true style of the era. On later vessels these were usually straight supports but *Dias*'s were nicely shaped with bulb-like features indicating the flair of the original design. For Lyle, who examined every detail, it was more than evident that this little ship, a wonderful example from a bygone era of British engineering and workmanship, deserved a better future, rather than being left to languish and slowly deteriorate at Grytviken.

At the beginning of February the engineers fabricated fittings to remove the fuel oil from the bunker tanks. By the end of the first day steam was circulating into the tanks by way of the original heating coils and *Dias* was towed to the nearby Tijuca Jetty whilst the oil was discharged into the Brecknock. There was a lot of oil and by 6 February almost 30 cubic metres had been removed from the twin fuel tanks. The manhole covers were now unbolted and compressed air blown through to remove any toxic fumes. After this the tanks were pressure washed followed by steam cleaning and hand mopping of the last residues of oily water.

A week later *Dias*, despite stormy days of rain and sleet, was declared totally free of oil and inspected by Gordon Liddle, the manager of the GSGSSI. He was overwhelmed by the cleanliness of the vessel overall and remarked that he had seen more oil on a full English breakfast.[24] Throughout the worst of the weather the old trawler had remained securely moored to the Tijuca Jetty and although she had ranged a bit during the worst of the storm she had hardly made even a cupful of water.

Whilst *Dias* was moored at Tijuca Jetty, the salvors were able to tackle *Albatros* which was also raised and cleaned. Preparations were then made to provide a new berth for the two vessels. During the final stages of salvage a very large basin was excavated on the shore by the side of the Harpon Quay with the aid of a large Volvo excavator. *Dias* was moved back alongside *Albatros* and both vessels were lashed firmly together in the hope that they would support each other on taking the ground when moving ahead into their new berth. Bridles and chains were then rigged to pull both vessels into the berth at the same time. Both vessels were pulled firmly ashore into the new basin by an old D6 caterpillar tractor which extorted a pull of around ten tons. The new basin was then backfilled against the foreparts of both hulls to assist with maintaining the perfectly upright position they had adopted.

The following four days were spent on final touches to *Dias*. Items of interest such as steam gauges, telegraphs and the like were removed and passed over to the South Georgia Museum for safekeeping and display, whilst Lyle ballasted *Dias* fully down to keep her in constant contact with the seabed, and the engine room was flooded to preserve the remaining internal features and ensure that oxygen did not accelerate the deterioration of the ferrous metal.[25]

The refloating of *Dias* prompted further interest in the vessel and back in Great Britain, this book's authors, Robb Robinson and Ian Hart, together with Tony Ellerbeck, Anthony Myers, Lyle Craigie-Halkett, and Paul Escreet of Specialist Marine Services Towage Ltd., amongst others, tried to get together a project aimed at returning the vessel to the United Kingdom. Robinson and Ellerbeck outlined their plans to a meeting of the South Georgia Association but, other than the creation of a website, those plans came to nothing, partly because of the then difficulty of finding an appropriate context for the vessel in Britain. Even so, these activities have led to a growing interest in the vessel and its story. At least three further models—one with a working steam engine—built by Alan Richardson who first saw the ship when in the Royal Fleet Auxiliary on a trip to South Georgia, have been built. In 2006 Robb Robinson also located *Viola*'s original bell in Norway and, after conducting a fund raising exercise, had this brought back to Hull and initially hung in the city's Fishgate Fishmarket. A couple of years later Robinson and Escreet—who was Chartering Manager of SMS Towage at the time of the Falklands War and had then played a significant role in facilitating the Admiralty's swift charter of the company's three tugs and their crews—were able to arrange the loan of the bell, together with a model of the vessel built by John Cherry of Hull, to the South Georgia Museum on condition it was rung on the deck of old trawler to mark the ninetieth anniversary of the Armistice, and also to commemorate the role that working fishermen and their fishing vessels played in the Great War.

In November 2008 a service was held in the church at Grytviken and attended by some of the passengers from a visiting cruise ship. Bell and ship were reunited for the first time in over eighty years. The bell was duly rung and its sounds echoed across not only across the waters of King Edward Cove but also back down many, many distant decades of life at sea.

EPILOGUE

VIOLA/DIAS

UNFATHOMABLE FEET OF SEA WATER have flowed under *Viola/Dias*'s keel since her launch and first tentative tow down the narrow River Hull back in January 1906. The lives and livelihoods of multitudes of mariners as well as many of their families and friends, up and down the length of the long Atlantic, have been tied up at one time or another with this little vessel over the subsequent decades.

From Grovehill Shipyard, Beverley by way of the Great War to Grytviken, South Georgia, *Viola/Dias*'s biography is a true twentieth century story of the sea. Her tale encapsulates so many aspects of humankind's timeless struggles with the oceans and of ordinary seafaring people living and earning their livelihoods in extraordinary circumstances.

Grytviken is a long way from the United Kingdom. Very far: not only in distance but in time. When *Viola/Dias* was launched the UK was the world's leading maritime nation, the country's Edwardian shipyards built more than three quarters of the world's tonnage of shipping, and the country boasted the largest and most modern fishing industry the world had ever seen. *Viola/Dias*'s subsequent career concisely encompasses so many dimensions of not only British twentieth century maritime history but also that of Norway, Argentina and indeed the world.

But what of the future of this little ship? *Viola/Dias* is currently relatively stable but her long term future is much more uncertain. Her funnel was removed for safety reasons a few years ago and has not been refitted. There seems only limited likelihood of resources being made available on South Georgia to ensure her preservation. She is almost the last intact survivor of more than 3,000 fishing vessels which, together with their crews, drawn from coastal communities across the United Kingdom, played an absolutely crucial role in ensuring Britain's vital sea lanes remained open throughout the war. Without these vessels our ability to continue to fight the war would almost certainly have been degraded. Their role and that of *Viola/Dias* in particular continues to be largely underplayed. Though a substantial fund of money was allocated for various commemorative projects through the Government's own Great War Centenary commemoration plans, none seems to be available to support this unique vessel's return, or even some form of restoration. Historic ships of all kinds are part of our island nation's built environment. Vessels such as *Viola/Dias* represent the everyday world of the working seafarer, the backbone of our country's trade and commerce—they formed its very fabric. Such ships deserve to be embraced, retained and maintained.

At this time you can still see *Viola/Dias*. Today, South Georgia is visited each austral summer by around 8,000 passengers on Antarctic cruise ship voyages. The South Georgia Museum at Grytviken, situated in the old whaling manager's house, is visited by many of these arrivals and contains a wonderful display telling you something of this little vessel and of its long voyage across the seas of a tumultuous century.

ACKNOWLEDGMENTS

It is not possible to acknowledge everyone who has supported, advised or encouraged the writing of this story of *Viola*. We would above all like to thank the many descendants of people associated with this little ship who have been so helpful in terms of supplying photographs, documents, recollections or oral information and technical advice, or who have materially helped in various aspects of the research. These include Harold Appleyard (World Ship Society), Mike Atkinson, Bob Burton, John Cherry, Peter Craven, Elsa Davidson, Trevor Doyle, Tony Ellerbeck, Paul Escreet, Odd Galteland (Norway), Jon Grobler, Pat Hindshaw, Berit Johnson, Lyle Craigie-Halkett, Phil Haskins, Alan Hopper, Phil Johnson, Ken Knox, Kim Lever, Professor Hugh Murphy, James Morley, Bruce Robinson, John Simpson, Brian Smith, Professor David J. Starkey, Dr Bernard Stonehouse, Eric Tharratt, Pat Tharratt and Billy Wells

Our thanks are also due to the staffs of the British Library, the Brynmor Jones Library at the University of Hull, the Hull History Centre, the National Archives, the Treasure House at Beverley, Scott Polar Research Institute, Shetland Museum and Archives, and the South Georgia Museum.

On a personal level our especial thanks go to Dilys Hart and Wendy Robinson—our wives—for their patience, advice and succour in times of stress.

Finally, we would wish to recognise our particular debt of gratitude to Peter Chapman of the East Yorkshire Family History Society, who has not only proved absolutely invaluable in terms of genealogical research but has also unearthed some hitherto unknown information on some of the many people associated with *Viola* over her remarkable and lengthy career.

Robb Robinson and Ian Hart

NOTES

Chapter I

1   B. Stonehouse, *Encyclopedia of Antarctica and the Southern Oceans* (Wiley, 2002), 243-4.

2   R. Headland, *The Island of South Georgia* (Cambridge University Press, 1992), 76-80

3   R. Perkins, *Operation Paraquat* (Picton, 1986), 209.

4   *Eastern Morning News*, 20 February, 1906.

5   R. Robinson, *Far Horizons: From Hull to the Ends of the Earth* (2010), 237.

6   I. B. Hart, *PESCA: A History of the Pioneer Modern Whaling Company in the Antarctic* (Adrian Ellis, 2001), 442-3.

Chapter II

1   D. H. Cushing, *The Arctic Cod* (Pergamon, 1966) 7.

2   R. Robinson, *Trawling*, 12-13

3   R. Robinson, 'The North Sea Littoral and British Isles' in D.J.Starkey, I Heidbrink (eds) *A History of the North Sea Fisheries* Vol.2 (German Maritime Museum, Bremerhaven, 2012) 240.

4   G. L. Alward, *The Sea Fisheries of Great Britain and Ireland* (Grimsby, 1932)

5   W. Wood, *North Sea Fishers and Fighters* (Kegan Paul, 1911) 52.

6   Agreement between Robert Hellyer and William Addy for latter to buy fish, 24 February 1853. Copy in possession of author. I am grateful to Jon Grobbler for this copy.

7   HHC, Hull Custom House Vessel Register, 5 December, 1857.

8   See for example HHC, Hull Custom House Vessel Registers, 13 August, 1859, 6 March, 1860 and 21 June, 1872.

9   BMD, Birth Dec QTR 1846 District: Totnes Vol 9 Page 490

10   HHC, Hull Custom House Vessel Register, 7 March, 1870.

11   BPP, 1883, XVIII, *Report of the Board of Trade into the System of Deep Sea Trawling in the North Sea*, 7-8.

12   *Hull Times*, 15 March 1930.

13   *Hull Times*, 15 March 1930.

14 Bellamy, '*Some Aspects*', 360.

15 *Hull Daily Mail*, 21 February, 1905.

16 R. Robinson and I. B. Hart, 'Viola/Dias: The Working Life and Contexts of the Steam Trawler and Whaler' in *The Mariner's Mirror*, Vol 89 No. 3 (August, 2005), 328.

17 R. Robinson, *Far Horizons* (MHSC, 2010), 97-8.

18 Ibid, 47-9 and 233-6.

19 M Thompson, D. Newton, R. Robinson & T. Lofthouse, *Cook Welton & Gemmell* (Beverley, 1999), 5-10.

20 M. Thompson, D. Newton, R. Robinson & T. Lofthouse, *Cook Welton & Gemmell* (Beverley, 1999), 83.

21 HHC, Hull Custom House Vessel Register, 19 February, 1906.

22 Descriptions taken from loss reports on three sister vessels: *Lycurgus* and *Eudocia* (Board of Trade Loss Report s263 February 1909 and also the *Angus*, Board of Trade Loss Report s177 January, 1914. I am grateul to Alec Gill for bringing these to my attention.

CHAPTER III

1 HHC, DPF/23/1890 Running Agreement, *Viola*, 20 February, 1906.

2 *Daily News*, 7 January, 1899 and *Aberdeen Weekly Journal*, 8 April, 1899.

3 W. Wood, *North Sea Fishers and Fighters* (Kegan Paul, 1911), 143.

4 Log of Robert Glanville, Malet Lambert Local History Society (nd)

5 Reminiscences of Herbert Johnson. Tape, 1975, copy in possession of R. Robinson

6 E. J. Mather, *Nor'ard of the Dogger* (1889), 16.

7 A. G. Credland, *Earles of Hull* (Hull Museums, 1982), 63-4.

8 W. Wood, *North Sea Fishers and Fighters* (Kegan Paul, 1911), 236.

9 BPP, 1908 [Cd. 4304] Committee on Fishery Investigations. Minutes of evidence, q8744.

10 R. Robinson, *Trawling*, 10.

11 *Nottingham Evening Post*, 2 April, 1906 and A.Gill, *Lost Trawlers of Hull 1835-1937* (Beverley 1989), 71.

12 *Eastern Morning News*, 17 March 1906.

13 HHC, DPF/24/870 Running Agreement, *Viola,* 26 September, 1906.

14 HHC DPF/24/870 and DPF/24/159 Running Agreements, 26 September and 29 October, 1906.

15 HHC DPF/24/870 14 August, 1907.

16   HHC DPF 29/730 Running Agreement.

17   R. Robinson, *Trawling*, 79-80.

18   Reminiscences of Herbert Johnson

19   Reminiscences of William Wells, Tape, 1976 in possession of R. Robinson.

20   Robinson, *Far Horizons*, 63-9.

21   HHC, DPF 23/890, 7 August, 1907.

22   HHC, DPM/2 Hull Police Court Records, 22 September and 14 October, 1908.

23   John Hill was Robb Robinson's great grandfather.

24   *Hull Daily Mail*, 25 January, 1916.

25   *Hull Daily Mail*, 25 November, 1913.

26   Report on the Collision between the *Lycurgus* and *Eudocia* (s263) Marine Department, Board of Trade, Report Under Merchant Shipping Act, 1894

27   Herbert Johnson, former Hellyer skipper, tape recording of conversation 1975.

28   Report on the Loss of *Angus* (no 177) Marine Department, Board of Trade, Report Under Merchant Shipping Act, 1894. See also *Hull Daily Mail*, 1 December 1913 and Robinson, *Far Horizons*, 65.

29   A. Gill, *Lost Trawlers of Hull 1835-1937* (Beverley 1989), 64-79.

Chapter IV

1   *Hull Daily Mail*, 5 August 1914.

2   Herbert Johnson, former Hellyer skipper, tape recording of conversation 1975.

3   William Wells, former boxing fleet fisherman, tape recording of conversation.

4   *Hull Daily Mail*, 6 August 1914

5   Herbert Johnson, former Hellyer skipper, tape recording of conversation 1975.

6   *Hull Daily Mail*, 11 August, 1914.

7   Paul Kennedy, *The Rise and Fall of British Naval Mastery* (Penguin ed 1976), 244.

8   Paul G. Halpern, *A Naval History of World War I* (Maryland USA, 1994) 33.

9   U boat net, http://www.uboat.net/history/wwi/part2.htm (accessed 11 April, 2014)

10   Paul G. Halpern, *A Naval History of World War I* (Maryland, USA 1994), 29.

11   NA, RNR Service Record, Charles Allum, Catalogue Reference:BT/377/7

12   NA, RNR Service Records, William Blewitt, Edward Lodge, Thomas Gordon, George Tharratt and George Richards.

13   J. Thompson, *The War at Sea 1914* (London 2005), 149.

14   Burgh Police Station Records, Shetland, 12 November, 1914.

15   *Hull Daily Mail*, 6 September 1916.

16   NA, ADM 53/67617, 23 May 1915.

17   Archibald Hurd, *The Merchant Navy* Vol I, 379.

18   NA, ADM 53/67617, 1 – 30 June 1915.

19   James Miller, *The North Atlantic Front* (Edinburgh 2003), 27.

20   NA, ADM 53/67617, 2 June 1915.

21   R.H. Gibson and M. Prendegast, *The German Submarine War 1914-1918* (London 1931), 34-5.

22   Archibald Hurd, *The Merchant Navy* Vol I, 440-2.

23   E. Keble-Chatterton, *The Auxiliary Patrol* (London 1923), 83-4.

24   *Hull Daily Mail*, 25 June, 1915 and 9 December, 1918.

25   *Hull Daily Mail*, 5 September 1914.

26   Archibald Hurd, *The Merchant Navy* Vol I, 395-7.

27   Herbert Johnson, former Hellyer skipper, tape recording of conversation 1975.

28   U boat net, http://www.uboat.net/history/wwi/part2.htm (accessed 11 April, 2014).

29   R.H. Gibson and M. Prendegast, *The German Submarine War 1914-1918* (London 1931), 44-5.

30   E. Keble-Chatterton, *The Auxiliary Patrol* (London 1923), 84-5.

31   Archibald Hurd, *The Merchant Navy* Vol I, 440-2.

32   Paul G. Halpern, *A Naval History of World War I* (Maryland, USA 1994), 330.

33   Paul Kennedy, *The Rise and Fall of British Naval Mastery* (Penguin ed 1976), 248-9.

34   PRO. ADM 53/67617, 30 May 1915.

35   Auxiliary Patrol Red List, October 1916.

CHAPTER V

1   See for example, A. Firth, *East Coast War Channels in the First and Second World Wars* (English Heritage Project 6585) http://www.english-heritage.org.uk/publications/east-coast-war-channels-first-and-second-world-wars/ (accessed 23 June 2014).

2   The Unit system was abandoned early in 1917 and the trawlers in each patrol area were listed generally. MoD, Admiralty Library letter, ref D/NHB/22/1, 16 August, 2002.

3   *Newcastle Journal*, 21 June, 1917

4   *British Vessels Lost at Sea, 1914-1918*,HMSO, 1919.

5   C. Domville-Fife, *Submarine Warfare of Today* (London 1920), 71-3.

6   Arthur Hezlett, *The Submarine and Sea Power* (London 1967), 59.

7   C. Domville-Fife, *Submarine Warfare of Today* (London 1920), 78.

8   Arthur Hezlett, *The Submarine and Sea Power* (London 1967), 63.

9   Archibald Hurd, *The Merchant Navy* Vol III (London 1929), 44-5.

10 R. Young and P. Armstrong, *Silent Warriors: Submarine Wrecks of the United Kingdom*, Vol. One (Tempus, 2006), 45.

11 NA, BT/377/7, WSA 104, George Richards, RNR Service Record.

12 *Liverpool Daily Post*, 18 December 1917 and Commonwealth War Graves Commission.

13 NA, ADM 137/3986, April, 1917.

14 NA, ADM 137/3986, April, 1917.

15 *London Gazette*, 20 September, 1918 and ADM 171/84, 113.

16 NA, ADM 137/2653, Monthly Reports, December 1917.

17 NA, BT/377/7, WSA 260, Charles Allum, RNR Service Record.

18 NA, ADM 137/2653, Anti-Submarine Division, Monthly Report, 12 February 1918; Arthur Hezlett, *The Submarine and Sea Power* (London 1967), 96.

19 Marriage, Sept. Qtr, 1918, District, Tynemouth, Vol., 10b, page 568.

20 NA, ADM137/2653 Anti-Submarine Division, Monthly Report, June 1917.

21 NA, ADM137/2653 Anti-Submarine Division, Monthly Report, 26 March 1918.

22 NA, ADM137/2653 Anti-Submarine Division, Monthly Report, 28 March 1918.

23 NA, ADM137/2653 Anti-Submarine Division, Monthly Report, 27 July 1918.

24 NA, ADM137/2653 Anti-Submarine Division, Monthly Report, 15 August 1918.

25 NA, ADM137/2653 Anti-Submarine Division, Monthly Report, 13 August 1918.

26 Young and Armstrong, *Silent Warriors: Submarine Wrecks of the United Kingdom*, Vol. One (Tempus, 2006), 66-8.

27 *The Edinburgh Gazette*, 17 Aug., 1920.

28 Young and Armstrong, *Silent Warriors: Submarine Wrecks of the United Kingdom*, Vol. One (Tempus, 2006), 52-8.

29 NA, ADM 1/6553/65 Demobilising List of Auxiliary Patrol Vessels, Appendix IV.

30 Alec Gill, *Lost Trawlers of Hull 1835-1937* (Beverley 1989).

31 Min Agriculture and Fisheries, *Report on Sea Fisheries 1915 – 1918*; *Navy Losses and Merchant Shipping Losses* (HMSO, August 1919) and NA, BT/377/7, WSA 260, Charles Allum RNR Service Record.

CHAPTER VI

1   Young and Armstrong, *Silent Warriors: Submarine Wrecks of the United Kingdom*, Vol. One (Tempus, 2006), 60-65.

2   NA, BT 377/7, WSA 403, George William Tharratt, RNR Service Record.

3   NA, NA, BT 377/7WSA 403, George William Tharratt, RNR Service Record.

4   *Hull Daily Mail*, 16 April, 1917.

5   Wrecksite, http://www.wrecksite.eu/wreck.aspx?147067 (accessed, 27 April, 2014).

6   NA, J77/1374 C615594.

7   NA, BT 377/7WSA 403, George William Tharratt, RNR Service Record William Tharratt.

8   T. Dorling, *Swept Channels (1935)* 310-311.

9   NA, BT 377/7, Tharratt, RNR Service Record.

10 General Register Office, Copy of an Entry of Death, 56663507-1, 12 June, 1928.

11 Conversation with Eric Tharratt aged 97 in July 2014.

12 *Hull Daily Mail*, 20 and 21 February, 1919.

13 *Hull Daily Mail*, 11 April, 1919.

14 NA, BT/377/7, WSA 260, Charles Allum, RNR Service Record.

15 *Hull Daily Mail*, 15 and 17 February, 1919.

16 NA, ADM 1/8553/65 *Demobilising List of Auxiliary Patrol Vessels*, Appendix IV.

17 A. Credland (ed.) *United Towing, 1920 – 1990*, Beverley 1990, 11.

18 *Hull Daily Mail*, 6 March, 1906 and *The London Gazette*, 10 March, 1936.

19 Document in possession of R Robinson.

20 M. Thompson, D. Newton, R. Robinson & T. Lofthouse, *Cook Welton & Gemmell* (Beverley, 1999), 88-9.

21 Charles Allum Death Certificate IQ855483, 19 May 1953.

22 We are grateful to Kim Lever and other descendants of Charles Allum for this information and access to his surviving documentation.

23 Prospectus and invitation for shares in A/S Sandefjords Trawlfiskeselskap dated 20 February 1920 with a proposed share capital of between 125,000 and 250,000 Norwegian kroner as printed in *Sandefjords Blad*. The consortium comprised the following: Lars Thorsen, N. T. Nielsen-Alonso, Sigvald S. Myhre, O. Wegger, Hans Sperre, Carl Salvesen and G. A. Bøe.

24 R. Robinson and Ian B. Hart, 'Viola/Dias: the Working Life and Contexts of the Steam Trawler/Whaler and Sealer,' *The Mariner's Mirror*, Vol. 89, No. 3 (August, 2003) 331-2.

25 Veritas Register, Oslo, 1921, 19.

26 *Sandefjords Blad* 19 August 1920. We are grateful to Odd Galteland for this information.

27 *Sandefjords Blad* 6 December 1922.

28 R. Robinson and Ian B. Hart, 'Viola/Dias: the Working Life and Contexts of the Steam Trawler/Whaler and Sealer,' *The Mariner's Mirror*, Vol. 89, No. 3 (August, 2003), 331-2.

CHAPTER VII

1 Robb Robinson, *Far Horizons: From Hull to the Ends of the Earth* (Hull, 2010), 29.

2 Ibid., 32-4.

3 Gordon Jackson, *The British Whaling Trade* (London, 1978) 26.

4 Norges Skibsførere 1933-1935. (Stavanger 1935), 52.

5 Sigurd Risting, *Av Hvalfangstens Historie* (Kristiania, 1922), 478.

6 Sigurd Risting, *Hvalfangerflaaten – The Whaling Fleet, 1914.* (Sandefjord, 1914).

7 I. Hart & E. Edmundson. A *Historia da caça de baleias no Brasil* (A History of Whaling in Brazil) (São Paulo. In press, 2014)

8 Source: International Whaling Commission, Cambridge.

9 One of the other expedition catchers was named *Odd III* (135 gross tons). The name of the other catcher is not known. Notes taken by Odd Galteland, Sandefjord from Norsk Hvalfangst Tidende (1923) and other sources (2014).

10 In 1906 Nilsen was the master of the Chilean registered whale factory ship *Gobernador Bories*, which was the first factory ship to use the harbour at Port Foster, Deception Island, South Shetland Islands as a base for an Antarctic whaling expedition. Norges Skibsførere 1933-1935. (Stavanger,1935).

11 J.N.Tonnessen and A.O. Johnsen, *The History of Modern Whaling* (London, 1982), 214.

12 There is some confusion in Norwegian shipping records as to whether the ship was renamed *Dias* or *Diaz*. The Norwegian Whaling Register for 1926 and 1928 gives the name with a 'z', whereas Det Norske Veritas for 1925, 1926 and 1927 gives the name with an 's'.

13 Notes taken by Odd Galteland, Sandefjord from *Norsk Hvalfangst Tidende* and other sources (2014).

14 Framnæs Mekaniske Værksted docking records 1927 gives her name as Kapduen and that she was renamed Dias following completion of the conversion to a sealing vessel.

15 Much of this information relating to the Compañia Argentina de Pesca S.A. here and elsewhere in this Chapter is taken from Ian B. Hart, *Pesca – A History of the Pioneer Modern Whaling Company in the Antarctic.* (Salcombe, 2001 & 2004).

16   The *Consort*, 73 tons gross, O.N. 82461, was built in 1879 by John C. Tolman, New-haven, Sussex as a Dandy-rigged ketch for The Hull Steam Fishing & Ice Company, Hull in which Robert Hellyer and Richard Thomas Vivian held shareholdings. After a period of trading between Chile and the Falkland Islands 1905-07, she was wrecked off the coast of Chile in September 1907.

17   Ian B. Hart, *Whaling in the Falkland Islands Dependencies 1904-1931*. (Newton St. Margarets, 2006).

Chapter VIII

1   Ludwig Kohl-Larsen, *South Georgia: Gateway to Antarctica* (Germany, 1930, translated and republished, Huntingdon, 2003).

2   R. M. Laws, The Southern Elephant Seal (Mirounga leonina Linn.) at South Georgia, *Norsk Hvalfangst Tidende* (The Norwegian Whaling Gazette), 49, 1960.

3   L. Harrison Matthews, *Sea Elephant* (London, 1952), 12.

4   Much of this information about sealing vessels, sealing skippers and their length of service is taken from the archives of the Compañia Argentina de Pesca S.A. held at The Scott Polar Research Institute, Cambridge.

5   Kohl-Larsen, *South Georgia*, 240.

6   Conversation recalled by Lyle Craigie-Halkett in July 2014.

7   Report on S/S Dias expedition to Patagonia and Tierra del Fuego, 6.2.1930.

Chapter IX

1   See for example, *Yorkshire Evening Post*, 22nd Nov., 1930.

2   Robinson, *Far Horizons*, 234-5.

Chapter XI

1   The *Seiyo Maru* sailed with a cargo of 2,530 metric tons of whale oil, 290 metric tons of sperm oil and 1,663 metric tons of seal oil. This was the last shipment of whale and seal products to leave Grytviken.

2   Much of this information relating to the Compañia Argentina de Pesca S.A. and Albion Star (South Georgia) Ltd. here and elsewhere in this Chapter is taken from Ian B. Hart, *Pesca – A History of the Pioneer Modern Whaling Company in the Antarctic*. (Salcombe, 2001 & 2004).

3   For a biography of Edward B. Binnie see Ian Hart, *Antarctic Magistrate – a life through the lens of a camera*, Pequena (2009).

4   R. Headland, *The Island of South Georgia* (Cambridge, 1984)

5 A.B. Dickinson, *Seal Fisheries of the Falkland Islands and Dependencies: An Historical Review* (IMEHA, 2007), 170.

6 An unpublished account of Endurance and South Georgia in 1982, written by Tony Ellerbeck.

7 This name was initially given to the islands by the French.

8 P.Calvert, 'Sovereignty and the Falkland Crisis' in *The Falkland Islands Journal*, 1987, p. 5-6, reprinted from article originally published in *International Affairs*, 1883 Vol. 59, No. 3.

9 S. A. Royle, 'The Falkland Islands, 1833 – 1876: The Establishment of a Colony' in *The Falkland Islands Journal*, 1987, p. 16 (published by permission of the *Geographical Journal*).

10 Robinson, *Far Horizons*, 95.

11 B. Stonehouse, *The Last Continent: Discovering Antarctica* (SCP, 2002), 96.

12 L. Freedman, *The Official History of the Falklands Campaign*, Volume 1 (2004), 11.

13 R. Perkins, *Operation Paraquat* (Picton, 1986), 31.

14 Headland, *South Georgia*, 243-5.

15 Perkins, *Operation Paraquat*, 70-3.

16 Headland, *South Georgia*, 243-5.

17 Tony Ellerbeck unpublished account.

18 Tony Ellerbeck unpublished account.

19 Headland, *South Georgia*, 243-5

20 Headland, *South Georgia*, 243-5.

21 I am grateful to Tony Ellerbeck for information about the period in which Endurance acted as harbour master.

22 Lyle Craigie-Halkett Personal Recollections Paper 2014 (copy in possession of R. Robinson).

23 For an full account of Risdon Beazley and the scope of its salvage opeartions see R.Martin and L. Craigie-Halkett, *Risdon Beazley: Marine Salvor* (2006)

24 Lyle Craigie-Halkett, 'Abandoned Whalers Salvaged at South Georgia,' in *Sea Breezes*, June 2010, 34-6.

25 Much of the account of the salvage is taken from Lyle Craigie-Halkett's Personal Recollections document and from his *Sea Breezes* article.

BIBLIOGRAPHY

Anon, *British Vessels Lost at Sea 1914-18* (HMSO, 1918).

Anon, *Norges Skibsførere 1933-1935* (Stavanger, 1935).

G. L. Alward, *The Sea Fisheries of Great Britain and Ireland* (Grimsby, 1932).

P.Calvert, 'Sovereignty and the Falkland Crisis' in *The Falkland Islands Journal*, 1987.

E. Keble-Chatterton, *The Auxiliary Patrol* (London 1923).

A.G. Credland, *Earles of Hull* (Hull Museums, 1982).

A. G. Credland, A. Ford, *United Towing, 1920 - 1990*, (Beverley, 1990).

D. H. Cushing, *The Arctic Cod* (London, 1966).

D. De Chair, *The Sea is Strong* (London, 1961).

A. B. Dickinson, *Seal Fisheries of the Falkland Islands and Dependencies: An Historical Review* (IMEHA, 2007).

C. Domville-Fife, *Submarine Warfare of Today* (London 1920).

T. Dorling, *Swept Channels* (1935).

L. Freedman, *The Official History of the Falklands Campaign*, Volume 1 (2004).

R. H. Gibson and M. Prendegast, *The German Submarine War* (London 1931).

Alec Gill, *Lost Trawlers of Hull 1835-1937* (Beverley 1989).

Lyle Craigie-Halkett, 'Abandoned Whalers Salvaged at South Georgia,' in *Sea Breezes*, June 2010.

Paul G. Halpern, *A Naval History of World War I* (Maryland USA, 1994).

Ian B. Hart, *PESCA - A History of the Pioneer Modern Whaling Company in the Antarctic*, (Aidan Ellis, 2001).

Ian B. Hart, *Whaling in the Falkland Islands Dependencies 1904-1931*. (Pequena, 2006).

Ian B. Hart, *Antarctic Magistrate – A life through the lens of a camera*, (Pequena, 2009).

I. Hart & E. Edmundson. *A História da caça de baleias no Brasil* (A History of Whaling in Brazil) (São Paulo. In press, 2014).

R. Headland, *The Island of South Georgia* (Cambridge University Press, 1992).

Arthur Hezlett, *The Submarine and Sea Power* (London 1967).

Archibald Hurd, *The Merchant Navy* Vol III (London 1929).

Gordon Jackson, *The British Whaling Trade* (London, 1978).

Paul Kennedy, *The Rise and Fall of British Naval Mastery* (Penguin ed 1976).

Ludwig Kohl-Larsen, *South Georgia: Gateway to Antarctica* (Germany, 1930, translated and republished, Huntingdon, 2003).

R. Martin and L. Craigie-Halkett, *Risdon Beazley: Marine Salvor* (2006).

E. J. Mather, *Nor'ard of the Dogger* (London, 1889).

L. Harrison Matthews, *Sea Elephant* (London, 1952).

L. Harrison Matthews, *Penguins, Whalers and Sealers* (New York, 1978).

L. Harrison Matthews, *South Georgia –The British Empire's SubAntarctic Outpost* (London, 1931).

James Miller, *The North Atlantic Front* (Edinburgh 2003).

R. Perkins, *Operation Paraquat* (Picton, 1986).

Sigurd Risting, *Av Hvalfangstens Historie* (Kristiania, 1922).

R. Robinson, *Trawling: The Rise and Fall of the British Trawl Fishery* (Exeter, 1985).

R. Robinson and I. B. Hart, 'Viola/Dias: The Working Life and Contexts of the Steam Trawler and Whaler' in *The Mariner's Mirror*, Vol 89 No. 3 (August, 2005).

R. Robinson, *Far Horizons: from Hull to the Ends of the Earth* (2010)

R. Robinson, 'The North Sea Littoral and British Isles' in D.J.Starkey, I Heidbrink (eds) *A History of the North Sea Fisheries* Vol.2 (German Maritime Museum, Bremerhaven, 2012).

S. A. Royle, 'The Falkland Islands, 1833 – 1876: The Establishment of a Colony' in *The Falkland Islands Journal*, 1987.

B. Stonehouse, *Encyclopedia of Antarctica and the Southern Oceans* (Wiley, 2002).

B. Stonehouse, *The Last Continent: Discovering Antarctica* (SCP, 2002).

J. Thompson, *The War at Sea 1914* (London 2005).

M. Thompson, D. Newton, R.Robinson & T. Lofthouse, *Cook Welton & Gemmell* (Hutton, 1999).

J. N.Tønnessen and A.O. Johnsen, *The History of Modern Whaling* (London, 1982).

J. N. Tønnessen, *Den Moderne Hvalfangsts Historie*, Vol. 3 (Sandefjord 1969).

W. Wood, *North Sea Fishers and Fighters* (Kegan Paul, 2011).

R. Young and P. Armstrong, *Silent Warriors: Submarine Wrecks of the United Kingdom*, Vol. One (Tempus, 2006).

NEWSPAPERS AND JOURNALS

Aberdeen Weekly Journal
Daily News
Eastern Morning News

The Edinburgh Gazette

Hull Daily Mail

Hull Times

Liverpool Daily Post

London Gazette

Newcastle Journal

Nottingham Evening Post

Sandefjords Blad

York Herald

Yorkshire Evening Post

Norsk Hvalfangst Tidende (The Norwegian Whaling Gazette)

PRINCIPAL PRIMARY SOURCES CONSULTED

BPP, 1883, XVIII, Report of the Board of Trade into the System of Deep Sea Trawling in the North Sea, British Parliamentary Papers.

BPP, 1908 [Cd. 4304] Committee on Fishery Investigations. Minutes of evidence.

Marine Department, Board of Trade, Report Under Merchant Shipping Act, 1894 British Parliamentary Papers.

British Parliamentary Papers, Reports of the Fishery Board for Scotland, 1914 - 1919.

British Parliamentary Papers, Report on the Sea Fisheries of England and Wales, 1915-1918.

HHC, Hull Custom House Vessel Register, Hull History Centre.

HHC, DPF/23 Fishing Vessel Running Agreements. Hull History Centre.

NA, RNR Service Records, Catalogue Reference:BT/377, National Archives.

NA, Log of MHT *Viola*, ADM 53/67617, National Archives.

NA, ADM137 Anti-Submarine Division, Monthly Reports, National Archives.

Veritas Register, Oslo.

Compañia Argentina de Pesca Sociedad Anónima Archive, Scott Polar Research Institute, Cambridge.

Compañia Argentina de Pesca Sociedad Anónima 1904-1929. 25th Anniversary book, (Buenos Aires, 1929).

International Whaling Commission. Catch Statistics (Cambridge and Sandefjord).

PHOTO CREDITS

INDEX